Joint Publication 3-13

Information Operations

27 November 2012
Incorporating Change 1
20 November 2014

BOOK CONTENTS

PREFACE

1. Scope

This publication provides joint doctrine for the planning, preparation, execution, and assessment of information operations across the range of military operations.

2. Purpose

This publication has been prepared under the direction of the Chairman of the Joint Chiefs of Staff. It sets forth joint doctrine to govern the activities and performance of the Armed Forces of the United States in joint operations and provides the doctrinal basis for US military coordination with other US Government departments and agencies during operations and for US military involvement in multinational operations. It provides military guidance for the exercise of authority by combatant commanders and other joint force commanders (JFCs) and prescribes joint doctrine for operations, education, and training. It provides military guidance for use by the Armed Forces in preparing their appropriate plans. It is not the intent of this publication to restrict the authority of the JFC from organizing the force and executing the mission in a manner the JFC deems most appropriate to ensure unity of effort in the accomplishment of the overall objective.

3. Application

a. Joint doctrine established in this publication applies to the Joint Staff, commanders of combatant commands, subunified commands, joint task forces, subordinate components of these commands, and the Services.

b. The guidance in this publication is authoritative; as such, this doctrine will be followed except when, in the judgment of the commander, exceptional circumstances dictate otherwise. If conflicts arise between the contents of this publication and the contents of Service publications, this publication will take precedence unless the Chairman of the Joint Chiefs of Staff, normally in coordination with the other members of the Joint Chiefs of Staff, has provided more current and specific guidance. Commanders of forces operating as part of a multinational (alliance or coalition) military command should follow multinational doctrine and procedures ratified by the United States. For doctrine and procedures not ratified by the United States, commanders should evaluate and follow the multinational command's doctrine and procedures, where applicable and consistent with United States law, regulations, and doctrine.

For the Chairman of the Joint Chiefs of Staff:

CURTIS M. SCAPARROTTI
Lieutenant General, U.S. Army
Director, Joint Staff

SUMMARY OF CHANGES
CHANGE 1 TO JOINT PUBLICATION 3-13
DATED 27 NOVEMBER 2012

- Describes techniques for assessing information related capabilities (IRC) and techniques for assessing the integration of the IRCs in support of the joint force commander's objectives.

- Expands guidance for the 8-step assessment process.

- Provides additional information about private sector assessment techniques, including the theory of change.

- Expands discussion of sound assessment with a focused, organized approach that is being developed in conjunction with the initial operation plan.

- Emphasizes the need for assessments to be periodically adjusted to avoid becoming obsolete.

TABLE OF CONTENTS

Other titles we publish on Amazon.com:

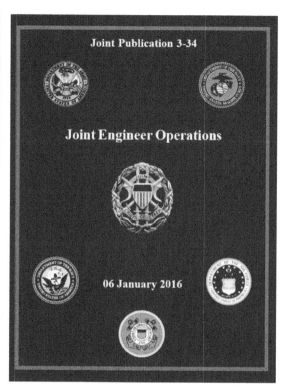

COAST GUARD HELICOPTER
RESCUE SWIMMER MANUAL

Distribution Statement A. Approved for public release. Distribution is unlimited.

COMDTINST M3710.4D
November 2018

EXECUTIVE SUMMARY
COMMANDER'S OVERVIEW

- **Provides an Overview of Information Operations (IO) and the Information Environment**

- **Describes IO and Its Relationships and Integration**

- **Addresses IO Authorities, Responsibilities, and Legal Considerations**

- **Explains Integrating Information-Related Capabilities into the Joint Operation Planning Process**

- **Covers Multinational Information Operations**

Overview

The ability to share information in near real time, anonymously and/or securely, is a capability that is both an asset and a potential vulnerability to us, our allies, and our adversaries.

The instruments of national power (diplomatic, informational, military, and economic) provide leaders in the US with the means and ways of dealing with crises around the world. Employing these means in the information environment requires the ability to securely transmit, receive, store, and process information in near real time. The nation's state and non-state adversaries are equally aware of the significance of this new technology, and will use information-related capabilities (IRCs) to gain advantages in the information environment, just as they would use more traditional military technologies to gain advantages in other operational environments. As the strategic environment continues to change, so does information operations (IO). Based on these changes, **the Secretary of Defense now characterizes IO as the integrated employment, during military operations, of IRCs in concert with other lines of operation to influence, disrupt, corrupt, or usurp the decision making of adversaries and potential adversaries while protecting our own.**

The Information Environment

The information environment is the aggregate of individuals, organizations, and systems that collect, process, disseminate, or act on information. This environment consists of three

The joint force commander's operational environment is the composite of the conditions, circumstances, and influences that affect employment of capabilities and bear on the decisions of the commander (encompassing physical areas and factors of the air, land, maritime, and space domains) as well as the information environment (which includes cyberspace).

interrelated dimensions, which continuously interact with individuals, organizations, and systems. These dimensions are known as physical, informational, and cognitive. The physical dimension is composed of command and control systems, key decision makers, and supporting infrastructure that enable individuals and organizations to create effects. The informational dimension specifies where and how information is collected, processed, stored, disseminated, and protected. The cognitive dimension encompasses the minds of those who transmit, receive, and respond to or act on information.

The Information and Influence Relational Framework and the Application of Information-Related Capabilities

IRCs are the tools, techniques, or activities that affect any of the three dimensions of the information environment. The joint force (means) employs IRCs (ways) to affect the information provided to or disseminated from the target audience (TA) in the physical and informational dimensions of the information environment to affect decision making.

Information Operations

Information Operations and the Information-Influence Relational Framework

The relational framework describes the application, integration, and synchronization of IRCs to influence, disrupt, corrupt, or usurp the decision making of TAs to create a desired effect to support achievement of an objective.

The Information Operations Staff and Information Operations Cell

Joint force commanders (JFCs) may establish an IO staff to provide command-level oversight and collaborate with all staff directorates and supporting organizations on all aspects of IO. Most combatant commands (CCMDs) include an IO staff to serve as the focal point for IO. Faced with an ongoing or emerging crisis within a geographic combatant commander's (GCC's) area of responsibility, a JFC can establish an IO cell to provide additional expertise and coordination across the staff and interagency.

Relationships and Integration

IO is not about ownership of individual capabilities but rather the use of those capabilities as force multipliers to create a desired effect. There are many military capabilities that contribute to IO and should be taken into consideration during the planning process. These include: strategic communication, joint interagency coordination group, public affairs, civil-military operations, cyberspace operations (CO), information assurance, space operations, military information support operations (MISO), intelligence, military deception, operations security, special technical operations, joint electromagnetic spectrum operations, and key leader engagement.

Authorities, Responsibilities, and Legal Considerations

Authorities

The authority to employ information-related capabilities is rooted foremost in Title 10, United States Code.

Department of Defense (DOD) and Chairman of the Joint Chiefs of Staff (CJCS) directives delegate authorities to DOD components. Among these directives, Department of Defense Directive 3600.01, *Information Operations*, is the principal IO policy document. Its joint counterpart, Chairman of the Joint Chiefs of Staff Instruction 3210.01, *Joint Information Operations Policy,* provides joint policy regarding the use of IRCs, professional qualifications for the joint IO force, as well as joint IO education and training requirements. Based upon the contents of these two documents, authority to conduct joint IO is vested in the combatant commander (CCDR), who in turn can delegate operational authority to a subordinate JFC, as appropriate.

Responsibilities

Under Secretary of Defense for Policy oversees and manages DOD-level IO programs and activities.

Under Secretary of Defense for Intelligence develops, coordinates, and oversees the implementation of DOD intelligence policy, programs, and guidance for intelligence activities supporting IO.

Joint Staff. As the Joint IO Proponent, the Deputy Director for Global Operations (J-39 DDGO) serves as the CJCS's focal point for IO and coordinates with the Joint Staff, CCMDs, and other organizations that have direct or supporting IO responsibilities.

Joint Information Operations Warfare Center (JIOWC) is a CJCS controlled activity reporting to the operations directorate of a joint staff via J-39 DDGO. The JIOWC supports the Joint Staff by ensuring operational integration of IRCs in support of IO, improving DOD's ability to meet CCMD IRC requirements, as well as developing and refining IRCs for use in support of IO across DOD.

Combatant Commands. The Unified Command Plan provides guidance to CCDRs, assigning them missions and force structure, as well as geographic or functional areas of responsibility. In addition to these responsibilities, the Commander, United States Special Operations Command, is also responsible for integrating and coordinating MISO. This responsibility is focused on enhancing interoperability and providing other CCDRs with MISO planning and execution capabilities. In similar fashion, the Commander, United States Strategic Command is responsible for advocating on behalf of the IRCs of electronic warfare and CO.

Service component command responsibilities include recommending to the JFC the proper employment of the Service component IRCs in support of joint IO.

Like Service component commands, **functional component commands** have authority over forces or in the case of IO, IRCs, as delegated by the establishing authority (normally a CCDR or JFC).

Legal Considerations

IO planners deal with legal considerations of an extremely diverse and complex nature. For this reason, joint IO planners should consult their staff judge advocate or legal advisor for expert advice.

Integrating Information-Related Capabilities into the Joint Operation Planning Process

Information Operations Planning

The IO cell chief is responsible to the JFC for integrating IRCs into the joint operation planning process (JOPP). Thus, the IO staff is responsible for coordinating and synchronizing IRCs to accomplish the JFC's objectives. The IO cell chief ensures joint IO planners adequately represent the IO cell within the joint planning group and other JFC planning processes. Doing so will help ensure that IRCs are integrated with all planning efforts. As part of JOPP, designation of release and execution authorities for IRCs is required. Normally, the JFC is designated in the execution order as the execution authority. Given the fact that IRC effects are often required across multiple operational phases, each capability requires separate and distinct authorities.

Information Operations Phasing and Synchronization

Through its contributions to the GCC's theater campaign plan, it is clear that joint IO is expected to play a major role in all phases of joint operations. This means that the GCC's IO staff and IO cell must account for logical transitions from phase to phase, as joint IO moves from the main effort to a supporting effort.

Multinational Information Operations

Other Nations and Information Operations

Multinational partners recognize a variety of information concepts and possess sophisticated doctrine, procedures, and capabilities. Given these potentially diverse perspectives regarding IO, it is essential for the multinational force commander (MNFC) to resolve potential conflicts as soon as possible. It is vital to integrate multinational partners into IO planning as early as possible to gain agreement on an integrated and achievable IO strategy.

Multinational Organization for Information Operations Planning

When the JFC is also the MNFC, the joint force staff should be augmented by planners and subject matter experts from the multinational force (MNF). MNF IO planners and IRC specialists should be trained on US and MNF doctrine, requirements, resources, and how the MNF is structured to integrate IRCs. IO planners should seek to accommodate the requirements of each multinational partner, within given constraints, with the goal of using all the available expertise and capabilities of the MNF.

Multinational Policy Coordination

The Joint Staff coordinates US positions on IO matters delegated to them as a matter of law or policy, and discusses them bilaterally, or in multinational organizations, to achieve interoperability and compatibility in fulfilling common requirements. Direct discussions regarding multinational IO planning in specific theaters are the responsibility of the GCC.

Information Operations Assessment

Information Operations assessment is iterative, continuously repeating rounds of analysis within the operations cycle in order to measure the progress of information related capabilities toward achieving objectives.

Assessment of IO is a key component of the commander's decision cycle, helping to determine the results of tactical actions in the context of overall mission objectives and providing potential recommendations for refinement of future plans. Assessments also provide opportunities to identify IRC shortfalls, changes in parameters and/or conditions in the information environment, which may cause unintended effects in the employment of IRCs, and resource issues that may be impeding joint IO effectiveness.

The Information Operations Assessment Process

A solution to these assessment requirements is the eight-step assessment process.

- Focused characterization of the information environment
- Integrate information operations assessment into plans and develop the assessment plan
- Develop information operations assessment information requirements and collection plans
- Build/modify information operations assessment baseline
- Coordinate and execute information operations and collection activities

- Monitor and collect focused information environment data for information operations assessment
- Analyze information operations assessment data
- Report information operations assessment results and recommendations

Measures and Indicators

Measures of performance (MOPs) and measures of effectiveness (MOEs) help accomplish the assessment process by qualifying or quantifying the intangible attributes of the information environment. The MOP for any one action should be whether or not the TA was exposed to the IO action or activity. MOEs should be observable, to aid with collection; quantifiable, to increase objectivity; precise, to ensure accuracy; and correlated with the progress of the operation, to attain timeliness. Indicators are crucial because they aid the joint IO planner in informing MOEs and should be identifiable across the center of gravity critical factors.

Considerations

Assessment teams may not have direct access to a TA for a variety of reasons. The goal of measurement is not to achieve perfect accuracy or precision—given the ever present biases of theory and the limitations of tools that exist—but rather, to reduce uncertainty about the value being measured.

CONCLUSION

This publication provides joint doctrine for the planning, preparation, execution, and assessment of information operations across the range of military operations.

Other books we publish on Amazon.com

Russia Land-Based Electronic Warfare/RUMINT

Customer reviews

★★★★☆ 4 out of 5

CHINA ELECTRONIC WARFARE WEAPONS/RUMINT

Customer reviews

★★★★☆ 4 out of 5

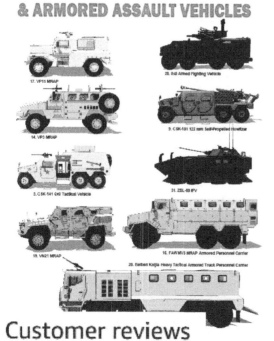

CHINA MRAPs, ARMORED CARS, ARMORED PERSONNEL CARRIERS & ARMORED ASSAULT VEHICLES

Customer reviews

★★★★★ 5 out of 5

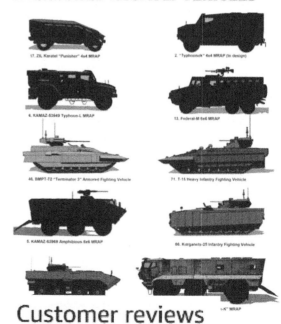

RUSSIA MRAPs, ARMORED CARS, ARMORED PERSONNEL CARRIERS & ARMORED ASSAULT VEHICLES

Customer reviews

★★★★★ 5 out of 5

CHAPTER I
OVERVIEW

"The most hateful human misfortune is for a wise man to have no influence."

Greek Historian Herodotus, 484-425 BC

1. Introduction

a. The growth of communication networks has decreased the number of isolated populations in the world. The emergence of advanced wired and wireless information technology facilitates global communication by corporations, violent extremist organizations, and individuals. The ability to share information in near real time, anonymously and/or securely, is a capability that is both an asset and a potential vulnerability to us, our allies, and our adversaries. Information is a powerful tool to influence, disrupt, corrupt, or usurp an adversary's ability to make and share decisions.

b. The instruments of national power (diplomatic, informational, military, and economic) provide leaders in the United States with the means and ways of dealing with crises around the world. Employing these means in the information environment requires the ability to securely transmit, receive, store, and process information in near real time. The nation's state and non-state adversaries are equally aware of the significance of this new technology, and will use information-related capabilities (IRCs) to gain advantages in the information environment, just as they would use more traditional military technologies to gain advantages in other operational environments. These realities have transformed the information environment into a battlefield, which poses both a threat to the Department of Defense (DOD), combatant commands (CCMDs), and Service components and serves as a force multiplier when leveraged effectively.

c. As the strategic environment continues to change, so does IO. Based on these changes, the Secretary of Defense now characterizes IO as the integrated employment, during military operations, of IRCs in concert with other lines of operation to influence, disrupt, corrupt, or usurp the decision making of adversaries and potential adversaries while protecting our own. This revised characterization has led to a reassessment of how essential the information environment can be and how IRCs can be effectively integrated into joint operations to create effects and operationally exploitable conditions necessary for achieving the joint force commander's (JFC's) objectives.

2. The Information Environment

The information environment is the aggregate of individuals, organizations, and systems that collect, process, disseminate, or act on information. This environment consists of three interrelated dimensions which continuously interact with individuals, organizations, and systems. These dimensions are the physical, informational, and cognitive (see Figure I-1). The JFC's operational environment is the composite of the conditions, circumstances, and influences that affect employment of capabilities and bear on the decisions of the commander

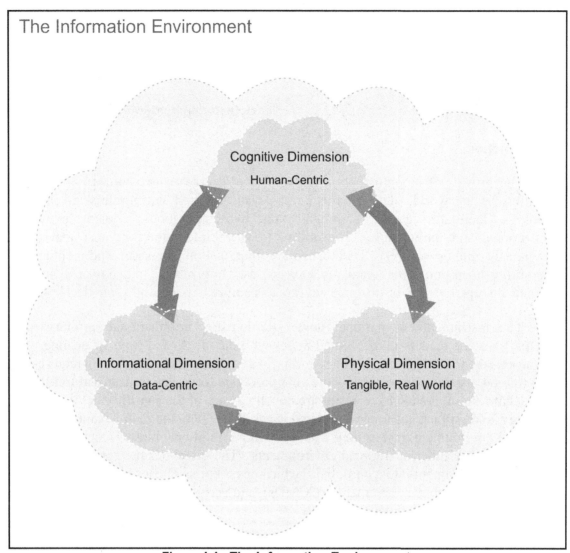

Figure I-1. The Information Environment

(encompassing physical areas and factors of the air, land, maritime, and space domains) as well as the information environment (which includes cyberspace).

a. **The Physical Dimension.** The physical dimension is composed of command and control (C2) systems, key decision makers, and supporting infrastructure that enable individuals and organizations to create effects. It is the dimension where physical platforms and the communications networks that connect them reside. The physical dimension includes, but is not limited to, human beings, C2 facilities, newspapers, books, microwave towers, computer processing units, laptops, smart phones, tablet computers, or any other objects that are subject to empirical measurement. The physical dimension is not confined solely to military or even nation-based systems and processes; it is a defused network connected across national, economic, and geographical boundaries.

b. **The Informational Dimension.** The informational dimension encompasses where and how information is collected, processed, stored, disseminated, and protected. It is the dimension where the C2 of military forces is exercised and where the commander's intent is conveyed. Actions in this dimension affect the content and flow of information.

c. **The Cognitive Dimension.** The cognitive dimension encompasses the minds of those who transmit, receive, and respond to or act on information. It refers to individuals' or groups' information processing, perception, judgment, and decision making. These elements are influenced by many factors, to include individual and cultural beliefs, norms, vulnerabilities, motivations, emotions, experiences, morals, education, mental health, identities, and ideologies. Defining these influencing factors in a given environment is critical for understanding how to best influence the mind of the decision maker and create the desired effects. As such, this dimension constitutes the most important component of the information environment.

3. The Information and Influence Relational Framework and the Application of Information-Related Capabilities

a. IRCs are the tools, techniques, or activities that affect any of the three dimensions of the information environment. They affect the ability of the target audience (TA) to collect, process, or disseminate information before and after decisions are made. The TA is the individual or group selected for influence. The joint force (means) employs IRCs (ways) to affect the information provided to or disseminated from the TA in the physical and informational dimensions of the information environment to affect decision making (see Figure I-2). The change in the TA conditions, capabilities, situational awareness, and in some cases, the inability to make and share timely and informed decisions, contributes to the desired end state. Actions or inactions in the physical dimension can be assessed for future operations. The employment of IRCs is complemented by a set of capabilities such as operations security (OPSEC), information assurance (IA), counterdeception, physical security, electronic warfare (EW) support, and electronic protection. These capabilities are critical to enabling and protecting the JFC's C2 of forces. Key components in this process are:

(1) **Information.** Data in context to inform or provide meaning for action.

(2) **Data.** Interpreted signals that can reduce uncertainty or equivocality.

(3) **Knowledge.** Information in context to enable direct action. Knowledge can be further broken down into the following:

(a) **Explicit Knowledge.** Knowledge that has been articulated through words, diagrams, formulas, computer programs, and like means.

(b) **Tacit Knowledge.** Knowledge that cannot be or has not been articulated through words, diagrams, formulas, computer programs, and like means.

(4) **Influence.** The act or power to produce a desired outcome or end on a TA.

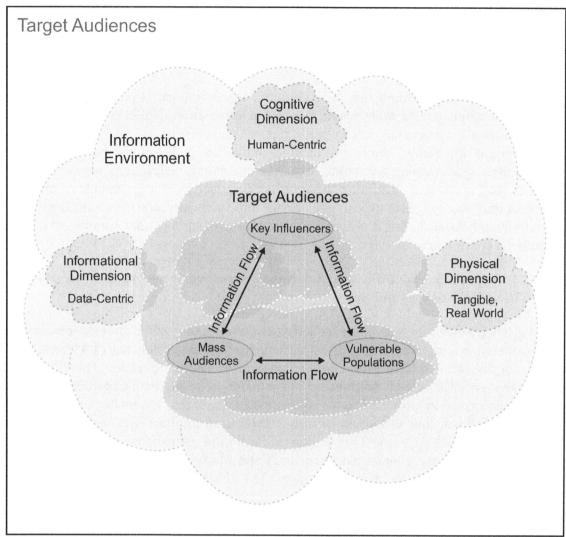

Figure I-2. Target Audiences

(5) **Means.** The resources available to a national government, non-nation actor, or adversary in pursuit of its end(s). These resources include, but are not limited to, public- and private-sector enterprise assets or entities.

(6) **Ways.** How means can be applied, in order to achieve a desired end(s). They can be characterized as persuasive or coercive.

(7) **Information-Related Capabilities.** Tools, techniques, or activities using data, information, or knowledge to create effects and operationally desirable conditions within the physical, informational, and cognitive dimensions of the information environment.

(8) **Target Audience.** An individual or group selected for influence.

(9) **Ends.** A consequence of the way of applying IRCs.

(10) Using the framework, the physical, informational, and cognitive dimensions of the information environment provide access points for influencing TAs (see Figure I-2).

b. The purpose of integrating the employment of IRCs is to influence a TA. While the behavior of individuals and groups, as human social entities, are principally governed by rules, norms, and beliefs, the behaviors of systems principally reside within the physical and informational dimensions and are governed only by rules. Under this construct, rules, norms, and beliefs are:

(1) **Rules.** Explicit regulative processes such as policies, laws, inspection routines, or incentives. Rules function as a coercive regulator of behavior and are dependent upon the imposing entity's ability to enforce them.

(2) **Norms.** Regulative mechanisms accepted by the social collective. Norms are enforced by normative mechanisms within the organization and are not strictly dependent upon law or regulation.

(3) **Beliefs.** The collective perception of fundamental truths governing behavior. The adherence to accepted and shared beliefs by members of a social system will likely persist and be difficult to change over time. Strong beliefs about determinant factors (i.e., security, survival, or honor) are likely to cause a social entity or group to accept rules and norms.

c. The first step in achieving an end(s) through use of the information-influence relational framework is to identify the TA. Once the TA has been identified, it will be necessary to develop an understanding of how that TA perceives its environment, to include analysis of TA rules, norms, and beliefs. Once this analysis is complete, the application of means available to achieve the desired end(s) must be evaluated (see Figure I-3). Such means may include (but are not limited to) diplomatic, informational, military, or economic actions, as well as academic, commercial, religious, or ethnic pronouncements. When the specific means or combinations of means are determined, the next step is to identify the specific ways to create a desired effect.

d. Influencing the behavior of TAs requires producing effects in ways that modify rules, norms, or beliefs. Effects can be created by means (e.g., governmental, academic, cultural, and private enterprise) using specific ways (i.e., IRCs) to affect how the TAs collect, process, perceive, disseminate, and act (or do not act) on information (see Figure I-4).

e. Upon deciding to persuade or coerce a TA, the commander must then determine what IRCs it can apply to individuals, organizations, or systems in order to produce a desired effect(s) (see Figure I-5). As stated, IRCs can be capabilities, techniques, or activities, but they do not necessarily have to be technology-based. Additionally, it is important to focus on the fact that IRCs may come from a wide variety of sources. **Therefore, in IO, it is not the ownership of the capabilities and techniques that is important, but rather their integrated application in order to achieve a JFC's end state.**

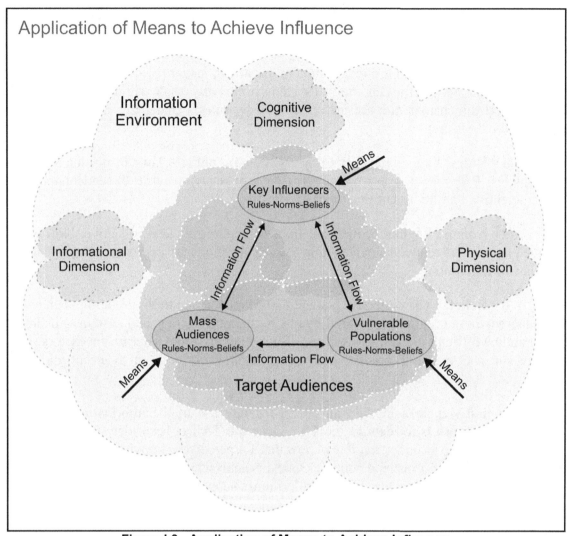

Figure I-3. Application of Means to Achieve Influence

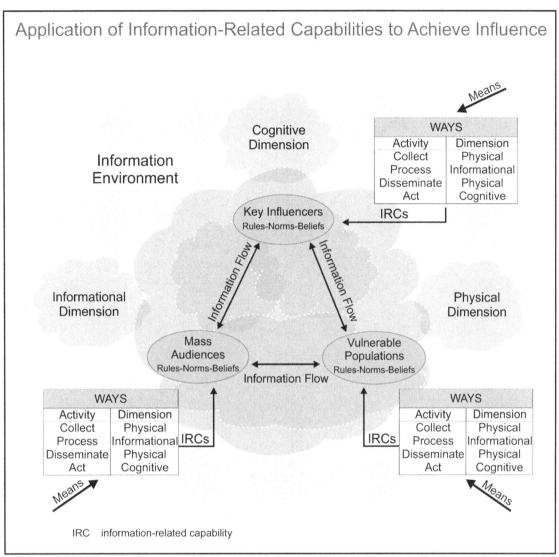

Figure I-4. Application of Information-Related Capabilities to Achieve Influence

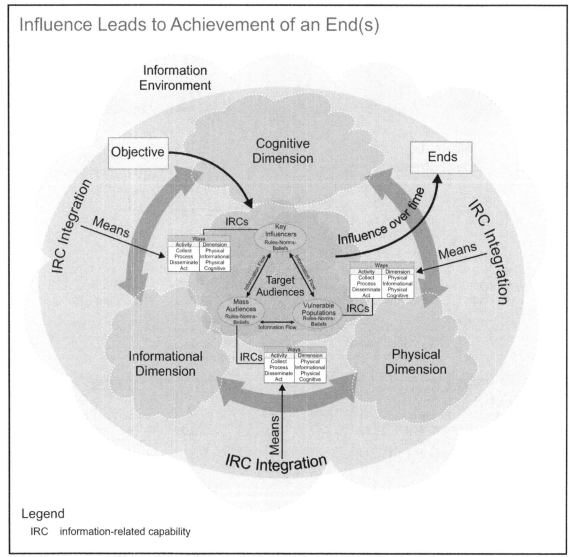

Figure I-5. Influence Leads to Achievement of an End(s)

CHAPTER II
INFORMATION OPERATIONS

"There is a war out there, old friend- a World War. And it's not about whose got the most bullets; it's about who controls the information."

Cosmo, in the 1992 Film "Sneakers"

1. Introduction

This chapter addresses how the integrating and coordinating functions of IO help achieve a JFC's objectives. Through the integrated application of IRCs, the relationships that exist between IO and the various IRCs should be understood in order to achieve an objective.

2. Terminology

a. Because IO takes place in all phases of military operations, in concert with other lines of operation and lines of effort, some clarification of the terms and their relationship to IO is in order.

(1) **Military Operations.** The US military participates in a wide range of military operations, as illustrated in Figure II-1. Phase 0 (Shape) and phase I (Deter) may include defense support of civil authorities, peace operations, noncombatant evacuation, foreign humanitarian assistance, and nation-building assistance, which fall outside the realm of major combat operations represented by phases II through V.

(2) **Lines of Operation and Lines of Effort.** IO should support multiple lines of operation and at times may be the supported line of operation. IO may also support numerous lines of effort when positional references to an enemy or adversary have little relevance, such as in counterinsurgency or stability operations.

b. IO integrates IRCs (ways) with other lines of operation and lines of effort (means) to create a desired effect on an adversary or potential adversary to achieve an objective (ends).

3. Information Operations and the Information-Influence Relational Framework

Influence is at the heart of diplomacy and military operations, with integration of IRCs providing a powerful means for influence. The relational framework describes the application, integration, and synchronization of IRCs to influence, disrupt, corrupt, or usurp the decision making of TAs to create a desired effect to support achievement of an objective. Using this description, the following example illustrates how IRCs can be employed to create a specific effect against an adversary or potential adversary.

Chapter II

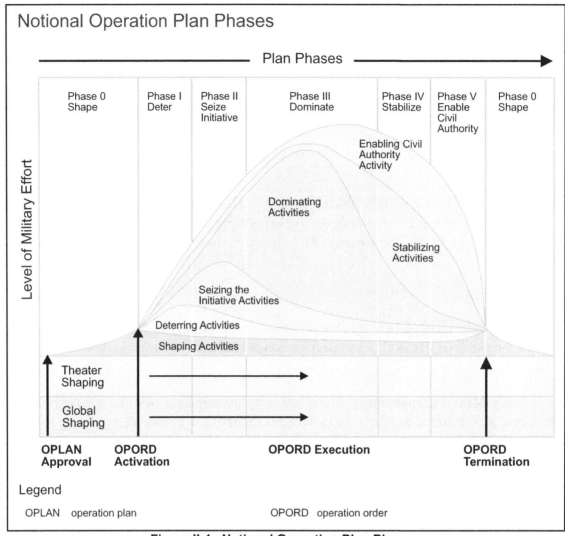

Figure II-1. Notional Operation Plan Phases

4. The Information Operations Staff and Information Operations Cell

Within the joint community, the integration of IRCs to achieve the commander's objectives is managed through an IO staff or IO cell. JFCs may establish an IO staff to provide command-level oversight and collaborate with all staff directorates and supporting organizations on all aspects of IO. Most CCMDs include an IO staff to serve as the focal point for IO. Faced with an ongoing or emerging crisis within a geographic combatant commander's (GCC's) area of responsibility (AOR), a JFC can establish an IO cell to provide additional expertise and coordination across the staff and interagency.

APPLICATION OF INFORMATION-RELATED CAPABILITIES TO THE INFORMATION AND INFLUENCE RELATIONAL FRAMEWORK

This example provides insight as to how information-related capabilities (IRCs) can be used to create lethal and nonlethal effects to support achievement of the objectives to reach the desired end state. The integration and synchronization of these IRCs require participation from not just information operations planners, but also organizations across multiple lines of operation and lines of effort. They may also include input from or coordination with national ministries, provincial governments, local authorities, and cultural and religious leaders to create the desired effect.

Situation: An adversary is attempting to overthrow the government of Country X using both lethal and nonlethal means to demonstrate to the citizens that the government is not fit to support and protect its people.

Joint Force Commander's Objective: Protect government of Country X from being overthrown.

Desired Effects:

1. Citizens have confidence in ability of government to support and protect its people.

2. Adversary is unable to overthrow government of Country X.

Potential Target Audience(s):

1. Adversary leadership (adversary).

2. Country X indigenous population (friendly, neutral, and potential adversary).

Potential Means available to achieve the commander's objective:

- Diplomatic action (e.g., demarche, public diplomacy)

- Informational assets (e.g., strategic communication, media)

- Military forces (e.g., security force assistance, combat operations, military information support operations, public affairs, military deception)

- Economic resources (e.g., sanctions against the adversary, infusion of capital to Country X for nation building)

- Commercial, cultural, or other private enterprise assets

Potential <u>Ways</u> (persuasive communications or coercive force):

- **Targeted radio and television broadcasts**

- **Blockaded adversary ports**

- **Government/commercially operated Web sites**

- **Key leadership engagement**

Regardless of the means and ways employed by the players within the information environment, the reality is that the strategic advantage rests with whoever applies their means and ways most efficiently.

a. **IO Staff**

(1) In order to provide planning support, the IO staff includes IO planners and a complement of IRCs specialists to facilitate seamless integration of IRCs to support the JFC's concept of operations (CONOPS).

(2) IRC specialists can include, but are not limited to, personnel from the EW, cyberspace operations (CO), military information support operations (MISO), civil-military operations (CMO), military deception (MILDEC), intelligence, and public affairs (PA) communities. They provide valuable linkage between the planners within an IO staff and those communities that provide IRCs to facilitate seamless integration with the JFC's objectives.

b. **IO Cell**

(1) The IO cell integrates and synchronizes IRCs, to achieve national or combatant commander (CCDR) level objectives. Normally, the chief of the CCMD's IO staff will serve as the IO cell chief; however, at the joint task force level, someone else may serve as the IO cell chief. Some of the functions of the IO cell chief are listed in Figure II-2.

(2) The IO cell comprises representatives from a wide variety of organizations to coordinate and integrate additional activities in support of a JFC. When considering the notional example in Figure II-3, note that the specific makeup of an IO cell depends on the situation. It may include representatives from organizations outside DOD, even allied or multinational partners.

Information Operations Cell Chief Functions

- Coordinate the overall information operations (IO) portion of the plan for the joint force commander (JFC).

- Coordinate IO issues within the joint force staff and with counterpart IO planners on the component staffs and supporting organizations.

- Coordinate employment of information-related capabilities and activities to support the JFC concept of operations.

- Recommend IO priorities to accomplish planned objectives.

- Determine the availability of information-related capability resources to carry out IO plans.

- Request planning support from organizations that plan and execute information-related capabilities.

- Serve as the primary "advocate" throughout the target nomination and review process for targets that, if engaged, will create a desired effect within the information environment.

- Coordinate the planning and execution of information-related capabilities among joint organizations (including components) and agencies that support IO objectives.

- Identify and coordinate intelligence and assessment requirements that support IO planning and associated activities.

- Coordinate support with the Joint Information Operations Warfare Center, Joint Warfare Analysis Center, and other joint centers and agencies.

Figure II-2. Information Operations Cell Chief Functions

5. Relationships and Integration

a. IO is not about ownership of individual capabilities but rather the use of those capabilities as force multipliers to create a desired effect. There are many military capabilities that contribute to IO and should be taken into consideration during the planning process.

(1) Strategic Communication (SC)

(a) The SC process consists of focused United States Government (USG) efforts to create, strengthen, or preserve conditions favorable for the advancement of national interests, policies, and objectives by understanding and engaging key audiences through the use of coordinated programs, plans, themes, messages, and products synchronized with the actions of all instruments of national power. SC is a whole-of-government approach, driven by interagency processes and integration that are focused upon effectively communicating national strategy.

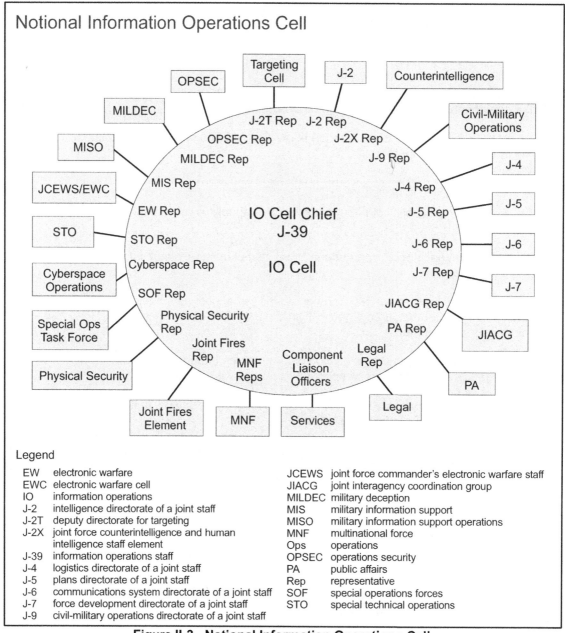

Figure II-3. Notional Information Operations Cell

(b) The elements and organizations that implement strategic guidance, both internal and external to the joint force, must not only understand and be aware of the joint force's IO objectives; they must also work closely with members of the interagency community, in order to ensure full coordination and synchronization of USG efforts. Hence, the JFC's IO objectives should complement the overall objectives in accordance with strategic guidance. The joint interagency coordination group (JIACG) representative within the IO cell facilitates coordination to comply with strategic guidance and facilitate SC.

(2) **Joint Interagency Coordination Group.** Interagency coordination occurs between DOD and other USG departments and agencies, as well as with private-sector entities, nongovernmental organizations, and critical infrastructure activities, for the purpose of accomplishing national objectives. Many of these objectives require the combined and coordinated use of the diplomatic, informational, military, and economic instruments of national power. Due to their forward presence, the CCMDs are well situated to coordinate activities with elements of the USG, regional organizations, foreign forces, and host nations. In order to accomplish this function, the GCCs have established JIACGs as part of their normal staff structures (see Figure II-4). The JIACG is well suited to help the IO cell with interagency coordination. Although IO is not the primary function of the JIACG, the group's linkage to the IO cell and the rest of the interagency is an important enabler for synchronization of guidance and IO.

(3) **Public Affairs**

(a) PA comprises public information, command information, and public engagement activities directed toward both the internal and external publics with interest in DOD. External publics include allies, neutrals, adversaries, and potential adversaries. When addressing external publics, opportunities for overlap exist between PA and IO.

(b) By maintaining situational awareness between IO and PA the potential for information conflict can be minimized. The IO cell provides an excellent place to coordinate IO and PA activities that may affect the adversary or potential adversary. Because there will be situations, such as counterpropaganda, in which the TA for both IO and PA converge, close cooperation and deconfliction are extremely important. Such coordination and deconfliction efforts can begin in the IO cell. However, since it involves more than just IO equities, final coordination should occur within the joint planning group (JPG).

(c) While the IO cell can help synchronize and deconflict specific IO-related and PA objectives, when implementing strategic guidance that affects the adversary, care must be taken to carefully follow all legal and policy constraints in conducting the different activities. For example, see Department of Defense Directive (DODD) S-3321.1, *Overt Psychological Operations Conducted by the Military Services in Peacetime and in Contingencies Short of Declared War.*

(4) **Civil-Military Operations**

(a) CMO is another area that can directly affect and be affected by IO. CMO activities establish, maintain, influence, or exploit relations between military forces, governmental and nongovernmental civilian organizations and authorities, and the civilian populace in a friendly, neutral, or hostile operational area in order to achieve US objectives. These activities may occur prior to, during, or subsequent to other military operations. In CMO, personnel perform functions normally provided by the local, regional, or national government, placing them into direct contact with civilian populations. This level of interaction results in CMO having a significant effect on the perceptions of the local populace. Since this populace may include potential adversaries, their perceptions are of great interest to the IO community. For this reason, CMO representation in the IO cell can

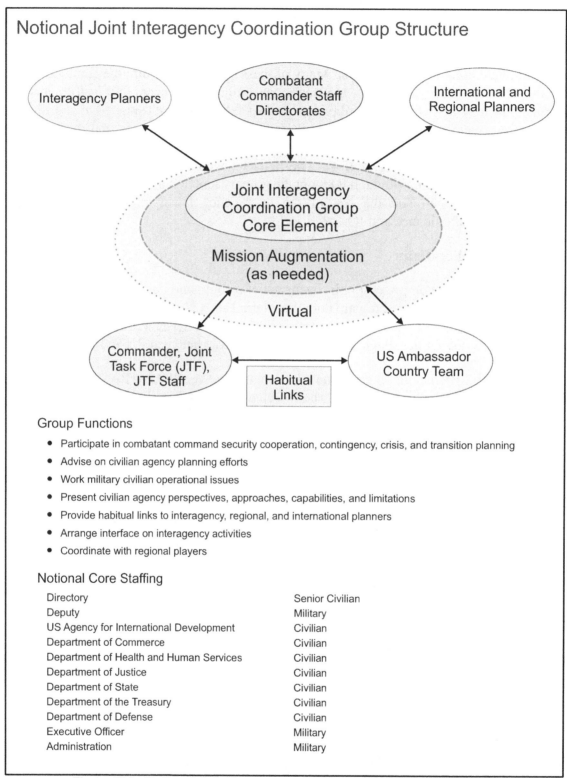

Figure II-4. Notional Joint Interagency Coordination Group Structure

assist in identifying TAs; synchronizing communications media, assets, and messages; and providing news and information to the local population.

(b) Although CMO and IO have much in common, they are distinct disciplines. The TA for much of IO is the adversary; however, the effects of IRCs often reach supporting friendly and neutral populations as well. In a similar vein, CMO seeks to affect friendly and neutral populations, although adversary and potential adversary audiences may also be affected. This being the case, effective integration of CMO with other IRCs is important, and a CMO representative on the IO staff is critical. The regular presence of a CMO representative in the IO cell will greatly promote this level of coordination.

(5) **Cyberspace Operations**

(a) Cyberspace is a global domain within the information environment consisting of the interdependent network of information technology infrastructures and resident data, including the Internet, telecommunications networks, computer systems, and embedded processors and controllers. CO are the employment of cyberspace capabilities where the primary purpose is to achieve objectives in or through cyberspace. Cyberspace capabilities, when in support of IO, deny or manipulate adversary or potential adversary decision making, through targeting an information medium (such as a wireless access point in the physical dimension), the message itself (an encrypted message in the information dimension), or a cyber-persona (an online identity that facilitates communication, decision making, and the influencing of audiences in the cognitive dimension). When employed in support of IO, CO generally focus on the integration of offensive and defensive capabilities exercised in and through cyberspace, in concert with other IRCs, and coordination across multiple lines of operation and lines of effort.

(b) As a process that integrates the employment of IRCs across multiple lines of effort and lines of operation to affect an adversary or potential adversary decision maker, IO can target either the medium (a component within the physical dimension such as a microwave tower) or the message itself (e.g., an encrypted message in the informational dimension). CO is one of several IRCs available to the commander.

For more information, see Joint Publication (JP) 3-12, Cyberspace Operations.

(6) **Information Assurance.** IA is necessary to gain and maintain information superiority. The JFC relies on IA to protect infrastructure to ensure its availability, to position information for influence, and for delivery of information to the adversary. Furthermore, IA and CO are interrelated and rely on each other to support IO.

(7) **Space Operations.** Space capabilities are a significant force multiplier when integrated with joint operations. Space operations support IO through the space force enhancement functions of intelligence, surveillance, and reconnaissance; missile warning; environmental monitoring; satellite communications; and space-based positioning, navigation, and timing. The IO cell is a key place for coordinating and deconflicting the space force enhancement functions with other IRCs.

(8) **Military Information Support Operations.** MISO are planned operations to convey selected information and indicators to foreign audiences to influence their emotions, motives, objective reasoning, and ultimately the behavior of foreign governments,

organizations, groups, and individuals. MISO focuses on the cognitive dimension of the information environment where its TA includes not just potential and actual adversaries, but also friendly and neutral populations. MISO are applicable to a wide range of military operations such as stability operations, security cooperation, maritime interdiction, noncombatant evacuation, foreign humanitarian operations, counterdrug, force protection, and counter-trafficking. Given the wide range of activities in which MISO are employed, the military information support representative within the IO cell should consistently interact with the PA, CMO, JIACG, and IO planners.

(9) **Intelligence**

(a) Intelligence is a vital military capability that supports IO. The utilization of information operations intelligence integration (IOII) greatly facilitates understanding the interrelationship between the physical, informational, and cognitive dimensions of the information environment.

(b) By providing population-centric socio-cultural intelligence and physical network lay downs, including the information transmitted via those networks, intelligence can greatly assist IRC planners and IO integrators in determining the proper effect to elicit the specific response desired. Intelligence is an integrated process, fusing collection, analysis, and dissemination to provide products that will expose a TA's potential capabilities or vulnerabilities. Intelligence uses a variety of technical and nontechnical tools to assess the information environment, thereby providing insight into a TA.

(c) A joint intelligence support element (JISE) may establish an IO support office (see Figure II-5) to provide IOII. This is due to the long lead time needed to establish information baseline characterizations, provide timely intelligence during IO planning and execution efforts, and to properly assess effects in the information environment. In addition to generating intelligence products to support the IO cell, the JISE IO support office can also work with the JISE collection management office to facilitate development of collection requirements in support of IO assessment efforts.

(10) **Military Deception**

(a) One of the oldest IRCs used to influence an adversary's perceptions is MILDEC. MILDEC can be characterized as actions executed to deliberately mislead adversary decision makers, creating conditions that will contribute to the accomplishment of the friendly mission. While MILDEC requires a thorough knowledge of an adversary or potential adversary's decision-making processes, it is important to remember that it is focused on desired behavior. It is not enough to simply mislead the adversary or potential adversary; MILDEC is designed to cause them to behave in a manner advantageous to the friendly mission, such as misallocation of resources, attacking at a time and place advantageous to friendly forces, or avoid taking action at all.

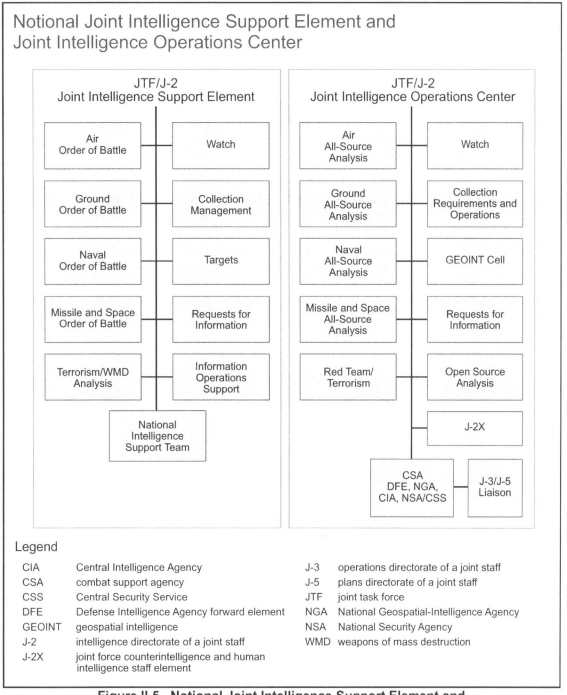

Figure II-5. Notional Joint Intelligence Support Element and
Joint Intelligence Operations Center

(b) When integrated with other IRCs, MILDEC can be a particularly powerful way to affect the decision-making processes of an adversary or potential adversary. The IO cell provides a coordinating mechanism for enabling or integrating MILDEC with other IRCs.

(c) MILDEC differs from other IRCs in several ways. Due to the sensitive nature of MILDEC plans, goals, and objectives, a strict need-to-know should be enforced.

(11) **Operations Security**

(a) OPSEC is a standardized process designed to meet operational needs by mitigating risks associated with specific vulnerabilities in order to deny adversaries critical information and observable indicators. OPSEC identifies critical information and actions attendant to friendly military operations to deny observables to adversary intelligence systems. Once vulnerabilities are identified, other IRCs (e.g., MILDEC, CO) can be used to satisfy OPSEC requirements. OPSEC practices must balance the responsibility to account to the American public with the need to protect critical information. The need to practice OPSEC should not be used as an excuse to deny noncritical information to the public.

(b) The effective application, coordination, and synchronization of other IRCs are critical components in the execution of OPSEC. Because a specified IO task is "to protect our own" decision makers, OPSEC planners require complete situational awareness, regarding friendly activities to facilitate the safeguarding of critical information. This kind of situational awareness exists within the IO cell, where a wide range of planners work in concert to integrate and synchronize their actions to achieve a common IO objective.

(12) **Special Technical Operations (STO).** IO need to be deconflicted and synchronized with STO. Detailed information related to STO and its contribution to IO can be obtained from the STO planners at CCMD or Service component headquarters. IO and STO are separate, but have potential crossover, and for this reason an STO planner is a valuable member of the IO cell.

(13) **Joint Electromagnetic Spectrum Operations (JEMSO)**

(a) All information-related mission areas increasingly depend on the electromagnetic spectrum (EMS). JEMSO, consisting of EW and joint EMS management operations, enable EMS-dependent systems to function in their intended operational environment. EW is the mission area ultimately responsible for securing and maintaining freedom of action in the EMS for friendly forces while exploiting or denying it to adversaries. JEMSO therefore supports IO by enabling successful mission area operations.

(b) EW activities are normally planned and managed by personnel dedicated to JEMSO and members of either the joint force commander's electronic warfare staff (JCEWS) or joint electronic warfare cell (EWC). The JCEWS or EWC integrates their efforts into the JFC's targeting cycle and coordinates with, the JFC's IO cell to align objective priorities and help synchronize EW employment with other IRCs.

For more information on EW, see JP 3-13.1, Electronic Warfare. *For more information on JEMSO, see JP 6-01,* Joint Electromagnetic Spectrum Management Operations.

(14) **Key Leader Engagement (KLE)**

(a) KLEs are deliberate, planned engagements between US military leaders and the leaders of foreign audiences that have defined objectives, such as a change in policy or supporting the JFC's objectives. These engagements can be used to shape and influence foreign leaders at the strategic, operational, and tactical levels, and may also be directed toward specific groups such as religious leaders, academic leaders, and tribal leaders; e.g., to solidify trust and confidence in US forces.

(b) KLEs may be applicable to a wide range of operations such as stability operations, counterinsurgency operations, noncombatant evacuation operations, security cooperation activities, and humanitarian operations. When fully integrated with other IRCs into operations, KLEs can effectively shape and influence the leaders of foreign audiences.

b. The capabilities discussed above do not constitute a comprehensive list of all possible capabilities that can contribute to IO. This means that individual capability ownership will be highly diversified. The ability to access these capabilities will be directly related to how well commanders understand and appreciate the importance of IO.

Other books we publish on Amazon.com

China Surface-to-Air Missile Systems

Customer reviews
4.5 out of 5

Russia Surface-to-Air Missile Systems

Customer reviews
4 out of 5

CHINA UAV, UCAV, SUICIDE DRONES & SPACEPLANES

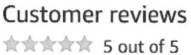

Customer reviews
5 out of 5

Armata Universal Combat Platform

Customer reviews
3.5 out of 5

CHAPTER III
AUTHORITIES, RESPONSIBILITIES, AND LEGAL CONSIDERATIONS

"Well may the boldest fear and the wisest tremble when incurring responsibilities on which may depend our country's peace and prosperity."

President James K. Polk, 1845 Inaugural Address

1. Introduction

This chapter describes the JFC's authority for the conduct of IO; delineates various roles and responsibilities established in DODD 3600.01, *Information Operations;* and addresses legal considerations in the planning and execution of IO.

2. Authorities

a. The authority to employ IRCs is rooted foremost in Title 10, United States Code (USC). While Title 10, USC, does not specify IO separately, it does provide the legal basis for the roles, missions, and organization of DOD and the Services. Title 10, USC, Section 164, gives command authority over assigned forces to the CCDR, which provides that individual with the authority to organize and employ commands and forces, assign tasks, designate objectives, and provide authoritative direction over all aspects of military operations.

b. DOD and Chairman of the Joint Chiefs of Staff (CJCS) directives delegate authorities to DOD components. Among these directives, DODD 3600.01, *Information Operations*, is the principal IO policy document. Its joint counterpart, Chairman of the Joint Chiefs of Staff Instruction (CJCSI) 3210.01, *Joint Information Operations Policy,* provides joint policy regarding the use of IRCs, professional qualifications for the joint IO force, as well as joint IO education and training requirements. Based upon the contents of these two documents, authority to conduct joint IO is vested in the CCDR, who in turn can delegate operational authority to a subordinate JFC, as appropriate.

c. The nature of IO is such that the exercise of operational authority inherently requires a detailed and rigorous legal interpretation of authority and/or legality of specific actions. Legal considerations are addressed in more detail later in this chapter.

3. Responsibilities

a. **Under Secretary of Defense for Policy (USD[P]).** The USD(P) oversees and manages DOD-level IO programs and activities. In this capacity, USD(P) manages guidance publications (e.g., DODD 3600.01) and all IO policy on behalf of the Secretary of Defense. The office of the USD(P) coordinates IO for all DOD components in the interagency process.

b. **Under Secretary of Defense for Intelligence (USD[I]).** USD(I) develops, coordinates, and oversees the implementation of DOD intelligence policy, programs, and guidance for intelligence activities supporting IO.

c. **Joint Staff.** In accordance with the Secretary of Defense memorandum on *Strategic Communication and Information Operations in the DOD*, dated 25 January 2011, the Joint Staff is assigned the responsibility for joint IO proponency. CJCS responsibilities for IO are both general (such as establishing doctrine, as well as providing advice, and recommendations to the President and Secretary of Defense) and specific (e.g., joint IO policy). As the Joint IO Proponent, the Deputy Director for Global Operations (J-39 DDGO) serves as the CJCS's focal point for IO and coordinates with the Joint Staff, CCMDs, and other organizations that have direct or supporting IO responsibilities. Joint Staff J-39 DDGO also provides IO-related advice and advocacy on behalf of the CCMDs to the CJCS and across DOD. As designated in the Secretary of Defense memorandum on SC and IO, the Joint Staff also serves as the proponent for the IRCs of MILDEC and OPSEC.

d. **Joint Information Operations Warfare Center (JIOWC).** The JIOWC is a CJCS-controlled activity reporting to the operations directorate of a joint staff (J-3) via J-39 DDGO. The JIOWC supports the Joint Staff by ensuring operational integration of IRCs in support of IO, improving DOD's ability to meet CCMD IRC requirements, as well as developing and refining IRCs for use in support of IO across DOD. JIOWC's specific organizational responsibilities include:

(1) Provide IO subject matter experts and advice to the Joint Staff and the CCMDs.

(2) Develop and maintain a joint IO assessment framework.

(3) Assist the Joint IO Proponent in advocating for and integrating CCMD IO requirements.

(4) Upon the direction of the Joint IO Proponent, provide support in coordination and integration of DOD IRCs for JFCs, Service component commanders, and DOD agencies.

e. **Combatant Commands.** The Unified Command Plan provides guidance to CCDRs, assigning them missions and force structure, as well as geographic or functional areas of responsibility. In addition to these responsibilities, the Commander, United States Special Operations Command, is also responsible for integrating and coordinating MISO. This responsibility is focused on enhancing interoperability and providing other CCDRs with MISO planning and execution capabilities. In similar fashion, the Commander, United States Strategic Command (USSTRATCOM) is responsible for advocating on behalf of the IRCs of EW and CO. The Commander, USSTRATCOM, is also focused on enhancing interoperability and providing other CCDRs with contingency EW expertise in support of their missions. For CO, the Commander, USSTRATCOM, synchronizes CO planning. CCDRs integrate, plan, execute, and assess IO when conducting operations or campaigns.

f. **Service Component Commands.** Service component command responsibilities are derived from their parent Service. These responsibilities include recommending to the JFC the proper employment of the Service component IRCs in support of joint IO. The JFC will execute IO using component capabilities.

g. **Functional Component Commands.** Like Service component commands, functional component commands have authority over forces or in the case of IO, IRCs, as delegated by the establishing authority (normally a CCDR or JFC). Functional component commands may be tasked to plan and execute IO as an integrated part of joint operations.

4. Legal Considerations

a. **Introduction.** US military activities in the information environment, as with all military operations, are conducted as a matter of law and policy. Joint IO will always involve legal and policy questions, requiring not just local review, but often national-level coordination and approval. The US Constitution, laws, regulations, and policy, and international law set boundaries for all military activity, to include IO. Whether physically operating from locations outside the US or virtually from any location in the information environment, US forces are required by law and policy to act in accordance with US law and the law of war.

b. **Legal Considerations.** IO planners deal with legal considerations of an extremely diverse and complex nature. Legal interpretations can occasionally differ, given the complexity of technologies involved, the significance of legal interests potentially affected, and the challenges inherent for law and policy to keep pace with the technological changes and implementation of IRCs. Additionally, policies are regularly added, amended, and rescinded in an effort to provide clarity. As a result, IO remains a dynamic arena, which can be further complicated by multinational operations, as each nation has its own laws, policies, and processes for approving plans. The brief discussion in this publication is not a substitute for sound legal advice regarding specific IRC- and IO-related activities. For this reason, joint IO planners should consult their staff judge advocate or legal advisor for expert advice.

c. **Implications Beyond the JFC.** Bilateral agreements to which the US is a signatory may have provisions concerning the conduct of IO as well as IRCs when they are used in support of IO. IO planners at all levels should consider the following broad areas within each planning iteration in consultation with the appropriate legal advisor:

(1) Could the execution of a particular IRC be considered a hostile act by an adversary or potential adversary?

(2) Do any non-US laws concerning national security, privacy, or information exchange, criminal and/or civil issues apply?

(3) What are the international treaties, agreements, or customary laws recognized by an adversary or potential adversary that apply to IRCs?

(4) How is the joint force interacting with or being supported by US intelligence organizations and other interagency entities?

Other books we publish on Amazon.com

Customer reviews

★★★★★ 4.6 out of 5

Customer reviews

★★★☆☆ 3 out of 5

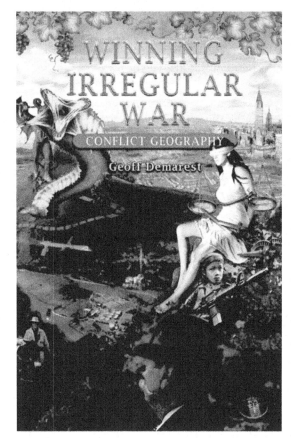

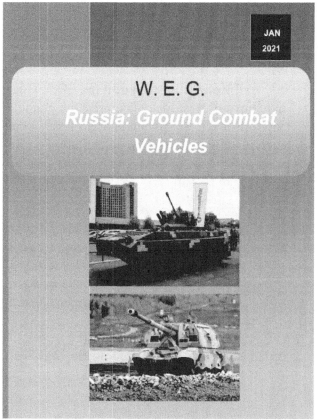

CHAPTER IV
INTEGRATING INFORMATION-RELATED CAPABILITIES INTO THE JOINT OPERATION PLANNING PROCESS

> *"Support planning is conducted in parallel with other planning and encompasses such essential factors as IO [information operations], SC [strategic communication]…"*
>
> **Joint Publication 5-0,** *Joint Operation Planning*, **11 August 2011**

1. Introduction

The IO cell chief is responsible to the JFC for integrating IRCs into the joint operation planning process (JOPP). Thus, the IO staff is responsible for coordinating and synchronizing IRCs to accomplish the JFC's objectives. Coordinated IO are essential in employing the elements of operational design. Conversely, uncoordinated IO efforts can compromise, complicate, negate, and pose risks to the successful accomplishment of the JFC and USG objectives. Additionally, when uncoordinated, other USG and/or multinational information activities, may complicate, defeat, or render DOD IO ineffective. For this reason, the JFC's objectives require early detailed IO staff planning, coordination, and deconfliction between the USG and partner nations' efforts within the AOR, in order to effectively synchronize and integrate IRCs.

2. Information Operations Planning

a. **The IO cell and the JPG.** The IO cell chief ensures joint IO planners adequately represent the IO cell within the JPG and other JFC planning processes. Doing so will help ensure that IRCs are integrated with all planning efforts. Joint IO planners should be integrated with the joint force planning, directing, monitoring, and assessing process.

b. **IO Planning Considerations**

(1) IO planners seek to create an operational advantage that results in coordinated effects that directly support the JFC's objectives. IRCs can be executed throughout the operational environment, but often directly impact the content and flow of information.

(2) IO planning begins at the **earliest stage** of JOPP and must be an integral part of, not an addition to, the overall planning effort. IRCs can be used in all phases of a campaign or operation, but their effective employment during the shape and deter phases can have a significant impact on remaining phases.

(3) The use of IO to achieve the JFC's objectives requires the ability to integrate IRCs and interagency support into a comprehensive and coherent strategy that supports the JFC's overall mission objectives. The GCC's theater security cooperation guidance contained in the theater campaign plan (TCP) serves as an excellent platform to embed specific long-term information objectives during phase 0 operations. For this reason, the IO

staff and IO cell should work closely with their plans directorate staff as well as the JIACG in the development of the security cooperation portion of the TCP.

(4) Many IRCs require long lead time for development of the joint intelligence preparation of the operational environment (JIPOE) and release authority. The intelligence directorate of a joint staff (J-2) identifies intelligence and information gaps, shortfalls, and priorities as part of the JIPOE process in the early stages of the JOPP. Concurrently, the IO cell must identify similar intelligence gaps in its understanding of the information environment to determine if it has sufficient information to successfully plan IO. Where identified shortfalls exist, the IO cell may need to work with J-2 to submit requests for information (RFIs) to the J-2 to fill gaps that cannot be filled internally.

(5) There may be times where the JFC may lack sufficient detailed intelligence data and intelligence staff personnel to provide IOII. Similarly, a JFC's staff may lack dedicated resources to provide support. For this reason, it is imperative the IO cell take a proactive approach to intelligence support. The IO cell must also review and provide input to the commander's critical information requirements (CCIRs), especially priority intelligence requirements (PIRs) and information requirements. The joint intelligence staff, using PIRs as a basis, develops information requirements that are most critical. These are also known as essential elements of information (EEIs). In the course of mission analysis, the intelligence analyst identifies the intelligence required to CCIRs. Intelligence staffs develop more specific questions known as information requirements. EEIs pertinent to the IO staff may include target information specifics, such as messages and counter-messages, adversary propaganda, and responses of individuals, groups, and organizations to adversary propaganda.

(6) As part of JOPP, designation of release and execution authorities for IRCs is required. For example, release authority provides approval for the employment of specific IRCs in support of a commander's objectives and normally specifies the allocation of specific offensive means and IRCs. For its part, the execution authority constitutes the authority to employ IRCs. Normally, the JFC is designated in the execution order as the execution authority. Given the fact that IRC effects are often required across multiple operational phases, each capability requires separate and distinct authorities.

c. **IO and the Joint Operation Planning Process**

Throughout JOPP, IRCs are integrated with the JFC's overall CONOPS (see Figure IV-1). An overview of the seven steps of JOPP follow; however, a more detailed discussion of the planning process can be found in JP 5-0, *Joint Operation Planning*.

(1) **Planning Initiation.** Integration of IRCs into joint operations should begin at step 1, planning initiation. Key IO staff actions during this step include the following:

(a) Review key strategic documents.

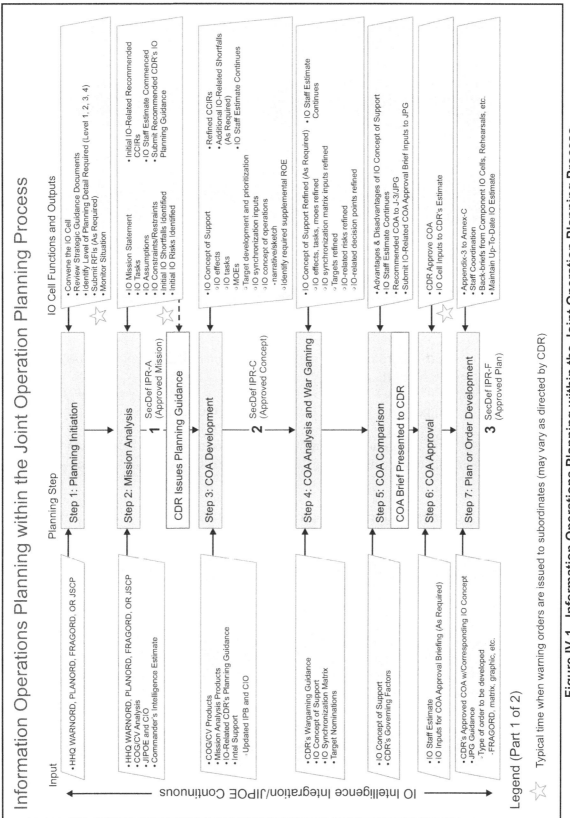

Figure IV-1. Information Operations Planning within the Joint Operation Planning Process

Information Operations Planning within the Joint Operation Planning Process (continued)

Legend (Part 2 of 2)

CCIR	commander's critical information requirement	J-3	operations directorate of a joint staff
CDR	commander	JIPOE	joint intelligence preparation of the
CIO	combined information overlay		operational environment
COA	course of action	JPG	joint planning group
COG	center of gravity	JSCP	Joint Strategic Capabilities Plan
CV	critical vulnerability	MOE	measure of effectiveness
FRAGORD	fragmentary order	PLANORD	planning order
HHQ	higher headquarters	RFI	request for information
IPB	intelligence preparation of the battlespace	ROE	rules of engagement
IPR	in-progress review	SecDef	Secretary of Defense
IO	information operations	WARNORD	warning order

Figure IV-1. Information Operations Planning within the Joint Operation Planning Process (cont'd)

(b) Monitor the situation, receive initial planning guidance, and review staff estimates from applicable operation plans (OPLANs) and concept plans (CONPLANs).

(c) Alert subordinate and supporting commanders of potential tasking with regard to IO planning support.

(d) Gauge initial scope of IO required for the operation.

(e) Identify location, standard operating procedures, and battle rhythm of other staff organizations that require integration and divide coordination responsibilities among the IO staff.

(f) Identify and request appropriate authorities.

(g) Begin identifying information required for mission analysis and course of action (COA) development.

(h) Identify IO planning support requirements (including staff augmentation, support products, and services) and issue requests for support according to procedures established locally and by various supporting organizations.

(i) Validate, initiate, and revise PIRs and RFIs, keeping in mind the long lead times associated with satisfying IO requirements.

(j) Provide IO input and recommendations to COAs, and provide resolutions to conflicts that exist with other plans or lines of operation.

(k) In coordination with the targeting cell, submit potential candidate targets to JFC or component joint targeting coordination board (JTCB). For vetting, validation, and deconfliction follow local targeting cell procedures because these three separate processes do not always occur at the JTCB.

(l) Ensure IO staff and IO cell members participate in all JFC or component planning and targeting sessions and JTCBs.

(2) **Mission Analysis.** The purpose of step 2, mission analysis, is to understand the problem and purpose of an operation and issue the appropriate guidance to drive the remaining steps of the planning process. The end state of mission analysis is a clearly defined mission and thorough staff assessment of the joint operation. Mission analysis orients the JFC and staff on the problem and develops a common understanding, before moving forward in the planning process. During mission analysis, all staff sections, including the IO cell, will examine the mission from their own functional perspective and contribute the results of that analysis to the JPG. As IO impacts each element of the operational environment, it is important for the IO staff and IO cell during mission analysis to remain focused on the information environment. Key IO staff actions during mission analysis are:

(a) Assist the J-3 and J-2 in the identification of friendly and adversary center(s) of gravity and critical factors (e.g., critical capabilities, critical requirements, and critical vulnerabilities).

(b) Identify relevant aspects of the physical, informational, and cognitive dimensions (whether friendly, neutral, adversary, or potential adversary) of the information environment.

(c) Identify specified, implied, and essential tasks.

(d) Identify facts, assumptions, constraints, and restraints affecting IO planning.

(e) Analyze IRCs available to support IO and authorities required for their employment.

(f) Develop and refine proposed PIRs, RFIs, and CCIRs.

(g) Conduct initial IO-related risk assessment.

(h) Develop IO mission statement.

(i) Begin developing the initial IO staff estimate. This estimate forms the basis for the IO cell chief's recommendation to the JFC, regarding which COA it can best support.

(j) Conduct initial force allocation review.

(k) Identify and develop potential targets and coordinate with the targeting cell no later than the end of target development. Compile and maintain target folders in the Modernized Integrated Database. Coordinate with the J-2 and targeting cell for participation and representation in vetting, validation, and targeting boards (e.g., JTCB, joint targeting working group).

(l) Develop mission success criteria.

(3) **COA Development.** Output from mission analysis, such as initial staff estimates, mission and tasks, and JFC planning guidance are used in step 3, COA development. Key IO staff actions during this step include the following:

(a) Identify desired and undesired effects that support or degrade JFC's information objectives.

(b) Develop measures of effectiveness (MOEs) and measures of effectiveness indicators (MOEIs).

(c) Develop tasks for recommendation to the J-3.

(d) Recommend IRCs that may be used to accomplish supporting information tasks for each COA.

(e) Analyze required supplemental rules of engagement (ROE).

(f) Identify additional operational risks and controls/mitigation.

(g) Develop the IO CONOPS narrative/sketch.

(h) Synchronize IRCs in time, space, and purpose.

(i) Continue update/development of the IO staff estimate.

(j) Prepare inputs to the COA brief.

(k) Provide inputs to the target folder.

(4) **COA Analysis and War Gaming.** Based upon time available, the JFC staff should war game each tentative COA against adversary COAs identified through the JIPOE process. Key IO staff and IO cell actions during this step include the following:

(a) Analyze each COA from an IO functional perspective.

(b) Reveal key decision points.

(c) Recommend task adjustments to IRCs as appropriate.

(d) Provide IO-focused data for use in a synchronization matrix or other decision-making tool.

(e) Identify IO portions of branches and sequels.

(f) Identify possible high-value targets related to IO.

(g) Submit PIRs and recommend CCIRs for IO.

(h) Revise staff estimate.

(i) Assess risk.

(5) **COA Comparison.** Step 5, COA comparison, starts with all staff elements analyzing and evaluating the advantages and disadvantages of each COA from their respective viewpoints. Key IO staff and IO cell actions during this step include the following:

(a) Compare each COA based on mission and tasks.

(b) Compare each COA in relation to IO requirements versus available IRCs.

(c) Prioritize COAs from an IO perspective.

(d) Revise the IO staff estimate. During execution, the IO cell should maintain an estimate and update as required.

(6) **COA Approval.** Just like other elements of the JFC's staff, during step 6, COA approval, the IO staff provides the JFC with a clear recommendation of how IO can best contribute to mission accomplishment in the COA(s) being briefed. It is vital this recommendation is presented in a clear, concise manner that is not only able to be quickly grasped by the JFC, but can also be easily understood by peer, subordinate, and higher-headquarters command and staff elements. Failure to foster such an understanding of IO contribution to the approved COA can lead to poor execution and/or coordination of IRCs in subsequent operations.

(7) **Plan or Order Development.** Once a COA is selected and approved, the IO staff develops appendix 3 (Information Operations) to annex C (Operations) of the operation order (OPORD) or OPLAN. Because IRC integration is documented elsewhere in the OPORD or OPLAN, it is imperative that the IO staff conduct effective staff coordination within the JPG during step 7, plan or order development. Key staff actions during this step include the following:

(a) Refine tasks from the approved COA.

(b) Identify shortfalls of IRCs and recommend solutions.

(c) Facilitate development of supporting plans by keeping the responsible organizations informed of relevant details (as access restrictions allow) throughout the planning process.

(d) Advise the supported commander on IO issues and concerns during the supporting plan review and approval process.

(e) Participate in time-phased force and deployment data refinement to ensure IO supports the OPLAN or CONPLAN.

(f) Assist in the development of OPLAN or CONPLAN appendix 6 (IO Intelligence Integration) to annex B (Intelligence).

d. **Plan Refinement.** The information environment is continuously changing and it is critical for IO planners to remain in constant interaction with the JPG to provide updates to OPLANs or CONPLANs.

e. **Assessment of IO.** Assessment is integrated into all phases of the planning and execution cycle, and consists of assessment activities associated with tasks, events, or programs in support of joint military operations. Assessment seeks to analyze and inform on the performance and effectiveness of activities. The intent is to provide relevant feedback to decision makers in order to modify activities that achieve desired results. Assessment can also provide the programmatic community with relevant information that informs on return on investment and operational effectiveness of DOD IRCs. It is important to note that integration of assessment into planning is the first step of the assessment process. Planning for assessment is part of broader operational planning, rather than an afterthought. Iterative in nature, assessment supports the Adaptive Planning and Execution process, and provides feedback to operations and ultimately, IO enterprise programmatics.

For more on assessments, see JP 5-0, Joint Operation Planning.

f. **Relationship Between Measures of Performance (MOPs) and MOEs.** Effectiveness assessment is one of the greatest challenges facing a staff. Despite the continuing evolution of joint and Service doctrine and the refinement of supporting tactics, techniques, and procedures, assessing the effectiveness of IRCs continues to be challenging. MOEs attempt to accomplish this assessment by quantifying the intangible attributes within the information environment, in order to assess the effectiveness of IRCs against an adversary or potential adversary. Figures IV-2 and IV-3 are tangible examples of MOP and MOE sources that an IO planner would have to rely on for feedback.

(1) MOPs are criteria used to assess friendly accomplishment of tasks and mission execution.

Examples of Measures of Performance Feedback

- Numbers of populace listening to military information support operations (MISO) broadcasts
- Percentage of adversary command and control facilities attacked
- Number of civil-military operations projects initiated/number of projects completed
- Human intelligence reports number of MISO broadcasts during Commando Solo missions

Figure IV-2. Examples of Measures of Performance Feedback

Possible Sources of Measures of Effectiveness Feedback

- Intelligence assessments (human intelligence, etc.)
- Open source intelligence
- Internet (newsgroups, etc.)
- Military information support operations, and civil-military operations teams (face to face activities)
- Contact with the public
- Press inquiries and comments
- Department of State polls, reports and surveys (reports)
- Open Source Center
- Nongovernmental organizations, intergovernmental organizations, international organizations, and host nation organizations
- Foreign policy advisor meetings
- Commercial polls
- Operational analysis cells

Figure IV-3. Possible Sources of Measures of Effectiveness Feedback

(2) In contrast to MOPs, MOEs are criteria used to assess changes in system behavior, capability, or operational environment that are tied to measuring the attainment of an end state, achievement of an objective, or creation of an effect. Ultimately, MOEs determine whether actions being executed are creating desired effects, thereby accomplishing the JFC's information objectives and end state.

(3) MOEs and MOPs are both crafted and refined throughout JOPP. In developing MOEs and/or MOPs, the following general criteria should be considered:

(a) **Ends Related.** MOEs and/or MOPs should directly relate to the objectives and desired tasks required to accomplish effects and/or performance.

(b) **Measurable.** MOEs should be *specific, measurable,* and *observable.* Effectiveness or performance is measured either quantitatively (e.g., counting the number of attacks) or qualitatively (e.g., subjectively evaluating the level of confidence in the security forces). In the case of MOEs, **a baseline measurement must be established prior to the execution, against which to measure system changes.**

(c) **Timely.** A time for required feedback should be clearly stated for each MOE and/or MOP and a plan made to report within that specified time period.

(d) **Properly Resourced.** The collection, analysis, and reporting of MOE or MOP data requires personnel, financial, and materiel resources. The IO staff or IO cell

---

should ensure that these resource requirements are built into IO planning during COA development and closely coordinated with the J-2 collection manager to ensure the means to assess these measures are in place.

(4) **Measure of Effectiveness Indicators.** An MOEI is a unit, location, or event observed or measured, that can be used to assess an MOE. These are often used to add quantitative data points to qualitative MOEs and can assist an IO staff or IO cell in answering a question related to a qualitative MOE. The identification of MOEIs aids the IO staff or IO cell in determining an MOE and can be identified from across the information environment. MOEIs can be independently weighted for their contribution to an MOE and should be based on separate criteria. Hundreds of MOEIs may be needed for a large scale contingency. Examples of how effects can be translated into MOEIs include the following:

(a) **Effect:** Increase in the city populace's participation in civil governance.

1. **MOE:** (Qualitative) Metropolitan citizens display increased support for the democratic leadership elected on 1 July. (What activity trends show progress toward or away from the desired behavior?)

2. **MOEI:**

a. A decrease in the number of anti-government rallies/demonstrations in a city since 1 July (this indicator might be weighted heavily at 60 percent of this MOE's total assessment based on rallies/demonstrations observed.)

b. An increase in the percentage of positive new government media stories since 1 July (this indicator might be weighted less heavily at 20 percent of this MOE's total assessment based on media monitoring.)

c. An increase in the number of citizens participating in democratic functions since 1 July (this indicator might be weighted at 20 percent of this MOE's total assessment based on government data/criteria like voter registration, city council meeting attendance, and business license registration.)

(b) **Effect:** Insurgent leadership does not orchestrate terrorist acts in the western region.

1. **MOE:** (Qualitative) Decrease in popular support toward extremists and insurgents.

2. **MOEI:**

a. An increase in the number of insurgents turned in/identified since 1 October.

b. An increase in the amount of money disbursed to citizens from the "rewards program" since 1 October.

c. The percentage of blogs supportive of the local officials.

3. Information Operations Phasing and Synchronization

Through its contributions to the GCC's TCP, it is clear that joint IO is expected to play a major role in all phases of joint operations. This means that the GCC's IO staff and IO cell must account for logical transitions from phase to phase, as joint IO moves from the main effort to a supporting effort. Regardless of what operational phase may be underway, it is always important for the IO staff and IO cell to determine what legal authorities the JFC requires to execute IRCs during the subsequent operations phase.

a. **Phase 0–Shape.** Joint IO planning should focus on supporting the TCP to deter adversaries and potential adversaries from posing significant threats to US objectives. Joint IO planners should access the JIACG through the IO cell or staff. Joint IO planning during this phase will need to prioritize and integrate efforts and resources to support activities throughout the interagency. Due to competing resources and the potential lack of available IRCs, executing joint IO during phase 0 can be challenging. For this reason, the IO staff and IO cell will need to consider how their IO activities fit in as part of a whole-of-government approach to effectively shape the information environment to achieve the CCDR's information objectives.

b. **Phase I–Deter.** During this phase, joint IO is often the main effort for the CCMD. Planning will likely emphasize the JFC's flexible deterrent options (FDOs), complementing US public diplomacy efforts, in order to influence a potential foreign adversary decision maker to make decisions favorable to US goals and objectives. Joint IO planning for this phase is especially complicated because the FDO typically must have a chance to work, while still allowing for a smooth transition to phase II and more intense levels of conflict, if it does not. Because the transition from phase I to phase II may not allow enough time for application of IRCs to create the desired effects on an adversary or potential adversary, the phase change may be abrupt.

c. **Phase II-Seize Initiative.** In phase II, joint IO is supporting multiple lines of operation. Joint IO planning during phase II should focus on maximizing synchronized IRC effects to support the JFC's objectives and the component missions while preparing the transition to the next phase.

d. **Phase III–Dominate.** Joint IO can be a supporting and/or a supported line of operation during phase III. Joint IO planning during phase III will involve developing an information advantage across multiple lines of operation to execute the mission.

e. **Phase IV–Stabilize.** CMO, or even IO, is likely the supported line of operation during phase IV. Joint IO planning during this phase will need to be flexible enough to simultaneously support CMO and combat operations. As the US military and interagency information activity capacity matures and eventually slows, the JFC should assist the host-nation security forces and government information capacity to resume and expand, as necessary. As host nation information capacity improves, the JFC should be able to refocus joint IO efforts to other mission areas. Expanding host-nation capacity through military and interagency efforts will help foster success in the next phase.

f. **Phase V-Enable Civil Authority.** During phase V, joint IO planning focuses on supporting the redeployment of US forces, as well as providing continued support to stability operations. IO planning during phase V should account for interagency and country team efforts to resume the lead mission for information within the host nation territory. The IO staff and cell can anticipate the possibility of long term US commercial and government support to the former adversary's economic and political interests to continue through the completion of this phase.

CHAPTER V
MULTINATIONAL INFORMATION OPERATIONS

"In order more effectively to achieve the objectives of this Treaty, the Parties, separately and jointly, by means of continuous and effective self-help and mutual aid, will maintain and develop their individual and collective capacity to resist armed attack."

Article 3, The North Atlantic Treaty, April 4, 1949

1. Introduction

Joint doctrine for multinational operations, including command and operations in a multinational environment, is described in JP 3-16, *Multinational Operations*. The purpose of this chapter is to highlight specific doctrinal components of IO in a multinational environment (see Figure V-1). In doing so, this chapter will build upon those aspects of IO addressed in JP 3-16. Additional data regarding IO in a multinational environment can be found in Allied Joint Publication (AJP)-3.10, *Allied Joint Doctrine for Information Operations*. This chapter includes IO coordination processes, staff requirements, planning formats, and matrices for staff and commanders involved in a multinational operation.

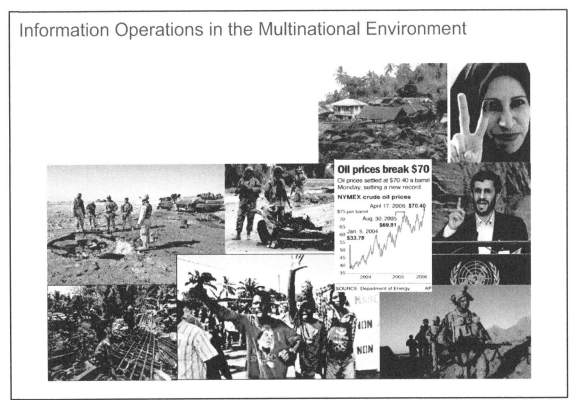

Figure V-1. Information Operations in the Multinational Environment

2. Other Nations and Information Operations

a. Multinational partners recognize a variety of information concepts and possess sophisticated doctrine, procedures, and capabilities. Given these potentially diverse perspectives regarding IO, it is essential for the multinational force commander (MNFC) to resolve potential conflicts as soon as possible. It is vital to integrate multinational partners into IO planning as early as possible to gain agreement on an integrated and achievable IO strategy. Initial requirements for coordinating, synchronizing, and when required integrating other nations into the US IO plan include:

(1) Clarifying all multinational partner information objectives.

(2) Understanding all multinational partner employment of IRCs.

(3) Establishing IO deconfliction procedures to avoid conflicting messages.

(4) Identifying multinational force (MNF) vulnerabilities as soon as possible.

(5) Developing a strategy to mitigate MNF IO vulnerabilities.

(6) Identifying MNF IRCs.

b. Regardless of the maturity of each partner's IO strategy, doctrine, capabilities, tactics, techniques, or procedures, every multinational partner can contribute to MNF IO by providing regional expertise to assist in planning and conducting IO. Multinational partners have developed unique approaches to IO that are tailored for specific targets in ways that may not be employed by the US. Such contributions complement US IO expertise and IRCs, potentially enhancing the quality of both the planning and execution of multinational IO.

3. Multinational Information Operations Considerations

a. Military operation planning processes, particularly for IO, whether JOPP based or based on established or agreed to multinational planning processes, include an understanding of multinational partner(s):

(1) Cultural values and institutions.

(2) Interests and concerns.

(3) Moral and ethical values.

(4) ROE and legal constraints.

(5) Challenges in multilingual planning for the employment of IRCs.

(6) IO doctrine, techniques, and procedures.

b. Sharing of information with multinational partners.

(1) Each nation has various IRCs to provide, in support of multinational objectives. These nations are obliged to protect information that they cannot share across the MNF. However, to plan thoroughly, all nations must be willing to share appropriate information to accomplish the assigned mission.

(2) Information sharing arrangements in formal alliances, to include US participation in United Nations missions, are worked out as part of alliance protocols. Information sharing arrangements in ad hoc multinational operations where coalitions are working together on a short-notice mission must be created during the establishment of the coalition.

(3) Using National Disclosure Policy (NDP) 1, *National Policy and Procedures for the Disclosure of Classified Military Information to Foreign Governments and International Organizations*, and Department of Defense Instruction (DODI) O-3600.02, *Information Operations (IO) Security Classification Guidance (U)*, as guidance, the senior US commander in a multinational operation must provide guidelines to the US-designated disclosure representative on information sharing and the release of classified information or capabilities to the MNF. NDP 1 provides policy and procedures in the form of specific disclosure criteria and limitations, definition of terms, release arrangements, and other guidance. The disclosure of classified information is never automatic. It is not necessary for MNFs to be made aware of all US intelligence, capabilities, or procedures that are required for planning and execution of IO. The JFC should request approval from higher command authorities to release information that has not been previously cleared for multinational partners.

(4) Information concerning US persons may only be collected, retained, or disseminated in accordance with law and regulation. Applicable provisions include: the Privacy Act, Title 5, USC, Section 552a; DODD 5200.27, *Acquisition of Information Concerning Persons and Organizations not Affiliated with the Department of Defense*; Executive Order 12333, *United States Intelligence Activities*; and DOD 5240.1-R, *Procedures Governing the Activities of DOD Intelligence Components that Affect United States Persons.*

4. Planning, Integration, and Command and Control of Information Operations in Multinational Operations

a. The role of IO in multinational operations is the prerogative of the MNFC. The mission of the MNF determines the role of IO in each specific operation.

b. Representation of key multinational partners in the MNF IO cell allows their expertise and capabilities to be utilized, and the IO portion of the plan to be better coordinated and more timely.

c. While some multinational partners may not have developed an IO concept or fielded IRCs, it is important that they fully appreciate the importance of the information in achieving the MNFC's objectives. For this reason, every effort should be made to provide basic-level IO training to multinational partners serving on the MNF IO staff. In cases where this is not possible, it may be necessary for the MNF headquarters staff to assist the subordinate MNFCs in planning and conducting IO.

d. MNF headquarters staff could be organized differently; however, as a general rule, an information operations coordination board (IOCB) or similar organization may exist (see Figure V-2). The IOCB is normally responsible for preparing inputs to relevant MNF headquarters internal and external processes such as joint targeting and provides a forum to outline current and future application of IRCs designed to achieve MNFC's objectives. A wide range of MNF headquarters staff organizations should participate in IOCB deliberations to ensure their input and subject matter expertise can be applied to satisfy a requirement in order to achieve MNFC's objectives.

e. Besides the coordination activities highlighted above, the IOCB should also participate in appropriate joint operations planning groups (JOPGs) and should take part in early discussions, including mission analysis. An IO presence on the JOPG is essential, as it is the IOCB which provides input to the overall estimate process in close coordination with other members of the MNF headquarters staff.

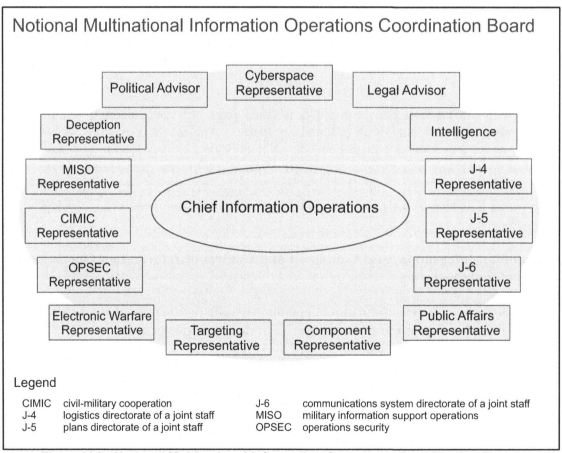

Figure V-2. Notional Multinational Information Operations Coordination Board

5. Multinational Organization for Information Operations Planning

a. When the JFC is also the MNFC, the joint force staff should be augmented by planners and subject matter experts from the MNF. MNF IO planners and IRC specialists should be trained on US and MNF doctrine, requirements, resources, and how the MNF is structured to integrate IRCs. IO planners should seek to accommodate the requirements of each multinational partner, within given constraints, with the goal of using all the available expertise and capabilities of the MNF.

b. In the case where the JFC is not the MNFC, it may be necessary for **the J-3 to brief the MNFC and staff on the advantages of integrating US IO processes and procedures to achieve MNF objectives.** The JFC should propose organizing a multinational IO staff using organizational criteria discussed earlier. If this is not acceptable to the MNFC, the JFC should assume responsibility for implementing IO within the joint force as a part of multinational operations to support multinational mission objectives.

6. Multinational Policy Coordination

The development of capabilities, tactics, techniques, procedures, plans, intelligence, and communications support applicable to IO requires coordination with the responsible DOD components and multinational partners. Coordination with partner nations above the JFC/MNFC level is normally effected within existing defense arrangements, including bilateral arrangements. **The Joint Staff coordinates US positions on IO matters** delegated to them as a matter of law or policy, and discusses them bilaterally, or in multinational organizations, to achieve interoperability and compatibility in fulfilling common requirements. Direct discussions regarding multinational IO planning in specific theaters are the responsibility of the GCC.

Other books we publish on Amazon.com

CHAPTER VI
INFORMATION OPERATIONS ASSESSMENT

"Not everything that can be counted, counts, and not everything that counts can be counted."

Dr. William Cameron, *Informal Sociology:*
A Casual Introduction to Sociological Thinking, **1963**

1. Introduction

a. This chapter provides a framework to organize, develop, and execute assessment of IO, as conducted within the information environment. The term "assessment" has been used to describe everything from analysis (e.g., assessment of the enemy) to an estimate of the situation (pre-engagement assessment of blue and red forces). Within the context of this chapter, assessment is the determination of the progress toward achieving commander's objectives or attaining an end state, and focuses on the tactical and operational levels of assessment that assist and inform the JFC's decision making. Assessment considerations should be thoroughly integrated into IO planning.

b. Assessment of IO is a key component of the commander's decision cycle, helping to determine the results of tactical actions in the context of overall mission objectives and providing potential recommendations for refinement of future plans. The decision to adapt plans or shift resources is based upon the integration of intelligence in the operational environment and other staff estimates, as well as input from other mission partners, in pursuit of the desired end state.

c. Assessments also provide opportunities to identify IRC shortfalls, changes in parameters and/or conditions in the information environment, which may cause unintended effects in the employment of IRCs, and resource issues that may be impeding joint IO effectiveness.

2. Understanding Information Operations Assessment

a. Assessment consists of activities associated with tasks, events, or programs in support of the commander's desired end state. IO assessment is iterative, continuously repeating rounds of analysis within the operations cycle in order to measure the progress of IRCs toward achieving objectives. The assessment process begins with the earliest stages of the planning process and continues throughout the operation or campaign and may extend beyond the end of the operation to capture long-term effects of the IO effort. Integrating assessment from the start, to ensure future assessment requirements, enables the IO planner to ensure that desirable effects that support the commander's objectives are well-defined and measurable and provide feedback to commanders, operators, and planners as operations evolve.

b. Analysis of the information environment should begin before operations start, in order to establish baselines from which to measure change. During operations, data is continuously collected, recharacterizing our understanding of the information environment and providing the ability to measure changes and determine whether desired effects are being created.

3. Purpose of Assessment in Information Operations

Assessments help commanders better understand current conditions. The commander uses assessments to determine how the operation is progressing and whether the operation is creating the desired effects. Assessing the effectiveness of IO activities challenges both the staff and commander. There are numerous venues for informing and receiving information from the commander; they provide opportunities to identify IRC shortfalls and resource issues that may be impeding joint IO effectiveness.

4. Impact of the Information Environment on Assessment

a. Operation assessments in IO differ from assessments of other operations because the success of the operation mainly relies on nonlethal capabilities, often including reliance on measuring the cognitive dimension, or on nonmilitary factors outside the direct control of the JFC. This situation requires an assessment with a focused, organized approach that is developed in conjunction with the initial planning effort. It also requires a clear vision of the end state, an understanding of the commander's objectives, and an articulated statement of the ways in which the planned activities achieve objectives.

For more discussion of objective and effects, see JP 5-0, Joint Operation Planning.

b. The information environment is a complex entity, an "open system" affected by variables that are not constrained by geography. The mingling of people, information, capabilities, organizations, religions, and cultures that exist inside and outside a commander's operational area are examples of these variables. These variables can give commanders and their staffs the appreciation that the information environment is turbulent—constantly in motion and changing—which may make analysis seem like a daunting task, and make identifying an IRC (or IRCs) most likely to create a desired effect, feel nearly impossible. In a complex environment, seemingly minor events can produce enormous outcomes, far greater in effect than the initiating event, including secondary and tertiary effects that are difficult to anticipate and understand. This complexity is why assessment is required and why there may be specific capabilities required to conduct assessment and subsequent analysis.

c. A detailed study and analysis of the information environment affords the planner the ability to identify which forces impact the information environment and find order in the apparent chaos. Often the complexity of the information environment relative to a specific operational area requires assets and capabilities that exceed the organic capability of the command, making the required exhaustive study an impossible task. The gaps in capability and information are identified by planners and are transformed into information requirements and requests, request for forces and/or augmentation, and requests for support from external agencies. Examples of capabilities, forces, augmentation, and external support include specialized software, behavioral scientists, polling, social-science studies, operational research specialists, statisticians, demographic data held by commercial industry, reachback support to other mission partners, military information support personnel, access to external DOD databases, and support from academia. But the presence of sensitive variables can be a catalyst for exponential changes in outcomes, as in the aforementioned secondary and tertiary effects. Joint IO planners should be cautious about making direct causal statements, since many nonlinear feedback loops can render direct causal statements inaccurate. Incorrect assumptions about causality in a complex system can have disastrous effects on the planning of future operations and open the assessment to potential discredit, because counterexamples may exist.

5. The Information Operations Assessment Process

a. Integrating the employment of IRCs with other lines of operation is a unique requirement for joint staffs and is a discipline that is comparatively new. The variety of IRCs is broad, with specific capabilities having unique purposes and focus. For example, an EW asset may be able to focus on disrupting a very specific piece of adversary hardware while a team from the Army's military information support groups may sit down with the former president of a country to convince him to communicate a radio message to the people. The broad range of information-related activities occurring across the three dimensions of the information environment (physical, informational, and cognitive) demand a specific, validated, and formal assessment process to determine whether these actions are contributing towards the fulfillment of an objective. With the additional factor that some actions result in immediate effect (e.g., jamming a radio frequency or entire band [frequency modulation]) and others may take years or generations to fully create (e.g., eliminating police extortion of tourists), the assessment process must be able to report incremental effects in each dimension. In particular, when assessing the effect of an action or series of actions on behavior, the effects may need to be measured in terms such as cognitive, affective, and action or behavioral. Put another way, we may need to assess how a group thinks, feels, and acts, and whether those behaviors are a result of our deliberate actions intended to produce that effect, an unintended consequence of our actions, a result of another's action or activity, or a combination of all of these. A solution to these assessment requirements is the eight-step assessment process identified in Figure VI-1.

Information Operations Assessment Framework	
Step 1	Analyze the information environment
Step 2	Integrate information operations assessment into plans and develop the assessment plan
Step 3	Develop information operations assessment information requirements and collection plans
Step 4	Build/modify information operations assessment baseline
Step 5	Coordinate and Execute Information Operations and Coordinate Intelligence Collection Activities
Step 6	Monitor and collect focused information environment data for information operations assessment
Step 7	Analyze information operations assessment data
Step 8	Report assessment results and make recommendations

Figure VI-1. Information Operations Assessment Framework

b. **Step 1—Analyze the Information Environment**

(1) As the entire staff conducts analysis of the operational environment, the IO staff focuses on the information environment. This analysis occurs when planning for an operation begins or, in some cases, prior to planning for an operation, e.g., during routine analysis in support of theater security cooperation plan activities. It is a required step for viable planning and provides necessary data for, among other things, development of MOEs, determining potential target audiences and targets, baseline data from which change can be measured. Analysis is conducted by interdisciplinary teams and staff sections. The primary product of this step is a description of the information environment. This description should include categorization or delineation of the physical, informational, and cognitive dimensions.

(2) Analysis of the information environment identifies key functions and systems within the operational environment. The analysis provides the initial information to identify decision makers (cognitive), factors that guide the decision-making process (informational), and infrastructure that supports and communicates decisions and decision making (physical).

(3) Gaps in the ability to analyze the information environment and gaps in required information are identified and transformed into information requirements and requests, requests for forces and/or augmentation, and requests for support from external agencies. The information environment is fluid. Technological, cultural, and infrastructure changes, regardless of their source or cause, can all impact each dimension of the information environment. Once the initial analysis is complete, periodic analyses must be conducted to capture changes and update the analysis for the commander, staff, other units, and unified action partners. As assessments are executed and the subsequent data retrieved and analyzed, the effects of our actions on the information are codified. This information is captured, and updates the analysis of the information environment, as well. Much like a running estimate, the analysis of the information environment becomes a living document, continuously updated to provide a current, accurate picture.

c. **Step 2—Integrate Information Operations Assessment into Plans and Develop the Assessment Plan**

(1) Early integration of assessments into plans is paramount, especially in the information environment. One of the first things that must happen during planning is to ensure that the objectives to be assessed are clear, understandable, and measureable. Equally important is to consider as part of the assessment baseline, a control set of conditions within the information environment from which to assess the performance of the tasks assigned to any given IRC, in order to determine their potential impact on IO. In order to assess progress on the objectives, they should portray a progression from the baseline toward the desired end state. The end state should be realistic and attainable. During this step, several tasks occur; after identifying the commander's objectives and end state that are supportable by integrating IRCs with other lines of effort, supporting objectives and tasks are developed. This is followed by developing an initial assessment plan, which includes MOEs and impact indicators. Planners should also be aware that while each staff section participates in the planning process, quite often portions of individual staff sections are simultaneously working

on the steps of the planning process in greater depth and detail, not quite keeping pace with the entire staff effort as they work on subordinate and supporting staff tasks. The intelligence staff's efforts to analyze the operational environment are an example of this, as is the operations staff function of integrating IRCs.

(2) In order to achieve the objectives, specific effects need to be identified. It is during COA development, Step 3 of JOPP, that specific tasks are determined that will create the desired effects, based on the commander's objectives. Effects should be clearly distinguishable from the objective they support as a condition for success or progress and not be misidentified as another objective. These effects ultimately support tasks to influence, disrupt, corrupt, or usurp the decision making of our adversaries, or to protect our own. Effects should provide a clear and common description of the desired change in the information environment.

UNDERSTANDING TASK AND OBJECTIVE, CAUSE AND EFFECT INTERRELATIONSHIPS

Understanding the interrelationships of the tasks and objectives, and the desired cause and effect, can be challenging for the planner. Mapping the expected change (a theory of change) provides the clear, logical connections between activities and desired outcomes by defining intermediate steps between current situation and desired outcome and establishing points of measurement. It should include clearly stated assumptions that can be challenged for correctness as activities are executed. The ability to challenge assumptions in light of executed activities allows the joint information operations planner to identify flawed connections between activity and outcome, incorrect assumptions, or the presence of spoilers. For example:

Training and arming local security guards increases their ability and willingness to resist insurgents, which will increase security in the locale. Increased security will lead to increased perceptions of security, which will promote participation in local government, which will lead to better governance. Improved security and better governance will lead to increased stability.

- Logical connection between activities and outcomes

    – Activity: training and arming local security guards

    – Outcome: increased ability to resist insurgents

- Clearly stated assumptions

    – Increased ability and willingness to resist increases security in the locale

    – Increased security leads to increased perceptions of security

- **Intermediate steps and points of measurement**

  - **Measures of performance regarding training activities**

  - **Measures of effectiveness (MOEs) regarding willingness to resist**

  - **MOEs regarding increased local security**

(3) This expected change shows a logical connection between activities (training and arming locals) and desired outcomes (increased stability). It makes some assumptions, but those assumptions are clearly stated, so they can be challenged if they are believed to be incorrect. Further, those activities and assumptions suggest obvious things to measure, such as performance of the activities (the training and arming) and the outcome (change in stability). They also suggest measurement of more subtle elements of all the intermediate logical nodes such as capability and willingness of local security forces, change in security, change in perception of security, change in participation in local government, change in governance, and so on. Better still, if one of those measurements does not yield the desired result, the joint IO planner will be able to ascertain where in the chain the logic is breaking down (which hypotheses are not substantiated). They can then modify the expected change and the activities supporting it, reconnecting the logical pathway and continuing to push toward the objectives.

(4) Such an expected change might have begun as something quite simple: training and arming local security guards will lead to increased stability. While this gets at the kernel of the idea, it is not particularly helpful for building assessments. Stopping there would suggest only the need to measure the activity and the outcome. However, it leaves a huge assumptive gap. If training and arming security guards goes well, but stability does not increase, there will be no apparent reason why. To begin to expand on a simple expected change, the joint IO planner should ask the question, "Why? How might A lead to B?" (In this case, how would training and arming security guards lead to stability?) A thoughtful answer to this question usually leads to recognition of another node to the expected change. If needed, the question can be asked again relative to this new node, until the expected change is sufficiently articulated.

(5) Circumstances on the ground might also require the assumptions in an expected change to be more explicitly defined. For example, using the expected change articulated in the above example, the joint IO planner might observe that in successfully training and arming local security guards, they are better able to resist insurgents, leading to an increased perception of security, as reported in local polls. However, participation in local government, as measured through voting in local elections and attendance at local council meetings, has not increased. The existing expected change and associated measurements illustrate where the chain of logic is breaking down (somewhere between perceptions of security and participation in local governance), but it does not (yet) tell why that break is occurring. Adjusting the expected change by identifying the incorrect assumption or spoiling factor preventing the successful connection between security and local governance will also help improve achievement of the objective.

d. **Step 3—Develop Information Operations Assessment Information Requirements and Collection Plans**

(1) Critical to this step is ensuring that attributes are chosen that are relevant and applicable during the planning processes, as these will drive the determination of measures that display behavioral characteristics, attitudes, perceptions, and motivations that can be examined externally. Measures are categorized as follows:

(a) Qualitative—a categorical measurement expressed by means of a natural language description rather than in terms of numbers. Methodologies consist of focus groups, in-depth interviews, ethnography, media content analysis, after-action reports, and anecdotes (individual responses sampled consistently over time).

(b) Quantitative—a numerical measurement expressed in terms of numbers rather than means of a natural language description. Methodologies consist of surveys, polls, observational data (intelligence, surveillance, and reconnaissance), media analytics, and official statistics.

(2) An integrated collection management plan ensures that assessment data gathered at the tactical level is incorporated into operational planning. This collection management plan needs to satisfy information requirements with the assigned tactical, theater, and national intelligence sources and other collection resources. Just as crucial is realizing that not every information requirement will be answered by the intelligence community and therefore planners must consider collaborating with other sources of information. Planners must discuss collection from other sources of information with the collection manager and unit legal personnel to ensure that the information is included in the overall assessment and the process is in accordance with intelligence oversight regulations and policy.

(3) Including considerations for assessment collection in the plan will facilitate the return of data needed to accomplish the assessment. Incorporating the assessment plan with the directions to conduct an activity will help ensure that resource requirements for assessment are acknowledged when the plan is approved. The assessment plan should, at a minimum, include timing and frequency of data collection, identify the party to conduct the collection, and provide reporting instructions.

(4) A well-designed assessment plan will:

(a) Develop the commander's assessment questions.

(b) Document the expected change.

(c) Document the development of information requirements needed specifically for IO.

(d) Define key terms embedded within the end state with regard to the actors or TAs, operational activities, effects, acceptable conditions, rates of change, thresholds of success/failure, and technical/tactical triggers.

(e) Verify tactical objectives—support operational objectives.

(f) Identify strategic and operational considerations—in addition to tactical considerations, linking assessments to lines of operation and the associated desired conditions.

(g) Identify key nodes and connections in the expected change to be measured.

(h) Document collection and analysis methods.

(i) Establish a method to evaluate triggers to the commander's decision points.

(j) Establish methods to determine progress towards the desired end state.

(k) Establish methods to estimate risk to the mission.

(l) Develop recommendations for plan adjustments.

(m) Establish the format for reporting assessment results.

e. **Step 4—Build/Modify Information Operations Assessment Baseline.** A subset of JIPOE, the baseline is part of the overall characterization of the information environment that was accomplished in Step 1. It serves as a reference point for comparison, enabling an assessment of the way in which activities create desired effects. The baseline allows the commander and staff to set goals for desired rates of change within the information environment and establish thresholds for success and failure. This focuses information and intelligence collection on answering specific questions relating to the desired outcomes of the plan.

f. **Step 5—Coordinate and Execute Information Operations and Coordinate Intelligence Collection Activities**

(1) With information gained in steps 1 and 4, the joint IO planner should be able to build an understanding of the TA. This awareness will yield a collection plan that enables the joint IO planner to determine whether or not the TA is "seeing" the activities/actions presented. The collection method must perceive the TA reaction. IO planners, assessors, and intelligence planners need to be able to communicate effectively to accurately capture the required intelligence needed to perform IO assessments.

(2) Information requirements and subsequent indicator collection must be tightly managed during employment of IRCs in order to validate execution and to monitor TA response. In the information environment, coordination and timing are crucial because some IRCs are time sensitive and require immediate indicator monitoring to develop valid assessment data.

g. **Step 6—Monitor and Collect Information Environment Data for Information Operations Assessment**

(1) Monitoring is the continuous process of observing conditions relevant to current operations. Assessment data are collected, aggregated, consolidated and validated. Gaps in the assessment data are identified and highlighted in order to determine actions needed to alleviate shortfalls or make adjustments to the plan. As information and intelligence are collected during execution, assessments are used to validate or negate assumptions that define cause (action) and effect (conclusion) relationships between operational activities, objectives, and end states.

(2) If anticipated progress toward an end state does not occur, then the staff may conclude that the intended action does not have the intended effect. The uncertainty in the information environment makes the use of critical assumptions particularly important, as operation planning may need to be adjusted for elements that may not have initially been well understood when the plan was developed.

h. **Step 7—Analyze Information Operations Assessment Data**

(1) If available, personnel trained or qualified in analysis techniques should conduct data analysis. Analysis can be done outside the operational area by leveraging reachback capabilities. One of the more important factors for analysis is that it is conducted in an unbiased manner. This is more easily accomplished if the personnel conducting analysis are not the same personnel who developed the execution plan. Assessment data are analyzed and the results are compared to the baseline measurements and updated continuously as the staff continues its analysis of the information environment. These comparisons help the staff determine whether the information environment has changed and if so, the degree and area of that change, or if it remains unchanged. These changes are indications of effects on or in the information environment and help determine whether progress is being made toward achieving objectives. Assessment remains an iterative process. When problems or errors are found in the data, feedback about what occurred and where adjustments are necessary must be reported, as appropriate.

(2) Deficiency analysis must also occur in this step. If no changes were observed in the information environment, then a breakdown may have occurred somewhere. The plan might be flawed, execution might not have been successful, collection may not have been accomplished as prescribed, or more time may be needed to observe any changes.

i. **Step 8—Report Assessment Results and Make Recommendations**

As expressed earlier in this chapter, assessment results enable staffs to ensure that tasks stay linked to objectives and objectives remain relevant and linked to desired end states. They provide opportunities to identify IRC shortfalls and resource issues that may be impeding joint IO effectiveness. These results may also provide information to agencies outside of the command or chain of command. The primary purpose of reporting the results is to inform the command and staff concerning the progress of objective achievement and the effects on the information environment, and to enable decision making. The published assessment plan, staff standard operating procedures, battle rhythm, and orders are documents in which commanders can dictate how often assessment results are provided and the format in which they are reported. In designated venues and in the required format, the

IO staff reports progress and makes recommendations. They record the decision made and implement those decisions continuing the iterative assessment process.

6. Barriers to Information Operations Assessment

a. The preceding IO assessment methodology can support all operations, and most barriers to assessment can be overcome simply by considering assessment requirements as the plan is developed. But whatever the phase type of operation, the biggest barriers to assessment are generally self-generated.

b. Some of the self-generated barriers to assessment include the failure to establish objectives that are actually measurable, the failure to collect baseline data against which "post-test" data can be compared, and the failure to plan adequately for the collection of assessment data, including the use of intelligence assets.

c. There are other factors that complicate IO assessment. Foremost, it may be difficult or impossible to directly relate behavior change to an individual act or group of actions. Also, the logistics of data capture are not simple. Contingencies and operations in uncertain or hostile environments present unique challenges in terms of operational tempo and access to conduct assessments. Depending on the phase of the conflict, the operational tempo might present unique challenges to access or assessment. Rapidly changing conditions might also affect the accuracy and volume of data able to be collected. The cognitive biases of the analyst may also act as a barrier to influence accuracy.

7. Organizing for Operation Assessments

a. Integrating assessment into the planning effort is normally the responsibility of the lead planner, with assistance across the staff. The lead planner understands the complexity of the plan and decision points established as the plan develops. The lead planner also understands potential indicators of success or failure. For IO-specific assessments planning regarding collecting and analyzing the success of the IO message, the organization responsible for IO should build the IO assessment framework into the plan. This framework must include collection and reporting responsibilities.

b. As a plan becomes operationalized, the overall assessment responsibility typically transitions from the lead planner to the J-3. The IO lead provides the necessary IO-related information and analysis to guide the assessment and recommendations for implementing specific changes to better accomplish the mission.

c. When appropriate, the commander can establish an assessments cell or team to manage assessments activities. When utilized, this cell or team must have appropriate access to operational information, appropriate access to the planning process, and the representation of other staff elements, to include IRCs.

8. Measures and Indicators

a. As emphasized in Chapter IV, "Integrating Information-Related Capabilities into the Joint Operation Planning Process," paragraph 2.f., "Relationship Between Measures of

Performance (MOPs) and Measures of Effectiveness (MOEs)," MOPs and MOEs help accomplish the assessment process by qualifying or quantifying the intangible attributes of the information environment. This is done to assess the effectiveness of activities conducted in the information environment and to establish a direct cause between the activity and the effect desired.

b. MOPs should be developed during the operation planning process, should be tied directly to operation planning, and at a minimum, assess completion of the various phases of an activity or program. Further, MOPs should assess any action, activity, or operation at which IO actions or activities interact with the TA. For certain tasks there are TA capabilities (voice, text, video, or face-to-face). For instance, during a leaflet-drop, the point of dissemination of the leaflets would be an action or activity. The MOP for any one action should be whether or not the TA was exposed to the IO action or activity.

(1) For each activity phase, task, or touch point, a set of MOPs based on the operational plan outlined in the program description should be developed. Task MOPs are measured via internal reporting within units and commands. Touch-point MOPs can be measured in one of several ways. Whether or not a TA is aware of, interested in, or responding to, an IRC product or activity, can be directly ascertained by conducting a survey or interview. This information can also be gathered by direct observational methods such as field reconnaissance, surveillance, or intelligence collection. Information can also be gathered via indirect observations such as media reports, online activity, or atmospherics.

(2) The end state of operation planning is a multi-phased plan or order, from which planners can directly derive a list of MOPs, assuming a higher echelon has not already designated the MOPs.

c. MOEs need to be specific, clear, and observable to provide the commander effective feedback. In addition, there needs to be a direct link between the objectives, effects, and the TA. Most of the IRCs have their own doctrine and discuss MOEs with slightly different language, but with ultimately the same functions and roles.

(1) In line with JP 5-0, *Joint Operation Planning*, development of MOEs and their associated impact indicators (derived from measurable supporting objectives) must be done during the planning process. By determining the measure in the planning process, planners ensure that organic assets and enablers, such as intelligence assets, are identified to assist in evaluating MOEs in the conduct of IO.

(2) In developing IO MOEs, the following general guidelines should be considered. First, they should be related to the end state; that is, they should directly relate to the desired effects. They should also be measurable quantitatively or qualitatively. In order to measure effectiveness, *a baseline measurement must exist or be established prior to execution, against which to measure system changes.* They should be within a defined periodical or conditional assessment framework (i.e., the required feedback time, cyclical period, or conditions should be clearly stated for each MOE and a deadline made to report within a specified assessment period, which clearly delineates the beginning, progression, and termination of a cycle in which the effectiveness of the operations is to be assessed). Finally,

they need to be properly resourced. The collection, collation, analysis and reporting of MOE data requires personnel, budgetary, and materiel resources. IO staffs, along with their counterparts at the component level, should ensure that these resource requirements are built into the plan during its development.

(3) The more specific the MOE, the more readily the intelligence collection manager can determine how best to collect against the requirements and provide valuable feedback pertaining to them. The ability to establish MOEs and conduct combat assessment for IO requires observation and collection of information from diverse, nebulous and often untimely sources. These sources may include: human intelligence; signals intelligence; air and ground-based intelligence; surveillance and reconnaissance; open-source intelligence, including the Internet; contact with the public; press inquiries and comments; Department of State polls; reports and surveys; nongovernmental organizations; international organizations; and commercial polls.

(4) One of the biggest challenges with MOE development is the difficulty of defining variables and establishing causality. Therefore, it is more advisable to approach this from a correlational, versus a causality perspective, where unrealistic "zero-defect" predictability gives way to more attainable correlational analysis, which provides insights to the likelihood of particular events and effects given a certain criteria in terms of conditions and actors in the information environment. While the *Joint Munitions Effectiveness Manual* provides a certain level of predictability, which supports causality in the employment of certain munitions with desired effects, such methodology is not analogous to assessments within the information environment, as evidence seems to point out that correlation of indicators and events have proven more accurate than the evidence to support cause and effects relationships, particularly when it comes to behavior and intangible parameters of the cognitive elements of the information environment. IRCs, however, are directed at TAs and decision makers, and the systems that support them, making it much more difficult to establish concrete causal relationships, especially when assessing foreign public opinion or human behavior. Unforeseen factors can lead to erroneous interpretations, for example, a traffic accident in a foreign country involving a US service member or a local civilian's bias against US policies can cause a decline in public support, irrespective of otherwise successful IO.

(5) If IO effects and supporting IO tasks are not linked to the commander's objectives, or are not clearly written, measuring their effectiveness is difficult. Clearly written IO tasks must be linked to the commander's objectives to justify resources to measure their contributing effects. If MOEs are difficult to write for a specific IO effect, the effect should be reevaluated and a rewrite considered. When attempting to describe desired effects, it is important to keep the effect impact in mind, as a guide to what must be observed, collected, and measured. In order to effectively identify the assessment methodology and to be able to recreate the process as part of the scientific method, MOE development must be written with a documented pathway for effect creation. This path should consist of indicators leading to the projected creation of the desired effect. MOEs should be observable, to aid with collection; quantifiable, to increase objectivity; precise, to ensure accuracy; and correlated with the progress of the operation, to attain timeliness.

d. Indicators are crucial because they aid the joint IO planner in informing MOEs and should be identifiable across the center of gravity critical factors. They can be independently weighted for their contribution to a MOE and should be based on separate criteria. A single indicator can inform multiple MOEs. Dozens of indicators will be required for a large-scale operation.

9. Considerations

a. In the information environment, it is unlikely that universal measures and indicators will exist because of varying perspectives. In addition, any data collected is likely to be incomplete. Assessments need to be periodically adjusted to the changing situation in order to avoid becoming obsolete. In addition, assessments will usually need to be supplemented by subjective constructs that are a reflection of the joint IO planner's scope and perspective (e.g., intuition, anecdotal evidence, or limited set of evidence).

b. Assessment teams may not have direct access to a TA for a variety of reasons. The goal of measurement is not to achieve perfect accuracy or precision—given the ever present biases of theory and the limitations of tools that exist—but rather, to reduce uncertainty about the value being measured. Measurements of IO effects on TA can be accomplished in two ways: direct observation and indirect observation. Direct observation measures the attitudes or behaviors of the TA either by questioning the TA or observing behavior firsthand. Indirect observation measures otherwise inaccessible attitudes and behaviors by the effects that they have on more easily measurable phenomena. Direct observations are preferable for establishing baselines and measuring effectiveness, while indirect observations reduce uncertainty in measurements, to a lesser degree.

10. Categories of Assessment

a. Operation assessment of IO is an evaluation of the effectiveness of operational activities conducted in the information environment. Operation assessments primarily document mission success or failure for the commander and staff. However, operation assessments inform other types of assessment, such as programmatic and budgetary assessment. Programmatic assessment evaluates readiness and training, while budgetary assessment evaluates return on investment.

b. When categorized by the levels of warfare, there exists tactical, operational and strategic-level assessment. Tactical-level assessment evaluates the effectiveness of a specific, localized activity. Operational-level assessment evaluates progress towards accomplishment of a plan or campaign. Strategic level assessment evaluates progress towards accomplishment of a theater or national objective. The skilled IO planner will link tactical actions to operational and strategic objectives.

Other books we publish on Amazon.com

Russia Surface Warships 2019-2020

Customer reviews
★★★★☆ 4.5 out of 5

CHINA SURFACE WARSHIPS 2019-2020

Customer reviews
★★★★☆ 4 out of 5

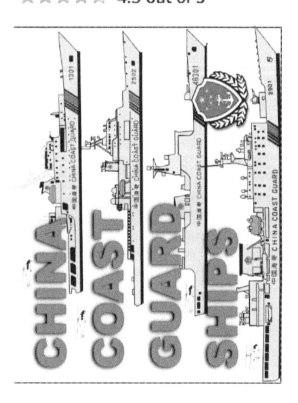

CHINA COAST GUARD SHIPS

NORTH KOREA SURFACE WARSHIPS 2019-2020

Customer reviews
★★★★★ 5 out of 5

APPENDIX A
REFERENCES

The development of JP 3-13 is based on the following primary references.

1. General

    a. *National Security Strategy.*

    b. *Unified Command Plan.*

    c. Executive Order 12333, *United States Intelligence Activities.*

    d. The Fourth Amendment to the US Constitution.

    e. *The Privacy Act*, Title 5, USC, Section 552a.

    f. *The Wiretap Act and the Pen/Trap Statute*, Title 18, USC, Sections 2510-2522 and 3121-3127.

    g. *The Stored Communications Act*, Title 18, USC, Sections 2701-2712.

    h. *The Foreign Intelligence Surveillance Act,* Title 50, USC.

2. Department of State Publications

Department of State Publication 9434, *Treaties In Force.*

3. Department of Defense Publications

    a. Secretary of Defense Memorandum dated 25 January 2011, *Strategic Communication and Information Operations in the DOD.*

    b. *National Military Strategy.*

    c. DODD S-3321.1, *Overt Psychological Operations Conducted by the Military Services in Peacetime and in Contingencies Short of Declared War.*

    d. DODD 3600.01, *Information Operations (IO).*

    e. DODD 5200.27, *Acquisition of Information Concerning Persons and Organizations not Affiliated with the Department of Defense.*

    f. DOD 5240.1-R, *Procedures Governing the Activities of DOD Intelligence Components that Affect United States Persons.*

    g. DODI O-3600.02, *Information Operation (IO) Security Classification Guidance.*

4. Chairman of the Joint Chiefs of Staff Publications

a. CJCSI 1800.01D, *Officer Professional Military Education Policy (OPMEP).*

b. CJCSI 3141.01E, *Management and Review of Joint Strategic Capabilities Plan (JSCP)-Tasked Plans.*

c. CJCSI 3150.25E, *Joint Lessons Learned Program.*

d. CJCSI 3210.01B, *Joint Information Operations Policy.*

e. Chairman of the Joint Chiefs of Staff Manual (CJCSM) 3122.01A, *Joint Operation Planning and Execution System (JOPES) Volume I, Planning Policies and Procedures.*

f. CJCSM 3122.02D, *Joint Operation Planning and Execution System (JOPES) Volume III, Time-Phased Force and Deployment Data Development and Deployment Execution.*

g. CJCSM 3122.03C, *Joint Operation Planning and Execution System (JOPES) Volume II, Planning Formats.*

h. CJCSM 3500.03C, *Joint Training Manual for the Armed Forces of the United States.*

i. CJCSM 3500.04F, *Universal Joint Task Manual.*

j. JP 1, *Doctrine for the Armed Forces of the United States.*

k. JP 1-02, *Department of Defense Dictionary of Military and Associated Terms.*

l. JP 1-04, *Legal Support to Military Operations.*

m. JP 2-0, *Joint Intelligence.*

n. JP 2-01, *Joint and National Intelligence Support to Military Operations.*

o. JP 2-01.3, *Joint Intelligence Preparation of the Operational Environment.*

p. JP 2-03, *Geospatial Intelligence Support to Joint Operations.*

q. JP 3-0, *Joint Operations.*

r. JP 3-08, *Interorganizational Coordination During Joint Operations.*

s. JP 3-10, *Joint Security Operations in Theater.*

t. JP 3-12, *Cyberspace Operations.*

u. JP 3-13.1, *Electronic Warfare.*

v. JP 3-13.2, *Military Information Support Operations.*

w. JP 3-13.3, *Operations Security.*

x. JP 3-13.4, *Military Deception.*

y. JP 3-14, *Space Operations.*

z. JP 3-16, *Multinational Operations.*

aa. JP 3-57, *Civil-Military Operations.*

bb. JP 3-60, *Joint Targeting.*

cc. JP 3-61, *Public Affairs.*

dd. JP 5-0, *Joint Operation Planning.*

ee. JP 6-01, *Joint Electromagnetic Spectrum Management Operations.*

5. Multinational Publication

AJP 3-10, *Allied Joint Doctrine for Information Operations.*

Other books we publish on Amazon.com

JAPAN SURFACE WARSHIPS 2019-2020

Customer reviews
★★★★⯪ 4.5 out of 5

TAIWAN SURFACE WARSHIPS 2019-2020

Customer reviews
★★★★☆ 4 out of 5

Turkey Surface Warships 2020-2025

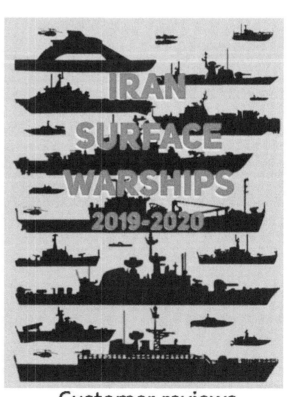

IRAN SURFACE WARSHIPS 2019-2020

Customer reviews
★★★★⯪ 4.5 out of 5

APPENDIX B
ADMINISTRATIVE INSTRUCTIONS

1. User Comments

Users in the field are highly encouraged to submit comments on this publication to: Joint Staff J-7, Deputy Director, Joint and Coalition Warfighting, Joint and Coalition Warfighting Center, ATTN: Joint Doctrine Support Division, 116 Lake View Parkway, Suffolk, VA 23435-2697. These comments should address content (accuracy, usefulness, consistency, and organization), writing, and appearance.

2. Authorship

The lead agent and the Joint Staff doctrine sponsor for this publication is the Director for Operations (J-3).

3. Supersession

This publication supersedes JP 3-13, 27 November 2012, *Information Operations.*

4. Change Recommendations

a. Recommendations for urgent changes to this publication should be submitted:

   TO: JOINT STAFF WASHINGTON DC//J7-JEDD//

b. Routine changes should be submitted electronically to the Deputy Director, Joint and Coalition Warfighting, Joint Doctrine Support Division and info the lead agent and the Director for Joint Force Development, J-7/JEDD.

c. When a Joint Staff directorate submits a proposal to the CJCS that would change source document information reflected in this publication, that directorate will include a proposed change to this publication as an enclosure to its proposal. The Services and other organizations are requested to notify the Joint Staff J-7 when changes to source documents reflected in this publication are initiated.

5. Distribution of Publications

Local reproduction is authorized and access to unclassified publications is unrestricted. However, access to and reproduction authorization for classified JPs must be in accordance with DOD Manual 5200.1, *Information Security Program: Overview, Classification, and Declassification.*

6. Distribution of Electronic Publications

a. Joint Staff J-7 will not print copies of JPs for distribution. Electronic versions are available on JDEIS at https://jdeis.js.mil (NIPRNET) and http://jdeis.js.smil.mil (SIPRNET), and on the JEL at http://www.dtic.mil/doctrine (NIPRNET).

b. Only approved JPs and joint test publications are releasable outside the CCMDs, Services, and Joint Staff. Release of any classified JP to foreign governments or foreign nationals must be requested through the local embassy (Defense Attaché Office) to DIA, Defense Foreign Liaison/IE-3, 200 MacDill Blvd., Joint Base Anacostia-Bolling, Washington, DC 20340-5100.

c. JEL CD-ROM. Upon request of a joint doctrine development community member, the Joint Staff J-7 will produce and deliver one CD-ROM with current JPs. This JEL CD-ROM will be updated not less than semiannually and when received can be locally reproduced for use within the CCMDs and Services.

GLOSSARY
PART I—ABBREVIATIONS AND ACRONYMS

AJP	allied joint publication
AOR	area of responsibility
C2	command and control
CCDR	combatant commander
CCIR	commander's critical information requirement
CCMD	combatant command
CJCS	Chairman of the Joint Chiefs of Staff
CJCSI	Chairman of the Joint Chiefs of Staff instruction
CJCSM	Chairman of the Joint Chiefs of Staff manual
CMO	civil-military operations
CO	cyberspace operations
COA	course of action
CONOPS	concept of operations
CONPLAN	concept plan
DOD	Department of Defense
DODD	Department of Defense directive
DODI	Department of Defense instruction
EEI	essential element of information
EMS	electromagnetic spectrum
EW	electronic warfare
EWC	electronic warfare cell
FDO	flexible deterrent option
GCC	geographic combatant commander
IA	information assurance
IO	information operations
IOCB	information operations coordination board
IOII	information operations intelligence integration
IRC	information-related capability
J-2	intelligence directorate of a joint staff
J-3	operations directorate of a joint staff
J-39 DDGO	Joint Staff, Deputy Director for Global Operations
JCEWS	joint force commander's electronic warfare staff
JEMSO	joint electromagnetic spectrum operations
JFC	joint force commander
JIACG	joint interagency coordination group
JIOWC	Joint Information Operations Warfare Center

JIPOE	joint intelligence preparation of the operational environment
JISE	joint intelligence support element
JOPG	joint operations planning group
JOPP	joint operation planning process
JP	joint publication
JPG	joint planning group
JTCB	joint targeting coordination board
KLE	key leader engagement
MILDEC	military deception
MISO	military information support operations
MNF	multinational force
MNFC	multinational force commander
MOE	measure of effectiveness
MOEI	measure of effectiveness indicator
MOP	measure of performance
NDP	national disclosure policy
OPLAN	operation plan
OPORD	operation order
OPSEC	operations security
PA	public affairs
PIR	priority intelligence requirement
RFI	request for information
ROE	rules of engagement
SC	strategic communication
STO	special technical operations
TA	target audience
TCP	theater campaign plan
USC	United States Code
USD(I)	Under Secretary of Defense for Intelligence
USD(P)	Under Secretary of Defense for Policy
USG	United States Government
USSTRATCOM	United States Strategic Command

PART II—TERMS AND DEFINITIONS

computer network attack. None. (Approved for removal from JP 1-02.)

computer network defense. None. (Approved for removal from JP 1-02.)

computer network exploitation. None. (Approved for removal from JP 1-02.)

computer network operations. None. (Approved for removal from JP 1-02.)

data. None. (Approved for removal from JP 1-02.)

data item. None. (Approved for removal from JP 1-02.)

defense information infrastructure. None. (Approved for removal from JP 1-02.)

defense support to public diplomacy. None. (Approved for removal from JP 1-02.)

global information infrastructure. None. (Approved for removal from JP 1-02.)

information-based processes. None. (Approved for removal from JP 1-02.)

information environment. The aggregate of individuals, organizations, and systems that collect, process, disseminate, or act on information. (JP 1-02. SOURCE: JP 3-13)

information operations. The integrated employment, during military operations, of information-related capabilities in concert with other lines of operation to influence, disrupt, corrupt, or usurp the decision-making of adversaries and potential adversaries while protecting our own. Also called **IO.** (Approved for incorporation into JP 1-02 with JP 3-13 as the source JP.)

information operations intelligence integration. The integration of intelligence disciplines and analytic methods to characterize and forecast, identify vulnerabilities, determine effects, and assess the information environment. Also called **IOII.** (Approved for inclusion in JP 1-02.)

information-related capability. A tool, technique, or activity employed within a dimension of the information environment that can be used to create effects and operationally desirable conditions. Also called **IRC.** (Approved for inclusion in JP 1-02.)

information security. None. (Approved for removal from JP 1-02.)

information superiority. The operational advantage derived from the ability to collect, process, and disseminate an uninterrupted flow of information while exploiting or denying an adversary's ability to do the same. (JP 1-02. SOURCE: JP 3-13)

information system. None. (Approved for removal from JP 1-02.)

national information infrastructure. None. (Approved for removal from JP 1-02.)

probe. None. (Approved for removal from JP 1-02.)

special information operations. None. (Approved for removal from JP 1-02.)

target audience. An individual or group selected for influence. Also called **TA.** (JP 1-02. SOURCE: JP 3-13)

JOINT DOCTRINE PUBLICATIONS HIERARCHY

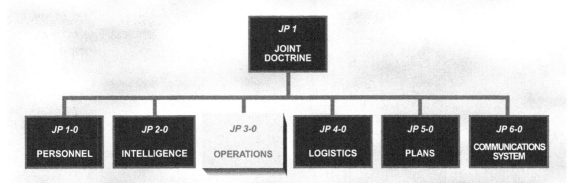

All joint publications are organized into a comprehensive hierarchy as shown in the chart above. **Joint Publication (JP) 3-13** is in the **Operations** series of joint doctrine publications. The diagram below illustrates an overview of the development process:

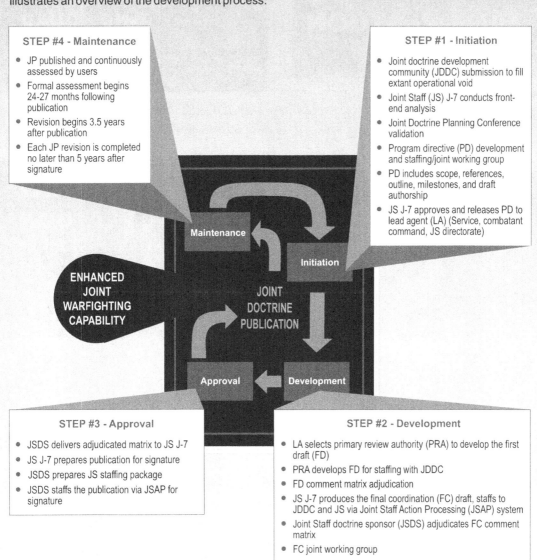

STEP #4 - Maintenance

- JP published and continuously assessed by users
- Formal assessment begins 24-27 months following publication
- Revision begins 3.5 years after publication
- Each JP revision is completed no later than 5 years after signature

STEP #1 - Initiation

- Joint doctrine development community (JDDC) submission to fill extant operational void
- Joint Staff (JS) J-7 conducts front-end analysis
- Joint Doctrine Planning Conference validation
- Program directive (PD) development and staffing/joint working group
- PD includes scope, references, outline, milestones, and draft authorship
- JS J-7 approves and releases PD to lead agent (LA) (Service, combatant command, JS directorate)

STEP #3 - Approval

- JSDS delivers adjudicated matrix to JS J-7
- JS J-7 prepares publication for signature
- JSDS prepares JS staffing package
- JSDS staffs the publication via JSAP for signature

STEP #2 - Development

- LA selects primary review authority (PRA) to develop the first draft (FD)
- PRA develops FD for staffing with JDDC
- FD comment matrix adjudication
- JS J-7 produces the final coordination (FC) draft, staffs to JDDC and JS via Joint Staff Action Processing (JSAP) system
- Joint Staff doctrine sponsor (JSDS) adjudicates FC comment matrix
- FC joint working group

Other books we publish on Amazon.com

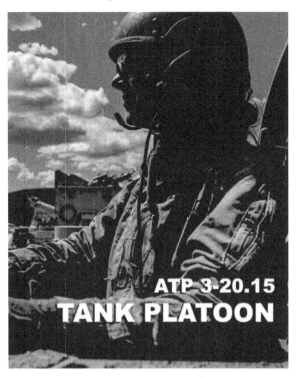

PODCAST: https://atp-3-2015-tank-platoon.castos.com

PODCAST: https://atp-3-218-infantry-platoon-and-squad.castos.com

Joint Publication 3-13.1

Electronic Warfare

08 February 2012

Other books we publish on Amazon.com

Translated from RUSSIAN 2021

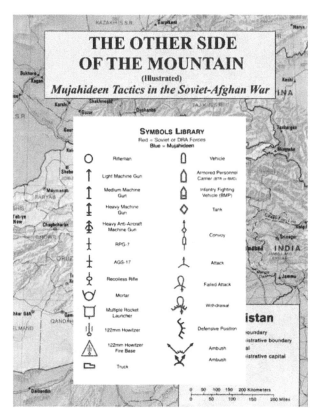

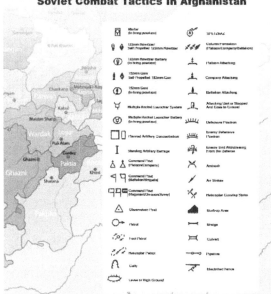

PREFACE

1. Scope

This publication provides joint doctrine for the planning, execution, and assessment of electronic warfare across the range of military operations.

2. Purpose

This publication has been prepared under the direction of the Chairman of the Joint Chiefs of Staff (CJCS). It sets forth joint doctrine to govern the activities and performance of the Armed Forces of the United States in joint operations and provides the doctrinal basis for interagency coordination and for US military involvement in multinational operations. It provides military guidance for the exercise of authority by combatant commanders and other joint force commanders (JFCs) and prescribes joint doctrine for operations, education, and training. It provides military guidance for use by the Armed Forces in preparing their appropriate plans. It is not the intent of this publication to restrict the authority of the JFC from organizing the force and executing the mission in a manner the JFC deems most appropriate to ensure unity of effort in the accomplishment of the overall objective.

3. Application

a. Joint doctrine established in this publication applies to the Joint Staff, commanders of combatant commands, subunified commands, joint task forces, subordinate components of these commands, and the Services.

b. The guidance in this publication is authoritative; as such, this doctrine will be followed except when, in the judgment of the commander, exceptional circumstances dictate otherwise. If conflicts arise between the contents of this publication and the contents of Service publications, this publication will take precedence unless the CJCS, normally in coordination with the other members of the Joint Chiefs of Staff, has provided more current and specific guidance. Commanders of forces operating as part of a multinational (alliance or coalition) military command should follow multinational doctrine and procedures ratified by the United States. For doctrine and procedures not ratified by the United States, commanders should evaluate and follow the multinational command's doctrine and procedures, where applicable and consistent with US law, regulations, and doctrine.

For the Chairman of the Joint Chiefs of Staff:

WILLIAM E. GORTNEY
VADM, USN
Director, Joint Staff

SUMMARY OF CHANGES
REVISION OF JOINT PUBLICATION 3-13.1
DATED 25 JANUARY 2007

- Adds a discussion on joint electromagnetic spectrum operations.

- Adds a discussion on the electromagnetic operational environment.

- Adds a discussion on electromagnetic battle management.

- Adds a discussion on joint electromagnetic spectrum management operations.

- Adds a discussion on electronic warfare's (EW's) relationship to irregular warfare, EW's relationship to space operations, EW's relationship to cyberspace operations, and EW's relationship to navigation warfare.

- Changes the electronic warfare coordination cell to the electronic warfare cell.

- Addresses component-level EW support activities referred to as EW elements: land-EW element, air-EW element, and maritime-EW element.

- Adds a discussion in Chapter III, "Planning Joint Electronic Warfare," on "chemical, biological, radiological, and nuclear considerations."

- Adds a discussion in Chapter IV, "Coordinating Joint Electronic Warfare," on EW and interagency coordination.

- Adds appendices: "Electronic Warfare Joint Munitions Effectiveness Manual Planning" and "SPECTRUM XXI."

- Changes the Appendix, "Joint Spectrum Center Support to Joint Electronic Warfare," to "Organizations Supporting Joint Electronic Warfare;" and adds discussions, on the Electromagnetic-Space Analysis Center, Global Positioning System Operations Center, Joint Electronic Warfare Center, Joint Navigation Warfare Center, and Information Operations Range in addition to the discussion on the Joint Spectrum Center.

- Deletes the Appendix, "Service Perspectives of Electronic Warfare" and added text to Chapter II, "Organizing for Joint Electronic Warfare," Paragraph 6, "Service Organization for Electronic Warfare."

- Adds definitions for the terms "electromagnetic battle management" and "electromagnetic spectrum control."

- **Modifies the definitions of the terms "directed-energy device," "directed-energy weapon," "electronic warfare reprogramming," "electro-optical-infrared countermeasure," "TABOO frequencies," and "verification."**

- **Assumes proponency for the terms "chaff," "countermeasures," "directed energy," "direction finding," "electronic probing," and "wartime reserve modes."**

- **Removes the terms "acoustical surveillance," "acoustic jamming," "barrage jamming," "control of electromagnetic radiation," "directed-energy protective measures," "emission control orders," "ferret," "imitative communications deception," "imitative electromagnetic deception," "information," "jamming," "manipulative electromagnetic deception," "meaconing," "pulse duration," "radar spoking," "scan," "scan period," " scan type," and "simulative electromagnetic deception" from Joint Publication 1-02, *Department of Defense Dictionary of Military and Associated Terms*.**

TABLE OF CONTENTS

CHAPTER V
MULTINATIONAL ASPECTS OF ELECTRONIC WARFARE

EXECUTIVE SUMMARY
COMMANDER'S OVERVIEW

- **Provides an Overview of Electronic Warfare**

- **Describes Organizing for Joint Electronic Warfare**

- **Explains Planning Joint Electronic Warfare**

- **Discusses Coordinating Joint Electronic Warfare**

- **Addresses Multinational Aspects of Electronic Warfare**

Overview of Electronic Warfare

Military operations are executed in an environment complicated by increasingly complex demands on the electromagnetic spectrum.

All modern forces depend on the electromagnetic spectrum (EMS). The military requirement for unimpeded access to, and use of, the EMS is the key focus for joint electromagnetic spectrum operations (JEMSO), both in support of military operations and as the focus of operations themselves. **Electronic warfare (EW) is essential for protecting friendly operations and denying adversary operations within the EMS throughout the operational environment.**

Military Operations and the Electromagnetic Environment

As with the operational environment, the goal of the joint force commander (JFC) is to shape and control the electromagnetic operational environment.

JEMSO are the coordinated efforts of EW and joint electromagnetic spectrum management operations (JEMSMO) to exploit, attack, protect, and manage the electromagnetic operational environment (EMOE). The impact of an EMOE upon the operational capability of military forces, equipment, systems, and platforms is referred to as electromagnetic environmental effects. It encompasses all electromagnetic (EM) disciplines to include electromagnetic compatibility; electromagnetic interference; EM vulnerability; electromagnetic pulse (EMP); electronic protection (EP); hazards of EM radiation to personnel, ordnance, and volatile materials; and natural phenomena effects such as sunspots, lightning, and precipitation static.

Role of Electronic Warfare Across the Range of Military Operations	The term EW refers to military action involving the **use of EM energy and directed energy (DE) to control the EMS or to attack the enemy. EW consists of three divisions:** electronic attack (EA), EP, and electronic warfare support (ES).
Electronic Attack	EA refers to the division of EW involving the use of **EM energy, DE, or antiradiation weapons** to attack personnel, facilities, or equipment with the intent of degrading, neutralizing, or destroying enemy combat capability and is considered a form of fires.
Electronic Protection	EP refers to the division of EW involving actions taken **to protect personnel, facilities, and equipment** from any effects of friendly, neutral, or enemy use of the EMS, as well as naturally occurring phenomena that degrade, neutralize, or destroy friendly combat capability.
Electronic Warfare Support	ES refers to the division of EW involving actions tasked by, or under direct control of, an operational commander to search for, intercept, identify, and locate or localize sources of intentional and unintentional radiated EM energy for the purpose of immediate threat recognition, targeting, planning, and conduct of future operations.
Principal Electronic Warfare Activities	The principal EW activities have been developed over time to exploit the opportunities and vulnerabilities inherent in the physics of EM energy. The principal activities used in EW include the following: countermeasures, EM battle management (EMBM), EM compatibility; EM deception; EM hardening, EM interference resolution, EM intrusion, EM jamming, EMP, EM spectrum control, electronic intelligence collection, electronic masking, electronic probing, electronic reconnaissance, electronics security, EW reprogramming, emission control, JEMSO, JEMSMO, low-observability/stealth, meaconing, navigation warfare (NAVWAR), precision geolocation, and wartime reserve modes.
Electronic Warfare Capabilities and Potential Effects	As an adaptive and responsive form of disruptive or destructive fires, EA's purpose is to gain and maintain friendly advantage within the EMOE and ensure requisite friendly access to the EMS. EW may adversely affect friendly forces when not properly integrated and coordinated. EW is employed to create decisive, standalone effects, or to support military operations by generating various levels of control, detection, denial,

deception, disruption, degradation, exploitation, protection, and destruction.

Electronic Warfare's Role in Irregular Warfare

During irregular warfare, adversaries may operate with unsophisticated electronic means to achieve their objectives. EW can influence the adversary, friendly population, and neutral population, with the joint force commander's (JFC's) information operations (IO) message, in effort to change/win popular support.

Electronic Warfare's Role in Information Operations

EW contributes to the success of IO by using offensive and defensive tactics and techniques in a variety of combinations to shape, disrupt, and exploit adversarial use of the EMS while protecting friendly freedom of action.

Electronic Warfare's Role in Space Operations

Since space-based operations depend on the EMS, EW must be considered. Most operations in space beyond uncontested communications, physical maneuvering, and uncontested EM collection involve some form of EW.

Electronic Warfare's Role in Cyberspace Operations

Since cyberspace requires both wired and wireless links to transport information, both offensive and defensive cyberspace operations may require use of the EMS for the enabling of effects in cyberspace. Due to the complementary nature and potential synergistic effects of EW and computer network operations, they must be coordinated to ensure they are applied to maximize effectiveness.

Electronic Warfare's Relationship to Navigation Warfare

EW produces NAVWAR effects by protecting or denying transmitted global navigation satellite system or other radio navigation aid signals.

Directed Energy

DE is an umbrella term covering technologies that produce concentrated EM energy and atomic or subatomic particles. A **DE weapon** is a system using DE primarily as a means to incapacitate, damage, disable, or destroy enemy equipment, facilities, and/or personnel.

Intelligence and Electronic Warfare Support

The distinction between whether a given asset is performing an ES mission or an intelligence mission is determined by who tasks or controls the collection assets, what they are tasked to provide, and for what purpose they are tasked. ES and signals intelligence (SIGINT) operations often share the same or similar assets and resources, and may be tasked to simultaneously collect information that meets both requirements.

Organizing for Joint Electronic Warfare

Responsibilities

How joint staffs are organized to plan and execute electronic warfare is a prerogative of the JFC.

EW planning and operations can be divided among multiple directorates of a joint staff based on long-, mid-, and near-term functionality and based upon availability of qualified EW personnel. **Long-range planning** of EW normally occurs under the plans directorate of a joint staff, while **near/mid-term planning and the supervision** of EW execution normally falls within the purview of the operations directorate of a joint staff (J-3).

Joint Electronic Warfare Organization

Joint Force Commander's EW Staff (JCEWS). The JCEWS is headed by the command electronic warfare officer (EWO), who is designated as the JCEWS chief. The JCEWS develops operation plans (OPLANs) and concept plans and monitors routine EW operations and activities.

Joint Electronic Warfare Cell. The JFC may designate and empower a joint electronic warfare cell (EWC) to organize, execute, and oversee conduct of EW.

Joint Frequency Management Organization

Each geographic combatant commander is specifically tasked by policy to establish a frequency management structure that includes a **joint frequency management office (JFMO)** and to establish procedures to support planned and ongoing operations. To accomplish these tasks, each supported combatant commander establishes a JFMO, typically under the cognizance of the communications system directorate of a joint staff, to **support joint planning, coordination, and operational control of the EMS** for assigned forces.

Organization of Intelligence Support to Electronic Warfare

At the national level, organizations and agencies such as the Central Intelligence Agency, National Security Agency/Central Security Service, National Geospatial-Intelligence Agency, and Defense Intelligence Agency are constantly seeking to identify, catalog, and update the electronic order of battle (EOB) of identified or potential adversaries. The joint intelligence operations center responds to theater-level EW-related intelligence requirements and forwards requests that require national-level assets to the defense collection coordination center or other national-level organizations according to established procedures. The intelligence directorate of a joint staff (J-2) [at the subordinate joint force level] normally assigns one or more members of the staff to act as a liaison between the J-2 section and the IO cell where EW planners are normally assigned.

Service Organization for Electronic Warfare

Each Service has a different approach to organizing its forces.

Army

The Army is organized to work in the structure of an electronic warfare working group with the foundation of the group centered on the EWO, the EW technician, and the EW specialist, who comprise the electronic warfare coordination cell (EWCC).

Marines

Marine EW assets are integral to the Marine air-ground task force (MAGTF). The MAGTF command element task organizes and coordinates EW systems to meet MAGTF EW needs and ultimately achieve the JFC's objectives.

Navy

Navy EW is executed by surface ships, aircraft, and submarines organized in strike groups. For each strike group, the IO warfare commander is responsible for coordinating and integrating EW, typically through the strike group EWO, into naval and joint operations.

Air Force

Within the Air Force component, dedicated EW support assets conduct a variety of EA, EP, and ES operations and support suppression of enemy air defenses (SEAD) and IO mission areas. These are all under the operational control of the commander, Air Force forces.

Planning Joint Electronic Warfare

Joint electronic warfare is centrally planned and directed and decentrally executed.

EW is a complex mission area that should be fully integrated with other aspects of joint operations in order to achieve its full potential. Such integration requires careful planning. EW planners must coordinate their planned activities with other aspects of military operations that use the EMS, as well as third party users that EW does not wish to disrupt.

Electronic Warfare Planning Considerations

Some of the considerations for planning EW in support of military operations include EMS management, EW support of SEAD, EW support against a nontraditional threat, EW reprogramming, electronic masking, interoperability, rules of engagement (ROE), unintended consequences, meteorological and oceanographic considerations, and chemical, biological, radiological, and nuclear considerations. Since EW activity may create effects within and throughout the entire EMS, joint EW planners must closely coordinate their efforts with those members of the joint staff who are concerned with managing military EMS use. EW activities frequently involve a unique set of complex issues. There are Department of Defense directives and instructions, laws, rules, law of armed conflict, and theater ROE that may affect EW activities. Commanders should seek legal review during all levels of EW planning and execution, to include development of theater ROE.

Joint Electronic Warfare Planning Process

In order to be fully integrated into other aspects of a planned operation, the EWC conducts joint EW planning beginning as early as possible and coordinates it with other aspects of the plan throughout the joint operation planning process. Proper EW planning requires understanding of the joint planning and decision-making processes; nature of time constrained operations; potential contributions of EW; and employment of joint EW. During execution, EW planners must monitor the plan's progress and be prepared to make modifications to the plan as the dynamics of the operation evolve.

Electronic Warfare Planning Guidance

Planning guidance for EW is included as tab D (EW) to appendix 3 (Information Operations) to annex C (Operations) of the OPLAN. EW plans should identify the desired EM profile; identify EW missions and tasks to Service or functional component commanders; evaluate adversary threats; and reflect the guidance, policies, and EW employment authorities.

Electronic Warfare Planning Aids

There are a number of automated planning tools available to help joint EW planners carry out their responsibilities. These tools can be divided into three broad categories: databases, planning process aids, and spatial and propagation modeling tools. **Databases** can assist EW planners by providing easy access to a wide variety of platform-specific technical data used in assessing the EW threat and planning appropriate friendly responses to that threat. **Planning process aids** include aids that automate OPLAN development and automated frequency management tools. Geographic information systems **[spatial and propagation modeling tools]** enable analysis and display of geographically referenced information.

Coordinating Joint Electronic Warfare

Once a plan has been approved and an operation has commenced, the preponderance of electronic warfare staff effort shifts to electromagnetic battle management.

EMBM includes continuous monitoring of the EMOE, EMS management, and the dynamic reallocation of EW assets based on emerging operational issues. Normally, this monitoring is performed by personnel on watch in the joint operations center (JOC).

Joint Electronic Warfare Coordination and Control

At combatant commands and subordinate unified commands, the J-3 is primarily responsible for the EW coordination function. The EW division of the J-3 staff should engage in the full range of EW functions to include deliberate planning; day-to-day planning and monitoring of routine theater EW activities in conjunction with the combatant command's theater campaign plan; and crisis action planning in preparation for EW as part of emergent joint operations. Since EW is concerned with **attacking personnel, facilities, or equipment (EA); protecting capabilities and EMS access (EP); and monitoring, exploiting, and targeting use of the EMS (ES),** EW staff personnel have a role in the **dynamic management** of the EMS, via tools and processes, during operations. A **comprehensive and well-thought-out joint restricted frequency list and emission control plan** are two significant tools that **permit flexibility of EW actions** during an operation without compromising friendly EMS use. The **electronic warfare control authority**, the senior EA authority in the operational area, develops guidance for performing EA on behalf of the JFC.

Service Component Coordination Procedures

Components requiring electronic warfare support from another component should be encouraged to directly coordinate that support when possible.

When the JFC has chosen to conduct operations through functional components, the functional component commanders will determine how their components are organized and what procedures are used. EW planners should coordinate with the functional component electronic warfare elements to determine how they are organized and what procedures are being used by functional component forces.

Army	The Army Service component command or Army component operations staff office (Army division or higher staff) plans, coordinates, and integrates EW requirements in support of the JFC's objectives.
Marines	The MAGTF headquarters EWCC, if established, or the MAGTF EWO, if there is no EWCC, is responsible for coordination of the joint aspects of MAGTF EW requirements.
Navy	The Navy operations directorate is responsible for all Navy EW efforts and provides coordination and tasking to task forces assigned.
Air Force	Air Force requirements for other component EW support are established through close coordination between the JFC's EWC and the commander, Air Force forces' operations directorate (or equivalent operations directorate) or plans directorate (or equivalent plans directorate), in coordination with the Director for Intelligence, A-2.
Special Operations Forces	Requirements from special operations units for EW support will be transmitted to the joint force special operations component command JOC for coordination with the joint force special operations component command IO cell.
United States Coast Guard	During both peacetime and war, joint operations may include United States Coast Guard (USCG) assets that possess EW capabilities. Coordination with USCG assets should be through assigned USCG liaison personnel or operational procedures specified in the OPLAN or operation order.
Electronic Warfare and Intelligence, Surveillance, and Reconnaissance Coordination	It is vital that all prudent measures are taken to **ensure EMS activities are closely and continuously deconflicted with ES** and intelligence collection activities. The J-2 must ensure that EW collection priorities and ES sensors are integrated into a **complete intelligence collection plan.**
Electronic Warfare and Interagency Coordination	Although there may not be intentional targeting of the EMS, inadvertent and unintentional interference may wreak havoc on the systems being used to support the execution of interagency operations. As such, constant and detailed coordination is essential between EW activities and relevant interagency organizations.

Multinational Aspects of Electronic Warfare

As in joint operations, electronic warfare is an integral part of multinational operations.

US planners should integrate US and partner nations' EW capabilities into an overall EW plan, provide partner nations with information concerning US EW capabilities, and provide EW support to partner nations. The planning of multinational force (MNF) EW is made more difficult because of security issues, different cryptographic equipment, differences in the level of training of involved forces, and language barriers.

Multinational Force Electronic Warfare Organization and Command and Control

The multinational force commander (MNFC) **provides guidance for planning and conducting EW operations to the MNF** through the operations directorate's combined EWCC.

Multinational Electronic Warfare Coordination Cell with Allies and Other Friendly Forces

The MNFC should include EWOs from supporting MNFs within the EWCC. Should this not be practical for security reasons or availability, the MNFC should, based on the mission, be prepared to provide EW support and the appropriate liaison officers to the multinational units.

Electronic Warfare Mutual Support

Exchange of SIGINT information in support of EW operations should be conducted in accordance with standard NATO, American, British, Canadian, Australian Armies Program, and Air and Space Interoperability Council procedures, as appropriate. **Exchange of EOB** in peacetime is normally achieved under bilateral agreement. **Reprogramming** of EW equipment is a national responsibility. However, the EWCC chief should be aware of reprogramming efforts being conducted within the MNF.

Releasability of Electronic Warfare Information to Multinational Forces

A clear, easily understood policy on the disclosure of EW information requested by multinational partners should be developed by the commander's foreign disclosure officer as early as possible.

CONCLUSION

This publication provides joint doctrine for the planning, execution, and assessment of electronic warfare across the range of military operations.

Other books we publish on Amazon.com

FM 7-22

HOLISTIC HEALTH AND FITNESS

Customer reviews

★★★★☆ 4.7 out of 5

ATP 7-22.02

HOLISTIC HEALTH AND FITNESS

Drills and Exercises

Customer reviews

★★★★★ 5 out of 5

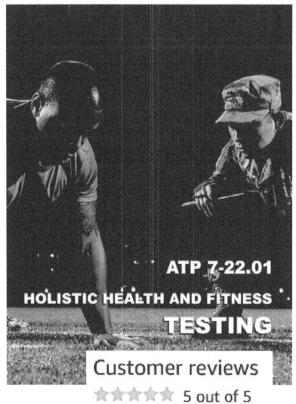

ATP 7-22.01

HOLISTIC HEALTH AND FITNESS

TESTING

Customer reviews

★★★★★ 5 out of 5

Army Combat Fitness Test

3.0

Includes:
ACFT 3.0 Scoring Standards
ACFT Performance Categories
Blank Test Scorecards

CHAPTER I
OVERVIEW OF ELECTRONIC WARFARE

"There is much more to electronic warfare than simply detecting enemy transmissions."

Martin Van Creveld
Technology and War, **1989**

1. Introduction

Military operations are executed in an environment complicated by increasingly complex demands on the electromagnetic spectrum (EMS). All modern forces depend on the EMS. The EMS is the entire range of electromagnetic (EM) radiation. At one end of the spectrum are gamma rays, which have the shortest wavelengths and high frequencies. At the other end are radio waves, which have the longest wavelengths and low frequencies. The EMS is used to organize and explain the types of EM energy that exist in our world and throughout the universe. Devices whose functions depend upon the EMS are used by both civilian and military organizations and individuals for **intelligence; communications; positioning, navigation, and timing (PNT); sensing; command and control (C2); attack; ranging; data transmission; and information storage and processing**. The military requirement for unimpeded access to, and use of, the EMS is the key focus for joint electromagnetic spectrum operations (JEMSO), both in support of military operations and as the focus of operations themselves. Electronic warfare (EW) is essential for protecting friendly operations and denying adversary operations within the EMS throughout the operational environment (OE).

2. Military Operations and the Electromagnetic Environment

a. The Electromagnetic Spectrum

(1) The EMS is a highly regulated continuum of EM waves arranged according to frequency and wavelengths. The EMS (Figure I-1) includes the full range of all possible frequencies of EM radiation.

(2) The use of the EMS is essential to control the OE during all military operations. The transfer of information from the collectors to the platforms will use the EMS. The EMS is constrained by both civil uses and adversary attempts to deny the use of the EMS—creating a congested and contested environment.

b. Joint Electromagnetic Spectrum Operations

(1) JEMSO includes all activities to successfully plan and execute joint or multinational operations in order to control the electromagnetic operational environment (EMOE).

(2) JEMSO are the coordinated efforts of EW and joint electromagnetic spectrum management operations (JEMSMO) to exploit, attack, protect, and manage the EMOE. They

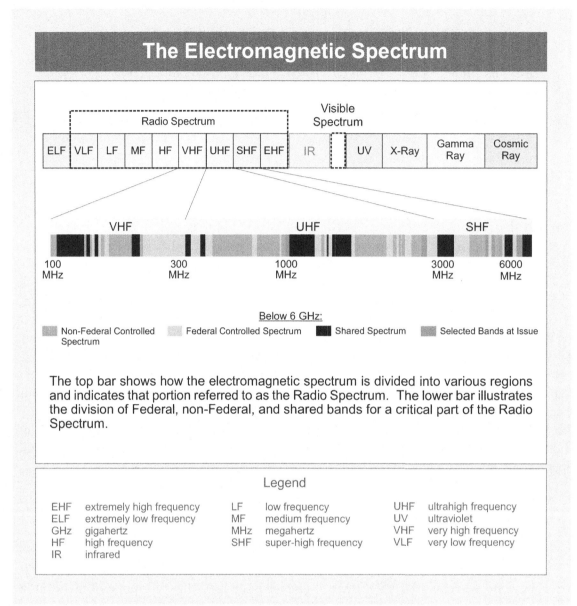

Figure I-1. The Electromagnetic Spectrum

enable EMS-dependent systems to function in the intended OE. JEMSO enable and support the six joint functions through all phases of military operations.

c. **The Electromagnetic Operational Environment**

(1) As discussed in Joint Publication (JP) 3-0, *Joint Operations*, the OE is the composite of the conditions, circumstances, and influences that affect employment of capabilities and bear on the decisions of the commander. It encompasses physical areas and factors (of the air, land, maritime, and space domains) and the information environment (which includes cyberspace) (see Figure I-2). The joint force commander (JFC) defines these areas with geographical boundaries in order to facilitate coordination, integration, and deconfliction of joint operations among joint force components and supporting commands.

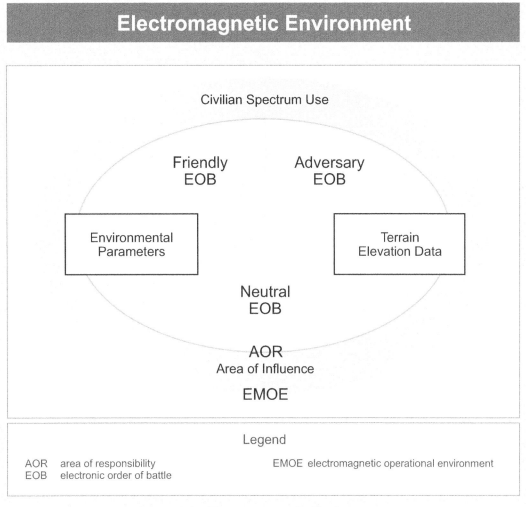

Figure I-2. Electromagnetic Environment

As with the OE, the goal of the JFC is to shape and control the EMOE. However, the electromagnetic environment (EME) in which this occurs transcends all physical domains and the information environment, and extends beyond defined borders or boundaries, thus complicating JEMSO. A variety of factors, including the types of equipment employed, users of the equipment (e.g., air, naval, and land forces), adversary capabilities, geography, and weather also significantly influence the conduct of JEMSO.

(2) The EME is described as the resulting product of the power and time distribution, in various frequency ranges, of the radiated or conducted EM emissions that may be encountered by a military force, system, or platform when performing its assigned mission in its intended OE. It is the sum of electromagnetic interference (EMI); electromagnetic pulse (EMP); hazards of EM radiation to personnel, ordnance, and volatile materials; and natural phenomena effects of sunspots, lightning, and precipitation static. Essentially, the EME is the global EM background.

(3) The EMOE is the background EME and the friendly, neutral, and adversarial electronic order of battle (EOB) within the EM area of influence associated with a given operational area (OA). This is the portion of the EME where JEMSO is conducted at a given time.

(4) EMS-dependent systems operate more efficiently in specific frequency bands depending on their function. These systems are also affected by different elements of the operating environment (e.g., jungle, urban, or harsh climatic environments). Examples include the adverse effects of fog, rain, and snow on super-high frequencies used for satellite communications (SATCOM); the effects of solar activities such as sunspots, solar flares, and atmospheric fluctuations on systems that use high frequency for propagation; and the effects of man-made interference from other transmitters, power lines, or static electricity on all systems.

d. **Electromagnetic Environmental Effects (E3).** The impact of an EMOE upon the operational capability of military forces, equipment, systems, and platforms is referred to as E3. It encompasses all EM disciplines to include electromagnetic compatibility (EMC); EMI; EM vulnerability; EMP; electronic protection (EP); hazards of EM radiation to personnel, ordnance, and volatile materials; and natural phenomena effects such as sunspots, lightning, and precipitation static. All EM-dependent systems are vulnerable, to some degree, to the effects of EM energy.

3. Role of Electronic Warfare Across the Range of Military Operations

a. The term EW refers to military action involving the **use of EM energy and directed energy (DE) to control the EMS or to attack the enemy. EW consists of three divisions:** electronic attack (EA), EP, and electronic warfare support (ES). DE is an umbrella term covering technologies that produce concentrated EM energy or atomic or subatomic particles. DE capabilities complement and optimize the use of EW because DE is an enabler for all mission areas. Figure I-3 depicts an overview of EW, the relationships of the three divisions, and the relationship of the divisions to principal EW activities.

b. **Electronic Attack.** EA refers to the division of EW involving the use of **EM energy, DE, or antiradiation weapons** to attack personnel, facilities, or equipment with the intent of degrading, neutralizing, or destroying enemy combat capability and is considered a form of fires (see JP 3-09, *Joint Fire Support*). EA:

(1) Includes actions taken to prevent or reduce an enemy's effective use of the EMS via employment of systems or weapons that use EM energy (e.g., jamming in the form of EM disruption, degradation, denial, and deception). EA includes both active EA, in which EA systems or weapons radiate in the EMS, as well as passive EA (non-radiating/re-radiating) such as chaff.

(2) Includes employment of systems or weapons that use radiated EM energy (to include DE) as their primary disruptive or destructive mechanism. Examples include lasers, electro-optical, infrared (IR), and radio frequency (RF) weapons such as high-power microwave (HPM) or those employing an EMP.

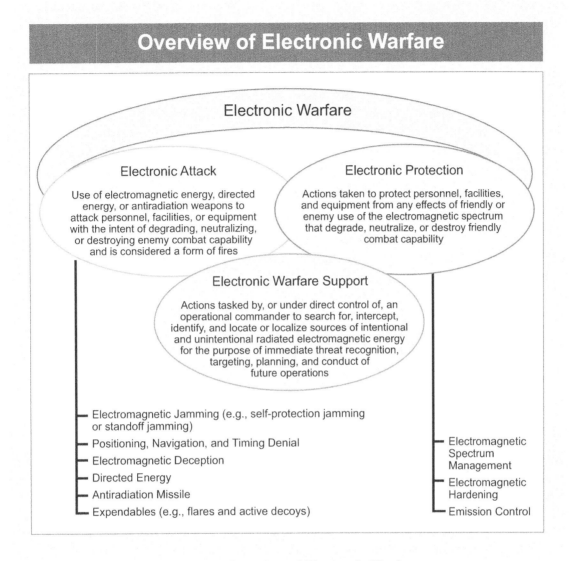

Figure I-3. Overview of Electronic Warfare

(3) Can be used for both offensive and defensive purposes.

(a) Offensive EA activities are generally conducted at the request and onset of friendly force engagement of the enemy. In many cases, these activities suppress a threat for only a limited period of time. Examples include employing self-propelled decoys; jamming an adversary's radar or C2 systems; using antiradiation missiles to suppress an adversary's air defenses; using electronic deception techniques to confuse an adversary's intelligence, surveillance, and reconnaissance (ISR) systems; and using DE weapons to disable an adversary's personnel, facilities, or equipment and disable or destroy material (e.g., satellites on orbit, airborne optical sensors, or massed land forces).

(b) Defensive EA activities use the EMS to protect personnel, facilities, capabilities and equipment. Examples include self-protection and force protection measures such as use of expendables (e.g., flares and active decoys), protection jammers and lasers, towed decoys, and DE IR countermeasures systems.

c. **Electronic Protection.** EP refers to the division of EW involving actions taken **to protect personnel, facilities, and equipment** from any effects of friendly, neutral, or enemy use of the EMS, as well as naturally occurring phenomena that degrade, neutralize, or destroy friendly combat capability. EP focuses on system or process attributes or capabilities. Inherent hardware features minimize the impact of unplanned/undesired EM signals on an EM-dependent system's operation. EP processes are designed to eliminate, reduce, or mitigate the impact of the same unplanned/undesired EM signals. These features and processes combine to allow friendly capabilities to continue to function, as intended, in contested and congested EMOEs.

(1) EP includes actions taken to ensure friendly use of the EMS, such as frequency agility in a radio, variable pulse repetition frequency in a radar, receiver/signal processing, spread spectrum technology, spectrum management processes, frequency coordination measures (e.g., joint restricted frequency list [JRFL]), Global Positioning System (GPS) signal protection measures, selective opacity (i.e., the phenomenon of not permitting the passage of EM radiation) of optical apertures, emission control (EMCON) procedures, and use of wartime reserve modes (WARMs).

(2) EP is not force protection or self-protection. EP is an EMS-dependent system's use of EM energy and/or physical properties to preserve itself from direct or environmental effects of friendly and adversary EW, thereby allowing the system to continue operating. The use of flare rejection logic on an IR missile (i.e., allowing the IR missile to continue to function despite an adversary's use of flares) is EP. The flare rejection technique ensures friendly use of the EMS to track the intended target despite the adversary's self-protection/defensive EA actions (i.e., the flare) to prevent or reduce friendly use of the EMS. Although defensive EA actions and EP both protect personnel, facilities, capabilities, and equipment, EP protects from the effects of EA (friendly and/or adversary) or EMI, while defensive EA is primarily used to protect against lethal attacks by denying adversary use of the EMS to target, guide, and/or trigger weapons.

d. **Electronic Warfare Support.** ES refers to the division of EW involving actions tasked by, or under direct control of, an operational commander to search for, intercept, identify, and locate or localize sources of intentional and unintentional radiated EM energy for the purpose of immediate threat recognition, targeting, planning, and conduct of future operations. ES prepares the EME for the commander to perform operational missions. ES synchronizes and integrates the planning and operational use of sensors, assets, and processes within a specific battle space to reduce uncertainties concerning the enemy, environment, time, and terrain. ES data can be used to produce signals intelligence (SIGINT), provide targeting for electronic or physical attack, and produce measurement and signature intelligence.

4. Principal Electronic Warfare Activities

The principal EW activities have been developed over time to **exploit the opportunities and vulnerabilities inherent in the physics of EM energy.** Although the basic physics of EM energy has remained constant, activities using convenient and affordable technology have changed dramatically and continue to be a challenge. The principal activities used in EW include the following:

a. **Countermeasures.** Countermeasures are that form of military science that, by the employment of devices and/or techniques, is designed to impair the operational effectiveness of enemy activity. Countermeasures can be active or passive and can be deployed preemptively or reactively. Examples include electro-optical-infrared (EO-IR) and RF countermeasures such as flares or chaff.

(1) **Electro-Optical-Infrared Countermeasures (EO-IR CMs).** Any device or technique employing EO-IR materials or technology that is intended to impair the effectiveness of enemy activity, particularly with respect to precision guided weapons and sensor systems. EO-IR CMs may use laser jammers, smokes/aerosols, signature suppressants, decoys, pyrotechnics/pyrophorics, high-energy lasers, or directed IR energy countermeasures.

(2) **Radio Frequency Countermeasures.** Devices and techniques that employ RF technology to impair the effectiveness of adversary activity (e.g., precision-guided or radio-controlled weapons, communications equipment, and sensor systems).

b. **Electromagnetic Battle Management (EMBM).** EMBM is the dynamic monitoring, assessing, planning and directing of JEMSO in support of the commander's scheme of maneuver. EMBM will proactively harness multiple platforms and diverse capabilities into a networked and cohesive sensor/decision/target/engagement system, as well as protect friendly use of the EMS while strategically denying benefits to the adversary.

c. **Electromagnetic Compatibility. EMC** is the ability of systems, equipment, and devices that utilize the EMS to operate in their intended OE **without suffering unacceptable degradation or causing unintentional degradation** because of EM radiation or response. EMC involves the application of sound EMS management: planning, coordinating, and managing joint use of the EMS through operational, engineering, and administrative procedures that ensure interference-free operation; and clear concepts and doctrine that maximize operational effectiveness.

d. **Electromagnetic Deception.** EM deception is the deliberate radiation, re-radiation, alteration, suppression, absorption, denial, enhancement, or reflection of EM energy in a manner **intended to convey misleading information to an enemy** or to enemy EM-dependent weapons, thereby degrading or neutralizing the enemy's combat capability. Among the types of EM deception are the following:

(1) **Manipulative.** This involves actions to eliminate revealing, or convey misleading, EM telltale indicators that may be used by hostile forces.

(2) **Simulative.** This involves actions to simulate friendly, notional, or actual capabilities to mislead hostile forces.

(3) **Imitative.** This involves actions to imitate enemy emissions to mislead hostile forces.

e. **Electromagnetic Hardening.** EM hardening consists of actions taken to protect personnel, facilities, and equipment by **filtering, attenuating, grounding, bonding, blanking, and shielding** against undesirable effects of EM energy. EM hardening is an EP activity.

f. **Electromagnetic Interference Resolution.** EMI resolution is the step-by-step process used to systematically diagnose the cause or source of EMI. EMI is any EM disturbance that **interrupts, obstructs, or otherwise degrades or limits the effective performance** of electronics and electrical equipment. It can be induced intentionally, as in some forms of EA, or unintentionally, as a result of spurious emissions and responses, intermodulation products, and inadequate EMS management.

g. **Electromagnetic Intrusion.** EM intrusion is the intentional insertion of EM energy into transmission paths in any manner, with the objective of **deceiving operators or causing confusion**.

h. **Electromagnetic Jamming.** EM jamming is the deliberate radiation, reradiation, or reflection of EM energy for the purpose of **preventing or reducing an enemy's effective use of the EMS,** and with the intent of degrading or neutralizing the enemy's combat capability.

i. **Electromagnetic Pulse.** EMP is EM radiation from a strong electronic pulse that can be produced by a nuclear explosion or generated conventionally that may couple with electrical or electronic systems to produce damaging current and voltage surges. EMP may be employed as a weapon (i.e., EA) or accounted for in the shielding and protection (i.e., EP) of friendly equipment, personnel, and facilities against its effects. EMP is one way that a nuclear detonation produces its damaging effects. The effects of EMP can extend to hundreds of kilometers depending on the height and yield of a nuclear burst. A high-altitude electromagnetic pulse (HEMP) can generate significant disruptive field strengths over a continental-size area. The portion of the EMS most affected by EMP and HEMP is the radio spectrum. Planning for communications system protection is significant when the potential for EMP is likely.

For more information on EMP considerations during military operations, refer to JP 3-11, Operations in Chemical, Biological, Radiological, and Nuclear (CBRN) Environments; *JP 3-41,* Chemical, Biological, Radiological, and Nuclear Consequence Management; *and Field Manual (FM) 3-11.4/Marine Corps Warfighting Publication (MCWP) 3-37.2/Navy Tactics, Techniques, and Procedures (NTTP) 3-11.27/Air Force Tactics, Techniques, and Procedures (Instruction) (AFTTP[I]) 3-2.46,* Multi-Service Tactics, Techniques, and Procedures for Nuclear, Biological, and Chemical Protection.

j. **Electromagnetic Spectrum Control**. Freedom of action in the EMOE is achieved through the coordinated execution of JEMSO with other lethal and nonlethal operations impacting the EMOE.

k. **Electronic Intelligence (ELINT) Collection**. ELINT, a subcomponent of SIGINT, is the **technical and geospatial intelligence derived from foreign noncommunications EM radiations** emanating from other than nuclear detonations or radioactive sources.

l. **Electronic Masking**. Electronic masking is the **controlled radiation of EM energy on friendly frequencies** in a manner to protect the emissions of friendly communications and electronic systems against enemy ES measures/SIGINT without significantly degrading the operation of friendly systems.

m. **Electronic Probing**. Electronic probing is the **intentional radiation designed to be introduced into the devices or systems of potential enemies** for the purpose of learning the functions and operational capabilities of the devices or systems.

n. **Electronic Reconnaissance**. Electronic reconnaissance is the **detection, location, identification, and evaluation of foreign EM radiations**.

o. **Electronics Security**. Electronics security is the protection resulting from all measures designed to **deny unauthorized persons information of value** that might be derived from their interception and study of communications and noncommunications EM radiations (e.g., radar).

p. **Electronic Warfare Reprogramming**. EW reprogramming is the **deliberate alteration or modification of EW or target sensing systems (TSSs)** in response to validated changes in equipment, tactics, or the EME. These changes may be the result of deliberate actions on the part of friendly, adversary, or third parties, or may be brought about by EMI or other inadvertent phenomena. The purpose of EW reprogramming is to maintain or enhance the effectiveness of EW and TSS equipment. EW reprogramming includes changes to self-defense systems, offensive weapons systems, and intelligence collection systems.

q. **Emission Control**. The selective and controlled use of EM, acoustic, or other emitters to **optimize C2 capabilities** while minimizing, for operations security (OPSEC):

(1) Detection by enemy sensors.

(2) Mutual interference among friendly systems.

(3) Enemy interference with the ability to execute a military deception (MILDEC) plan.

r. **Joint Electromagnetic Spectrum Operations**. JEMSO are the coordinated efforts of EW and JEMSMO to exploit, attack, protect, and manage the EMOE to achieve the commander's objectives.

s. **Joint Electromagnetic Spectrum Management Operations (JEMSMO).** Effective JEMSMO is integral to the successful execution of military operations. They consist of planning, coordinating, and managing joint use of the EMS through **operational, engineering, and administrative procedures.** The primary goal of JEMSMO is to enable electronic systems to perform their functions in the intended environment without causing or suffering unacceptable interference.

For more information on JEMSMO, refer to JP 6-01, Joint Electromagnetic Spectrum Management Operations.

t. **Low-Observability/Stealth.** All equipment, personnel, and facilities emit and reflect EM energy as discernible and often characteristic signatures (e.g., heat, light, magnetic, and RF) that can be collected and exploited. Assets involved in operations may incorporate low-observability/stealth EP attributes, thereby increasing their ability to operate in the physical domains by reducing the possibility of their detection and exploitation by adversaries. Low-observability/stealth and other signature reduction techniques also improve the effectiveness of EO-IR CMs.

u. **Meaconing.** Meaconing consists of receiving radio beacon signals and rebroadcasting them on the same frequency to confuse navigation. The meaconing stations cause inaccurate bearings to be obtained by aircraft or ground stations.

v. **Navigation Warfare (NAVWAR).** NAVWAR refers to deliberate defensive and offensive action to assure and prevent PNT information through coordinated employment of space, cyberspace, and EW operations.

w. **Precision Geolocation.** Precision geolocation involves planning, coordinating, and managing friendly assets to perform the function of geolocating enemy RF systems for the purposes of targeting, using EW assets among other sources of information, and intelligence data.

x. **Wartime Reserve Modes.** WARM are characteristics and operating procedures of sensors, communications, navigation aids, threat recognition, weapons, and countermeasures systems that **will contribute to military effectiveness if unknown to, or misunderstood by, opposing commanders** before they are used, but could be exploited or neutralized if known in advance. WARM are deliberately held in reserve for wartime or emergency use and seldom, if ever, applied or intercepted prior to such use.

5. Electronic Warfare Capabilities and Potential Effects

a. EW is conducted to secure and maintain freedom of action in the EMOE for friendly forces to deny the same to the adversary. As an adaptive and responsive form of disruptive or destructive fires, EA's purpose is to gain and maintain friendly advantage within the EMOE and ensure requisite friendly access to the EMS. EW can be applied from all physical domains by manned and unmanned systems. EW may adversely affect friendly forces when not properly integrated and coordinated. EW is employed to create decisive, standalone effects, or to support military operations by generating various levels of control, detection, denial, deception, disruption, degradation, exploitation, protection, and destruction. EW can further affect the OE by influencing both friendly and adversary leaders and population. EW plays a role at the tactical, operational, and strategic levels of war. Performing EA against an early warning radar, for example, has effects at all levels of war. Tactically, it affects cueing of engagement systems. Operationally, it affects the adversary's ability to mass and synchronize forces. Strategically, it prevents the adversary's senior leadership from maintaining a coherent picture of the national security environment. In another scenario, operational remediation of EMI against a national space-based asset (an EP-related process) would call for direction finding (DF) and geolocation of the source (through ES), and perhaps the decision to conduct EA on that source if attributed to hostile intent. While the actions described in this scenario occur within a tactical, time-sensitive context, the ramifications of the events could have strategic or operational-level significance. The value of EW is manifested fully only when commanders consider and employ capabilities across the OE.

b. EW is vital throughout all phases (shape, deter, seize initiative, dominate, stabilize, and enable civil authority) of an operation or campaign. EP attributes and processes are essential across all phases of conflict to ensure all EMS-dependent capabilities are able to operate effectively in operationally stressed EMOEs. During the shape and deter phases, ES assets contribute to the overall understanding of the OE. A judicious commander may employ EW to implement favorable intelligence preparation of the OE without prematurely crossing the threshold to conflict. The potential to employ nondestructive and nonlethal capabilities make EW assets vital to the preparation of the OE. Using EW, joint forces may set the conditions for combat when imminent and prosecute the attack once combat is under way. The ability to achieve an objective through nondestructive means may allow a more rapid transition from the seize initiative and dominate phases to support operations in the stabilize phase. EW may also employ destructive EM fires, decisive for achieving campaign objectives during the seize initiative and dominate phases. From the stabilize to enable civil authority phase, EW can foster restorative operations by offering nonlethal options such as force protection through ES to monitor subversive elements; EP for ensuring communications capabilities continue to function in EMOEs; EA to counter radio-controlled improvised explosive devices; or broadcasting selected themes and messages, to include civil defense messages, to assist civil authorities.

c. EW applications in support of homeland defense are vital to deter, detect, prevent, and defeat external threats such as ballistic missiles, aircraft (manned and unmanned), maritime vessels, land threats, hostile space systems, domestic/international terrorism, and cyberspace threats.

d. When used in support of a deterrence activity or operation, the role of EW goes beyond simply being available to support potential combat operations. EW can support the shaping of adversaries' perceptions and morale, as well as unit cohesion. EW applied toward deterrence objectives can sever lines of communications, logistics, C2, and other key functions while simultaneously protecting friendly capabilities. The physical presence of EW assets (e.g., airborne ES platforms), as well as enabling freedom of navigation activities, can reinforce the deterrent message.

e. **Control.** The overall goal of EW involves the use of EM energy and DE to control the EMS or to attack the enemy. Control of the EMS is achieved by effective management, coordination, and integration of friendly EMS-dependent systems (e.g., communications, ISR, EW, computer networks) while countering and exploiting adversary systems. EA limits adversary use of the EMS; EP secures use of the EMS for friendly forces; and ES enables the commanders to identify and monitor actions in the EMS throughout the OA. EMBM provides the enabling JEMSO processes to ensure effective control of the EMOE. Additionally, commanders should maximize integration among EW and their other combat capabilities as part of their combined arms operations. Activities in control of the EMS can include, but are not limited to:

(1) **Detection.** Detection is identification of potential enemy EM emissions through use of ES measures. It is the essential first step in any follow-on EW activity. Friendly forces must have the capability to detect and characterize interference as hostile jamming or unintentional EMI.

(2) **Exploitation.** Exploitation is taking full advantage of any information that has come to hand for tactical, operational, or strategic purposes. In an EW context, exploitation is ES that refers to taking full advantage of adversary radiated EM energy to identify, recognize, characterize, locate, and track EM radiation sources to support current and future operations. Data transmissions produce EM energy for exploitation by SIGINT, provide targeting for EM or destructive attacks, and develop awareness of operational trends. Examples of exploitation include geolocation of terrestrial EMI sources impacting space assets, terminal homing on adversary communication devices, determination of enemy indications and warnings, and geolocation of RF apertures in cyberspace for targeting. Exploitation may be enhanced or enabled by EA to stimulate target EMS-dependent systems.

(3) **Denial.** Denial is the prevention of access to or use of systems or services. This can be accomplished through numerous means (e.g., EW, computer network operations [CNO], destruction). Denial, in an EW context, is the prevention of an adversary from using EMS-dependent systems (e.g., communications equipment, radar) by affecting a particular portion of the EMS in a specific geographical area for a specific period of time. Denial prevents an adversary from acquiring accurate information about friendly forces. Denial is accomplished through EA techniques (degradation, disruption, or deception); expendable countermeasures; destructive measures; network applications; tactics, techniques, and procedures (TTP); and/or EMCON.

(4) **Disruption.** Disruption is to interrupt the operation of adversary EMS-dependent systems. The techniques interfere with the adversary's use of the EMS to limit the adversary's combat capabilities. A trained adversary operator may be able to thwart disruption through effective EP actions such as changing frequency, EM shielding, etc. The goal of disruption is to confuse or delay adversary action. Disruption is achieved with EM jamming, EM deception, and EM intrusion. These enhance attacks on hostile forces and act as force multipliers by increasing adversary uncertainty while reducing uncertainty for friendly forces. Advanced EA techniques offer the opportunity to nondestructively disrupt or degrade adversary infrastructure.

(5) **Degradation**. Degradation is to reduce the effectiveness or efficiency of adversary EMS-dependent systems. Degradation may confuse or delay the actions of an adversary, but a proficient operator may be able to work around the effects. Degradation is achieved with EM jamming, EM deception, and EM intrusion. Degradation may be the best choice to stimulate the adversary to determine the adversary's response or for EA conditioning.

(6) **Deception.** Deception is measures designed to mislead the adversary by manipulation, distortion, or falsification of evidence to induce the adversary to react in a manner prejudicial to the adversary's interests. Deception in an EW context presents adversary operators and higher-level processing functions with erroneous inputs, either directly through the sensors themselves or through EMS-based networks such as voice communications or data links. Through use of the EMS, EW manipulates the adversary's decision loop, making it difficult to establish an accurate perception of objective reality.

(7) **Destruction.** Destruction is to make the condition of a target so damaged that it can neither function as intended nor be restored to a usable condition. When used in the EW context, destruction is the use of EA to eliminate targeted adversary personnel, facilities, or equipment. Sensors and C2 nodes are lucrative targets because their destruction strongly influences the adversary's perceptions and ability to coordinate actions. Space assets on orbit, as well as computer services in cyberspace, are potentially lucrative targets as well. EW, through ES, supports destruction by providing actionable target locations and/or information. While destruction of adversary equipment is an effective means to permanently eliminate aspects of an adversary's capability, the duration of the effect on operations will depend on the adversary's ability to reconstitute.

(8) **Protection.** Protection is the preservation of the effectiveness and survivability of mission-related military and nonmilitary personnel, equipment, facilities, information, and infrastructure deployed or located within or outside the boundaries of a given OA. It involves the use of physical properties, operational TTP, as well as planning and employment processes to ensure friendly use of the EMS. This includes ensuring that EW activities do not electromagnetically destroy or degrade friendly intelligence sensors, communications systems, PNT capabilities, and other EMS-dependent systems and capabilities. Protection is achieved by component hardening, EMCON, EMS management and deconfliction, and other means to counterattack and defeat adversary attempts to control the EMS. Spectrum management and EW work collaboratively to accomplish active EMS deconfliction, which includes the capabilities to detect, characterize, geolocate, and mitigate EMI that affects operations. Additionally, structures such as a joint force commander's electronic warfare staff (JCEWS) or electronic warfare cell (EWC) enhance operational-level EP through coordination and integration of EW into the overall scheme of maneuver. It is not always possible to prevent the degradation of friendly systems from the effects of friendly forces' EW operations. In these cases, the JFC should make a determination on which system has a higher priority based on the capability provided by each system.

f. EA Delivery

EW effects can be generated from a variety of platforms including, but not limited to, aircraft, ground sites, maritime vessels, space assets, and cyberspace. In many cases, techniques and equipment that work in one arena will provide similar success in disparate environments. The same techniques and equipment for isolating the OE may be applicable regardless of whether the target is in a physical domain or the information environment (which includes cyberspace).

6. Electronic Warfare's Role in Irregular Warfare

EW plays a vital role in countering the adversary's use of the EMS during conventional operations or in irregular warfare (IW). During IW, adversaries may operate with unsophisticated electronic means to achieve their objectives. EW is an enabling capability that when integrated into the JFC's concept of operations (CONOPS) will improve the capacity of the joint forces, indigenous government, and its security forces' ability to wage IW. For this reason, it is important to integrate EW early during IW, especially as current and future uses of the EMS multiply. EW can influence the adversary, friendly population, and neutral population, with the JFC's information operations (IO) message, in effort to change/win popular support. Improper application or inadvertent targeting of friendly assets by EW forces may undermine popular support and legitimacy similar to kinetic collateral damage. Proper planning and deconfliction must be accomplished at all levels.

7. Electronic Warfare's Role in Information Operations

a. IO is the integrated employment, during military operations, of information-related capabilities in concert with other lines of operation (LOOs) to influence, disrupt, corrupt, or usurp the decision making of adversaries and potential adversaries while protecting those of friendly forces.

b. EW contributes to the success of IO by using offensive and defensive tactics and techniques in a variety of combinations to shape, disrupt, and exploit adversarial use of the EMS while protecting friendly freedom of action. Expanding reliance on the EMS for a wide range of purposes increases both the potential and the challenges of EW in IO. The increasing prevalence of wireless telephone and computer usage extends both the utility and threat of EW, offering opportunities to exploit an adversary's EM vulnerabilities and a requirement to identify and protect friendly communications from similar exploitation.

c. All EW activities conducted in joint operations should be coordinated through JCEWS or joint EWC. These staffs should integrate their efforts into the JFC's targeting cycle to coordinate nonlethal and lethal fires in strike operations. In addition, they should participate in, and coordinate with, the JFC's IO cell, to align objective priorities and help synchronize EW employment with information-related capabilities and operations.

For more information on IO, refer to JP 3-13, Information Operations.

8. Electronic Warfare's Role in Space Operations

Space operations and space control are enabled by EW. Since space-based operations depend on the EMS, EW must be considered. Most operations in space beyond uncontested communications, physical maneuvering, and uncontested EM collection involve some form of EW. For example, EA may be used to deny an adversary freedom of action in space by preventing the C2 of space assets or by preventing or negating the ability to use space systems and services for purposes hostile to the US. EP aids in the protection of space capabilities of national interest from adversary interference. Finally, ES may be used to maintain awareness of the location and status of friendly and adversary space assets or used to find and fix sources of EMI affecting friendly space-based assets.

For more information on space operations, refer to JP 3-14, Space Operations.

9. Electronic Warfare's Role in Cyberspace Operations

a. The advances in, and proliferation of, advanced technology have created an increasingly complex OE. Wired and wireless networks continue to evolve, and mobile computing devices continue to grow in both capability and number. Couple these emerging trends with an adversary's adaptive use of the EMS and the task becomes all the more challenging. Since cyberspace requires both wired and wireless links to transport information, both offensive and defensive cyberspace operations may require use of the EMS for the enabling of effects in cyberspace. Due to the complementary nature and potential synergistic effects of EW and CNO, they must be coordinated to ensure they are applied to maximize effectiveness. Cyberspace operations may be used to force an adversary from wired to wireless networks that are vulnerable to EA. EW may be used to set favorable conditions for cyberspace operations by stimulating networked sensors, denying wireless networks, or other related actions. In the defensive environment, EW systems may detect and defeat attacks across wireless access points.

b. Primary considerations of EW activities should be their intended and unintended effects on the information technology infrastructures of cyberspace and the broader range of communications architectures comprising the Department of Defense (DOD) information networks, including the possibility of EMI or EM fratricide on friendly communications. The increasing wireless and spaced-based communication path dependencies of cyberspace/DOD information networks infrastructure are susceptible to interference and attack from EW. Therefore, EW and spectrum management experts within the JCEWS or EWC must coordinate closely with the combatant command's theater network operations control center (TNCC) and designated joint frequency management office (JFMO). The TNCC coordinates with United States Cyber Command (USCYBERCOM) to deconflict the anticipated effects of friendly and, if possible, adversary EW operations on cyberspace/DOD information networks infrastructure. In support of United States Strategic Command's (USSTRATCOM's) Unified Command Plan-assigned mission, USCYBERCOM directs operation and defense of the DOD information networks.

c. Network operations (NETOPS) and computer network defense are continuous operations in cyberspace, just as EP and spectrum management are continuous operations in the EMS. NETOPS are the DOD-wide operational, organizational, and technical capabilities for operating and defending the DOD information networks. NETOPS include, but are not limited to, enterprise management, net assurance, and content management. A secure network is a necessary prerequisite to successful operations. Control of the EMS is a prerequisite to the security of DOD networks due to their increasing reliance on the EMS. EW provides the security for those networks in the EMS as the control and protection mechanism of JEMSO.

10. Electronic Warfare's Relationship to Nuclear Operations

Nuclear operations require a specialized focus, understanding, and an appropriate application of EW. EW during nuclear operations is essential to mission success and therefore must be organized, planned, and coordinated at the national and multinational levels.

11. Electronic Warfare's Relationship to Navigation Warfare

EW produces NAVWAR effects by protecting or denying transmitted global navigation satellite system (GNSS) or other radio navigation aid signals. Delivery of NAVWAR capabilities is also supported by efforts in space control, space force enhancement, and cyberspace operations. EA is used to create NAVWAR effects by degrading, disrupting, or deceptively manipulating PNT transmissions. EP is used to deliver NAVWAR capabilities protecting space, control, or user segments of the GPS/GNSS architecture from disruption or destruction. ES assists NAVWAR through DF and geolocation of intended or unintended transmissions that interfere with effective and timely PNT signal reception.

12. Directed Energy

a. DE is an umbrella term covering technologies that produce concentrated EM energy and atomic or subatomic particles. A **DE weapon** is a system using DE primarily as a means to incapacitate, damage, disable, or destroy enemy equipment, facilities, and/or personnel. **Directed-energy warfare (DEW)** is military action involving the use of DE weapons, devices, and countermeasures to incapacitate, cause direct damage or destruction of adversary equipment, facilities, and/or personnel, or to determine, exploit, reduce, or prevent hostile use of the EMS through damage, destruction, and disruption. It also includes actions taken to protect friendly equipment, facilities, and personnel and retain friendly use of the EMS. With the maturation of DE technology, weaponized DE systems are becoming more prolific, powerful, and a significant subset of the EW mission area. DE examples include active denial technology, lasers, RF weapons, and DE anti-satellite and HPM weapon systems.

b. DEW applications exist in their traditional EW roles as well as fitting into evolving fires applications. For example, a laser designed to blind or disrupt optical sensors is EA. A more powerful version of that laser could be targeted to destroy the aperture or chassis of a satellite on orbit, again performing EA. A laser warning receiver designed to detect and analyze a laser signal is ES, while a visor or goggle designed to filter out the harmful wavelength of laser light is EP.

c. The threat of an adversary's use of destructive DE weapons is growing. Intelligence efforts and assets can be tasked to collect information about this threat, and joint planning should include the development of courses of action (COAs) to mitigate the effects of an adversary's use of these weapons against friendly forces. Intelligence or other data concerning an adversary's deliberate use of a blinding laser weapon should be preserved as evidence of a possible violation of international law (e.g., Protocol IV of the 1980 Convention on Certain Conventional Weapons that prohibits the use of laser weapons with a combat function to cause permanent blindness).

d. DE weapons and devices create effects on designated targets, to include personnel and material. DE weapons may provide precise engagement on a target with limited or no collateral damage. DE weapons also support "escalation of force" efforts when directed by the JFC.

13. Intelligence and Electronic Warfare Support

Intelligence gathering comprises an important portion of the day-to-day activities of the intelligence community (IC) support to military operations. The distinction between whether a given asset is performing an ES mission or an intelligence mission is determined by who tasks or controls the collection assets, what they are tasked to provide, and for what purpose they are tasked. See Chairman of the Joint Chiefs of Staff Instruction (CJCSI) 3210.03C, *Joint Electronic Warfare Policy,* for a classified in-depth discussion of the relationship and distinctions between ES and SIGINT. In simpler terms, the distinction between ES and SIGINT is delineated by purpose, scope, and context. ES assets are tasked by operational commanders **to search for, intercept, identify, and locate or localize** sources of intentional or unintentional radiated EM energy. In contrast, SIGINT assets are tasked by Director, National Security Agency (NSA)/Chief, Central Security Service (CSS) or understanding or temporary SIGINT operational tasking authority by an operational commander. The purpose of ES tasking is **immediate threat recognition, planning, and conduct of future operations,** and other tactical actions such as threat avoidance, targeting, and homing. ES is intended to respond to an **immediate operational requirement.** ES and SIGINT operations often share the same or similar assets and resources, and may be tasked to simultaneously collect information that meets both requirements. That is not to say that data collected for intelligence cannot meet immediate operational requirements. Information collected for ES purposes is normally also processed by the appropriate parts of the IC for further exploitation after the operational commander's ES requirements are met. As such, it can be said that information collected from the EMS has "two lives." The first is as ES, unprocessed information used by operational forces to develop and maintain situational awareness for an operationally defined period of time. The second is as SIGINT, retained and processed under appropriate intelligence authorities in response to specified intelligence requirements. In cases where planned ES operations conflict with intelligence collection efforts, the commander with tasking authority will decide which mission has priority.

Other books we publish on Amazon.com

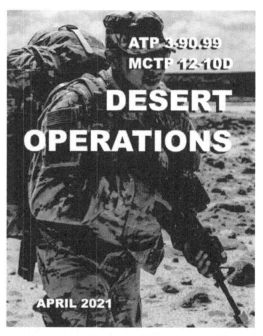

CHAPTER II
ORGANIZING FOR JOINT ELECTRONIC WARFARE

"The secret of all victory lies in the organization of the non-obvious."

Marcus Aurelius
Roman Emperor, A.D. 121–180

1. Introduction

How joint staffs are organized to plan and execute EW is a **prerogative of the JFC.** The size of the commander's staff, the mission or missions the joint force is tasked to accomplish, and the time allocated to accomplish the mission or missions are just some of the factors that affect the organization of the staff. This chapter discusses nominal **requirements, organizations, and staff functions** to plan and execute EW in joint operations. It also summarizes EMS management functions and joint-level organization of intelligence support to EW. A brief introduction to **how the Army, Marines, Navy, and Air Force are organized to plan and execute EW** is included to provide background on how joint staff EW functions interact with Service components.

2. Responsibilities

a. As with other combat, combat support, and combat service support functions, EW planning and operations can be divided among multiple directorates of a joint staff based on long-, mid-, and near-term functionality and based upon availability of qualified EW personnel. **Long-range planning** of EW normally occurs under the plans directorate of a joint staff (J-5), while **near/mid-term planning and the supervision** of EW execution normally falls within the purview of the operations directorate of a joint staff (J-3). All aspects of joint EW should be coordinated closely with joint force components. EA should be synchronized with the spectrum management office of the communications system directorate of a joint staff (J-6), and EA and ES activities with the collection management office of the intelligence directorate of a joint staff (J-2). The JRFL is prepared and promulgated by the J-6, coordinated through the EWC, and approved by the J-3. EA, EP, and ES functions significantly affect, and conversely are affected by, activities within the J-2, J-3, and J-6. Examples include ES for collection, management, and dissemination as well as all source analysis of information (J-2); overall EW operations to include OPSEC planning and integration within the IO division (J-3); and day-to-day operations of the DOD information networks, JRFL planning and integration, and EP considerations (J-6).

b. **J-3.** Authority for planning and supervising joint EW is **normally delegated by the JFC to the J-3.** When so authorized, the J-3 will have primary staff responsibility for **planning, coordinating, integrating, and monitoring execution of joint force EW operations.** The J-3 may delegate staff responsibility for EW as appropriate for the size of the staff and scope of J-3 responsibilities.

c. **Command Electronic Warfare Officer (EWO).** Normally, the command EWO is the **principal EW planner** on a joint staff. The scope and nature of the command EWO's responsibilities are dependent on the size of the staff, the OA of the JFC that the staff supports, and the type of mission or operation the staff must plan. The command EWO is part of the J-3 staff and coordinates internally with other staff organizations and outside organizations, as required.

3. Joint Electronic Warfare Organization

a. **Joint Force Commander's EW Staff.** The JCEWS is headed by the command EWO, who is designated as the JCEWS chief. The JCEWS develops operation plans (OPLANs) and concept plans (CONPLANs) and monitors routine EW operations and activities. It also focuses its efforts on potential contingency areas within the OA and develops the information and knowledge necessary to support contingency planning (e.g., JRFL development). The JCEWS maintains habitual relationships with key individuals (e.g., component liaison officers [LNOs]) and enabling organizations such as Service, functional, and multinational EW cells, the USSTRATCOM Joint Electronic Warfare Center (JEWC), Electromagnetic-Space Analysis Center (ESAC), Joint Spectrum Center (JSC), and Service spectrum management offices. The relationships are refined during training and exercises and optimized via a network of collaboration throughout planning, execution, and assessment.

(1) **Organization of the JCEWS.** The JCEWS should be a standing joint planning group (JPG) with multi-directorate membership. The JCEWS does not require that the headquarters' (HQ's) staff be augmented; rather, it uses existing staff members to participate in a staff organization that focuses on joint EW planning and execution. At a minimum, the JCEWS should consist of core membership from the combatant command/subordinate unified command HQ's J-2, J-3, and J-6. The J-3 and J-6 coordinate to synchronize EW activity that might affect the DOD information networks with USCYBERCOM, through the theater NETOPS centers and TNCCs. The JCEWS should also network with representatives from joint force components (Service and/or functional) and other supporting organizations or agencies. JCEWS membership should be a long-term assignment, and members should be designated spokespersons for their respective organizations. JCEWS membership may include:

(a) JCEWS chief (command EWO).

(b) Standing joint force HQ EW planner (may be dual-hatted as the deputy command EWO when assigned).

(c) JFMO representative.

(d) J-2 SIGINT collection manager.

(e) NSA Cryptologic Support Group (CSG) J-2 representative.

(f) Special technical operations (STO) planner.

(g) J-3 or space NAVWAR representative.

(h) Cyberspace representative.

(i) EM modeling and analysis engineer/representative.

(j) J-2 targets EW lead representative.

(2) JCEWS networked representation may include:

(a) Component EW planners.

(b) LNOs from subordinate and supporting commands.

b. **Joint Electronic Warfare Cell.** The JFC may designate and empower a joint EWC to organize, execute, and oversee conduct of EW. The JFC's decision to designate the joint EWC depends on the anticipated role of EW in the operation. To avoid confusion with the joint EWC (organizationally located with the JFC staff), component-level EW support activities are referred to as electronic warfare elements (EWEs). The land, air, and maritime component EWEs are designated as land-electronic warfare element (L-EWE), air-EWE, and maritime-EWE, respectively. When both the Army and Marine components provide L-EWEs, they should be referred to as Army L-EWE and Marine L-EWE, respectively, to avoid confusion. EWEs may be tasked temporarily with joint EWC responsibilities for the EW aspects of an operation until a joint EWC can be designated and sufficiently manned. The EWC may be part of the JFC's staff or assigned to the J-3. Supporting EWEs placed under a component command must guard against becoming focused on that component's EW issues to the exclusion of the other components. As soon as practical, the EWC should be aligned organizationally and, if possible, geographically colocated with the JFC.

(1) Members of a fully staffed joint EWC should include:

(a) EWC director (should be an EWO).

(b) EWC deputy director.

(c) EWC operations chief.

(d) EWC plans chief.

(e) EW duty officer(s).

(f) EW planner(s).

(g) Operations analyst(s).

(h) SIGINT and/or ELINT analyst(s).

(i) STO planner.

(j) Spectrum manager.

(k) EW asset LNOs.

(l) NAVWAR planner.

(m) Space representative.

(n) Cyberspace representative.

(o) Ground EW logistics planner.

(p) Electrical engineer/EM modeling analyst.

(q) Meteorological and oceanographic (METOC) officer.

(r) Joint interface control officer network manager.

(s) Ground EW asset manager.

(t) SIGINT planner(s).

(2) Joint EWC networked representation should include:

(a) Service/functional component LNOs.

(b) Other government department and agency representatives.

(c) Coalition partner representatives.

c. JCEWS and joint EWC responsibilities:

(1) Specific JCEWS functions and responsibilities:

(a) Maintain EW support to current theater OPLANs and CONPLANs.

(b) Prepare EW portion of estimates and tabs to joint force OPLANs.

(c) Formulate, recommend, and develop EW targets to support the JFC's OPLAN.

(d) Implement and manage EW policies.

(e) Develop and maintain contingency/EWC manning options and COAs.

(2) The following functions may be performed by the JCEWS and will transfer to the joint EWC once established by the JFC:

(a) Provide EW planning and coordination expertise to the JFC. Develop a daily EW battle rhythm that supports EW planning and operations requirements.

(b) Prepare the EW portion of estimates and tabs for operation orders (OPORDs) and identify authorities necessary to implement the OPORD.

(c) Identify requirements for intelligence support to joint EW operations, including assistance to the J-2 in planning the collection and dissemination of ES information.

(d) Define and develop intelligence requirements to support EW operations.

(e) Coordinate with intelligence organizations, collections managers, ISR assets, and national agencies when assessing adversary EW capabilities and limitations.

(f) Coordinate with appropriate DOD intelligence or ISR organizations and national agencies to weigh intelligence gain/loss (IGL) of EA or the physical destruction of targets, and if necessary, coordinate the resolution of these conflicts. Resolution of IGL conflicts resides with the J-3. Request support form J-2 targets if needed.

(g) Plan, coordinate, and assess offensive and defensive EA requirements.

(h) Maintain current assessment of EW resources available to the JFC (to include number, type, and status of EW assets) and analyze what resources are necessary to accomplish the JFC's objective.

(i) Assist JFC by recommending the level of EW support required of the component commanders.

(j) Prioritize EW targets based on JFC objectives, the EW plan, and available assets.

(k) Represent EW within the joint targeting coordination board (JTCB).

(l) Predict effects of friendly and enemy EW activity on joint and multinational operations using applicable modeling and simulation tools.

(m) Plan, coordinate, and assess EP (e.g., spectrum management procedures, EW deconfliction, and EMCON).

(n) Coordinate joint/urgent operational needs statements that affect the EMS.

(o) Coordinate entry of EW systems into the OA.

(p) Coordinate regularly with joint spectrum management element (JSME), and direct activities to resolve spectrum use conflicts resulting from EW activities.

(q) Carry out electronic warfare control authority (EWCA) responsibilities.

(r) Coordinate and monitor joint coordination of electronic warfare reprogramming (JCEWR) by identifying where EW reprogramming decisions and reprogramming actions affect joint force tactical operations and disseminating theater-wide EW plans, as required.

(s) Recommend and promulgate EW special instructions and rules of engagement (ROE).

(t) Plan, coordinate, integrate, and deconflict EW in current and future operations taking into consideration nontraditional capabilities (e.g., space, special operations, and STO) within the OA.

(u) Compile and coordinate EW support requests from all components according to the priorities set by the JFC.

(v) Coordinate, through the chain of command, to resolve any component or multinational EW requests that cannot be met at the JCEWS/EWC level.

(w) Monitor and adapt execution of EW plans in current operations and exercises.

(x) Reference lessons learned information systems during the planning process, archive EW planning and execution data, and document EW lessons learned in accordance with the joint lessons learned program. The Joint Lessons Learned Information System Web site can be found at https://www.jllis.mil or http://www.jllis.smil.mil.

(y) Coordinate actively with the J-6 to document incoming and outgoing EW and EMS-dependent systems so EMS databases can be accurately maintained.

(z) Coordinate, plan, and oversee execution of NAVWAR EW activities that ensure friendly force access to GPS/PNT sources while denying adversary access to GPS/GNSS/PNT sources.

(aa) Develop and coordinate corrective actions to be taken to maintain friendly force connectivity before, during, and after EW operations are employed.

(3) Joint EWC Support Requirements. When activated, the EWC should be located in, or have access to, a sensitive compartmented information facility (SCIF) to allow for appropriate security. Optimal EWC staffing will include STO cleared personnel in order to coordinate and deconflict STO issues and capabilities. The EWC will also require access to the administrative, intelligence, logistics, legal, and communications/network support made available to the J-3 staff.

(a) Administrative. Administrative support includes, but is not limited to, clerical assistance; classified material control; publications management; update, maintenance, and display of operational SIGINT data; and the provision of general administrative materials.

(b) Intelligence. The EWC will require direct access to all-source intelligence to maintain full knowledge of an adversary's intentions and capabilities. Intelligence support should include specific and detailed combat information, intelligence, and ES information (e.g., adversary electronic systems; scheme of maneuver; communications system capabilities and deployment; EMS-dependent weapon systems capabilities and deployment; PNT dependencies and EA capabilities; EW activities; and SIGINT collection plans). The J-2 and theater EW units should continually coordinate to ensure mission reports are received in a timely manner and disseminated to the staff and other agencies, as required.

(c) Logistics. Logistic support for the EWC includes, but is not limited to, storage containers for classified material, desks, maps, information display facilities, and messing and billeting of assigned personnel.

(d) Communications. The EWC should keep the J-6 aware of its communication/network requirements. These requirements depend directly on the level of EW activities involved in joint operations. Provisions must be made for secure, reliable, and timely communications support. The EWC should be able to communicate with both component EW authorities/agencies and appropriate external authorities concerning coordination of EW activities. The EWC must also be able to communicate with coalition partners within releasability restraints.

(e) Legal. Support for the joint EWC includes legal support to review and obtain the necessary authorities and to review the plan for compliance with ROE and applicable domestic and international law, including law of armed conflict (LOAC).

4. Joint Frequency Management Organization

Each geographic combatant commander (GCC) is specifically tasked by policy (CJCSI 3320.01C, *Electromagnetic Spectrum Use in Joint Military Operations*) to establish a frequency management structure that includes a **JFMO** and to **establish procedures** to support planned and ongoing operations. The supported combatant commander (CCDR) authorizes and controls use of EMS resources by the military forces under his command. Each supported GCC establishes a command policy on how the EMS will be used in his area of responsibility (AOR), obtains clearance (or approval) from host nations (HNs) for use of the EMS (through existing coordination procedures), and ensures assigned military forces are authorized sufficient use of the EMS to execute their designated missions. To accomplish these tasks, each supported CCDR establishes a JFMO, typically under the cognizance of the J-6, to **support joint planning, coordination, and operational control of the EMS** for assigned forces. A JSME may be established at any level of command. The combatant command JFMO, or the JSME within a joint task force (JTF), may be assigned from the J-6 staff, from a component's staff, or from an external organization such as the JSC (see Annex E, "Joint Spectrum Center," to Appendix B, "Organizations Supporting Joint Electronic Warfare"). In any event, the combatant command JFMO, or the JSME within a JTF, should be staffed with trained spectrum managers, preferably with experience in joint EMS use and knowledge of the EMS requirements of the combatant command component forces.

For more information on the basic process the combatant command JFMO or the JSME within a JTF uses to carry out its primary responsibilities, refer to Chapter III, "Planning Joint Electronic Warfare," and Chapter IV, "Coordinating Joint Electronic Warfare." For more information about the JFMO/JSME and their functions and processes, refer to Chairman of the Joint Chiefs of Staff Manual (CJCSM) 3320.01B, Joint Operations in the Electromagnetic Battlespace.

5. Organization of Intelligence Support to Electronic Warfare

a. **Intelligence support** to joint military operations is organized into four levels (see Figure II-1). Each of these levels is closely and continuously involved in providing support for EW.

b. **National-Level Intelligence Organizations.** At the national level, organizations and agencies such as the Central Intelligence Agency (CIA), NSA/CSS, National Geospatial-Intelligence Agency (NGA), and Defense Intelligence Agency (DIA) are constantly seeking to **identify, catalog, and update the EOB** of identified or potential adversaries. The ESAC

Organization of Intelligence Support to Electronic Warfare Operations

National-Level Intelligence Organizations

At the national level, organizations and agencies such as the Central Intelligence Agency, National Security Agency/Central Security Service, National Geospatial-Intelligence Agency, and Defense Intelligence Agency (DIA) are constantly seeking to identify, catalog, and update the electronic order of battle of identified or potential adversaries; analyzing and providing products on adversary electronic warfare (EW) doctrine and tactics; and providing much of the intelligence that is gathered about adversary electronic infrastructure.

Department of Defense (DOD)-Level Organizations

DIA is the lead DOD intelligence organization for coordinating intelligence support to meet combatant command requirements. Theater joint intelligence operations centers (JIOCs) will fully integrate all appropriate intelligence capabilities, e.g., planning, collection, exploitation, analysis, disclosure, disseminating, and intelligence support to EW and information operations (IO).

Combatant Command

At the combatant command level, the JIOC responds to theater-level EW intelligence requirements and forwards requests that require national-level assets to the National Military Joint Intelligence Center or other national-level organizations according to established procedures.

Subordinate Joint Force

Within the context of a geographic combatant command, individual subordinate intelligence directorate of a joint staff (J-2) organizational structures will be situation- and mission-dependent. The J-2 normally assigns one or more members of the staff to act as a liaison between the J-2 section and the IO cell where EW planners are normally assigned. This is to coordinate collection requirements and analytical support for compartmented and noncompartmented IO.

Figure II-1. Organization of Intelligence Support to Electronic Warfare Operations

serves as an operationally focused analytical clearinghouse for all EMS-related databases that provide intelligence support to EW. National-level organizations such as the National Air and Space Intelligence Center (NASIC), National Ground Intelligence Center (NGIC), and National Maritime Intelligence Center not only define EW target parameters and associated system performance, but also analyze and provide intelligence on adversary EW doctrine and tactics. National-level collection efforts also provide much of the intelligence gathered about adversary EM infrastructures. The DIA defense collection coordination center (DCCC) is the focal point for tasking national assets to collect intelligence in response to EW intelligence requirements. EW intelligence requirements that cannot be met by lower-level intelligence assets are forwarded to DCCC or other national-level organizations according to established procedures for prioritization and tasking to national assets.

For more information on the organization of national-level intelligence support, refer to JP 2-01, Joint and National Intelligence Support to Military Operations.

c. **Combatant Command.** At the combatant command level, intelligence support to military operations is focused in the **joint intelligence operations center (JIOC).** The JIOC responds to theater-level EW-related intelligence requirements and forwards requests that require national-level assets to the DCCC or other national-level organizations according to established procedures. EW planners at the combatant command level work with the command's J-2 staff to **satisfy EW intelligence requirements** according to command-specific procedures established by each CCDR.

For more information on theater-level intelligence support and multinational intelligence sharing, refer to JP 2-0, Joint Intelligence.

d. **Subordinate Joint Force.** The J-2 is the **primary point of contact** for providing intelligence support to joint EW. At the discretion of the JFC, a JTF **joint intelligence support element (JISE)** may be established to augment the subordinate joint force J-2 element. Under the direction of the joint force J-2, a JISE normally **manages the intelligence collection, production, and dissemination** of a joint force. The J-2 normally assigns one or more members of its staff to act as a liaison between the J-2 section of the staff and the EWC. The purpose of this liaison is to coordinate collection requirements and analytical support for compartmented and non-compartmented IO. Because of the close interrelationship between some ES and SIGINT activities, EW planners may find it necessary to work with a wide variety of personnel in the intelligence section of the staff.

For more information on how the IC is organized to support joint military operations, refer to JP 2-01, Joint and National Intelligence Support to Military Operations.

6. Service Organization for Electronic Warfare

a. Each Service has a different approach to organizing its forces. Therefore, a basic understanding of each Service's EW organization facilitates planning and coordination of EW at the joint level.

b. **Army**

(1) Army EW operations provide the land force commander with EW capabilities to fully support EMS operations, necessary to effectively conduct maneuver warfare on the modern battlefield. The ability to deny adversary use of the EMS, while preserving friendly EMS use, is imperative in the support of all six joint functions. Commanders and staffs determine which resident and joint force EW capabilities to leverage in support of operations. As commanders apply the appropriate level of EW effort, they can seize, retain, and exploit the initiative within their EMOE.

(2) The Army is organized to work in the structure of an electronic warfare working group (EWWG) with the foundation of the group centered on the EWO, the EW technician, and the EW specialist, who comprise the electronic warfare coordination cell (EWCC).

(3) The EWWG is comprised of, but not limited to, members of the following:

(a) Army component operations staff office (Army division or higher staff) (G-3)/S-3 (battalion or brigade operations staff office [Army battalion or regiment]).

(b) Army component intelligence staff office (Army division or higher staff) (G-2)/battalion or brigade intelligence staff office (Army battalion or regiment) (S-2).

(c) G-5 (Army component plans staff office [Army division or higher staff])/ S-5 (battalion or brigade plans staff office [Army battalion or regiment]).

(d) Army component communications staff office (Army division or higher staff) (G-6)/battalion or brigade communications staff office (Army battalion or regiment) (S-6).

(e) Army component information operations staff office (Army division or higher staff) (G-7)/ S-7 (battalion or brigade information operations staff office [Army battalion or regiment]).

(f) EWCC.

(g) Fires.

(h) Air LNO.

(i) STO/technical operations planner.

(j) Space operations.

(k) Maneuver LNOs.

(l) Special operations forces LNO.

(4) As a team lead by the EWO, the EWWG will provide the ground commander with available EW options, capabilities, and limitations during the military decision-making process to best organize all EW assets at the unit's disposal for full-spectrum operations. If assets are nonorganic to the unit, the EWO/EWCC has the knowledge, skills, and abilities to coordinate with higher headquarter to request the proper support at the proper time and location. It provides advice on technical and tactical employment of all assigned EW systems and tasked or requested nonorganic EW systems to include ES and EP activities. In coordination with G-2/S-2 and G-6/S-6, the EWCC identifies emerging EW threats or trends and develops mitigation measures to overcome new adversarial EW actions. It also recommends the use of ES for immediate target prosecution and triggering criteria and EP measures to provide resolution. As key EW planners and integrators, members of the EWCC provide EW input to the brigade ISR synchronization meeting, operations and intelligence working group, and targeting/planning meetings. As additional necessary tasks, the EWCC, or the EWCC in concert with the EWWG, will do the following:

(a) Generate and update EW staff estimates.

(b) Update and disseminate changes to the enemy tactical EW order of battle to include associated targeting information and necessary intelligence generation.

(c) Monitor and prioritize the processing of EA and review EW battle damage assessment.

(d) Coordinate with legal section to ensure EW operations comply with LOAC and ROE criteria.

(e) Advise members of the command group or staff on all matters concerning Army EW requests, requirements, and priorities.

(5) The EWO is part of the Army EWE of the fires functional cell at brigade and above. At the battalion level, an EW noncommissioned officer is part of the battalion staff. With responsibility for the overall planning, coordination, and supervision of Army EW actions, they are responsible for facilitating the internal (Army) and external (joint) integration, synchronization, and deconfliction of EW actions with the joint functions. The EWO reports through the chief of fires (fire support officer for brigade and below) for those EW actions. For planning, synchronizing, and deconflicting EW actions in support of EMS operations, the EWO coordinates with G-7, G-6, and G-2 elements, and the air LNO through the tactical air control party.

(6) Given the Army's dependence on cyberspace as well as the EMS, commanders must fully integrate cyberspace/electromagnetic activities within the overall operation. These activities employ a combined arms approach to operations in contested cyberspace and a congested EMS. Cyberspace/EM activities focus on seizing, retaining, and exploiting advantages in cyberspace and the EMS. Cyberspace/EM activities are divided into two lines of effort (LOEs). The cyberspace operations LOE aims to achieve objectives in and through cyberspace. The EW LOE aims to control the EMS or to attack the enemy. The Army's

EWE and working group will coordinate, plan, and integrate cyberspace/EM activities for the commander.

For more information on the joint functions, refer to JP 3-0, Joint Operations.

c. **Marine Corps**

(1) The Marine Corps employs EW as a part of maneuver warfare with the intent to disrupt the adversary's ability to command and control forces, thereby influencing the adversary's decision cycle. Marine EW assets are integral to the Marine air-ground task force (MAGTF). Marine EW units are found across the entire MAGTF. The MAGTF command element task organizes and coordinates EW systems to meet MAGTF EW needs and ultimately achieve the JFC's objectives.

(2) EW units are integrated into the commander's CONOPS and scheme of maneuver to enhance the MAGTF's inherent combined arms capabilities. Through this integration of aviation and ground EW capabilities, the MAGTF is able to exploit both the long- and short-term effects of EW, conducting active EA, EP, and ES operations to support the operational requirements of the MAGTF commander, as well as those of the JFC during joint operations.

(3) The MAGTF operations officer or one of the staff officers has responsibility for planning and coordinating MAGTF EW operations and activities. Ground-based EW is provided by the radio battalion (RADBN), and airborne EW is provided by EA-6Bs from the Marine tactical electronic warfare squadrons (VMAQs). The RADBN is organized and equipped to conduct tactical SIGINT and ground-based EA and ES in support of the MAGTF. To accomplish this mission, the RADBN provides the MAGTF with task-organized detachments. VMAQs conduct EW, tactical electronic reconnaissance, and ELINT operations in support of the MAGTF. With the employment of RADBNs and VMAQs, the Marine Corps possesses a unique capability to provide **EW support and SIGINT to the MAGTF commander and any subordinate elements** while also providing invaluable support and information to the JFC. The MAGTF commander will normally plan, synchronize, coordinate, and deconflict EW operations through an EWCC, which is under the cognizance of the fires or effects cells. The EWCC will have a resident EWO (serving as the MAGTF EWO) who is responsible for ensuring all EW plans are included in the appropriate OPLAN annex. The MAGTF EWO assumes overall responsibility for planning and coordinating EW operations. When participating in joint or multinational operations, the joint force air component commander (JFACC) (if established) will coordinate with the MAGTF for scheduling Marine Corps air assets in the air tasking order (ATO). When airborne assets are apportioned to support joint air operations, they will be monitored by the EWC for EW missions and be under tactical control of the JFACC.

d. **Navy**

(1) Navy EW is executed by surface ships, aircraft, and submarines organized in strike groups. For each strike group, the information operations warfare commander (IWC) is responsible for **coordinating and integrating** EW, typically through the strike group

EWO, into naval and joint operations. EW execution requires continual monitoring by EW personnel and is delegated to the EW control ship, usually an aircraft carrier or large deck amphibious ship serving with the strike group. Naval strike groups employ a variety of organic shipboard EW systems. Emphasis is on:

(a) ES to detect, identify, and locate potential threats and friendly forces, enhancing situational awareness.

(b) EA for self-protection, principally to defeat incoming anti-ship missiles and to deny adversary use of the EMS.

(c) Maintaining friendly force availability of EMS and space resources to ensure robust communication, surveillance, reconnaissance, data correlation, and navigation capabilities.

(2) Naval aviation is the primary means the Navy uses to project EW at extended ranges. Carrier and land-based EA-6B Prowlers and EA-18G Growlers use a variety of onboard systems to conduct EA (including both standoff and close-in jamming) and ES in support of suppression of enemy air defenses (SEAD), communications EA, and other IO taskings. Embarked airborne EA assets are normally under the direction of the strike warfare commander. When executing strike operations, air wing EA assets remain under the operational control of the strike warfare commander and come under the tactical control of the airborne mission commander. When participating in joint or multinational operations, the strike warfare commander is responsible for coordinating, with the JFACC or combined force air component commander, integration of air wing assets into the ATO. Additional EW tasking may originate with the EWC and be coordinated with the JFACC. When EA airborne assets are assigned ashore as part of an expeditionary force, they will be under the tactical control of the JFACC. Shore-based aircraft such as the EP-3E Aries II primarily provide Navy airborne ES. Either will be assigned national tasking or strike group tasking, or the JFACC will assign joint force tasking as scheduled by the ATO. Each will have tactical control of these aircraft.

(3) **Navy Coordination Procedures.** A maritime operations center (MOC) at each numbered fleet conducts operational-level coordination. The MOC IO cell is responsible for all Navy EW efforts and provides coordination and tasking to task forces assigned. Each MOC should have an EWO and a senior cryptologic technician—technical to conduct EW coordination as members of the IO cell and in liaison with other cells requiring EW expertise. The IWC at the strike group integrates and executes EW at the tactical level. When naval task forces are operating as a component of a joint force, the IWC provides an assessment of Navy EW capabilities to the other component operation centers and coordinates EW operations with appropriate component EW agencies.

For more information, refer to NTTP 3-51.1, Navy Electronic Warfare, *and NTTP 3-13.2,* Information Operations Warfare Commander's Manual.

e. **Air Force**

(1) Within the Air Force component, dedicated EW support assets conduct a variety of EA, EP, and ES operations and support SEAD and IO mission areas. These are all under the operational control of the **commander, Air Force forces (COMAFFOR).** The objective of all Air Force EW operations is to attack the adversary, enhance the effectiveness of other military operations, increase the probability of mission success, and increase aircraft survivability.

(2) The military significance of EW is directly related to the increase in mission effectiveness and to the reduction of risk associated with attaining air superiority. Air Force EW system development and employment focus on these tasks using an integrated mix of sensing, disruptive, and destructive EW systems to defeat hostile integrated air defenses. Disruptive EW systems (e.g., self-protection jamming and the EC-130H Compass Call) provide an immediate but perishable solution. ES systems (e.g., RC-135V/W and aircraft radar warning receivers) are key to successfully disrupting and/or destroying targets. Destructive systems provide a more permanent solution, but may take longer to achieve the desired results. The integrated use of disruptive and destructive systems offsets their individual disadvantages and results in a synergistic effect.

(3) Within the COMAFFOR HQ, the responsibility for providing EW support to joint operations lies within the operations directorate (A-3) and plans directorate (A-5). However, **functional planning for, directing, and providing of Air Force EW capabilities is normally conducted by the JFACC (when one is designated by the JFC)** through the joint air operations center's EWC. The EWC, as a part of the Air Force air and space operations center (AOC), coordinates with other planning and targeting activities to develop/monitor EW plans and operations in support of the JFC. The EWC consists of an EW plans element and an EW operations element. In response to the ATO, wing and unit staffs and individual aircrews conduct detailed tactical planning for specific EW missions. Due to the high demand for support from Air Force dedicated tactical systems, these systems are normally organized as separate EW wings and squadrons. For the same reason, within the Air Force component, Air Force EA and ES systems are normally organized within Air Force wings or squadrons. The COMAFFOR carefully allocates their employment through the ATO process in accordance with JFC priorities and in coordination with the JFC's EWC. Wing commanders are supported by staff defensive systems officers or EWOs. These officers work with the wing operations intelligence staff to analyze and evaluate the threat in the OA. The defensive systems officer, EWO, and electronic combat officer also plan available EW equipment employment and oversee radar warning receiver and EW systems reprogramming. In addition, they should participate in, and coordinate with, the JFC's IO cell, to align objectives and synchronize EW employment with other capabilities.

For more information on EW employment factors, refer to Air Force Tactics, Techniques, and Procedures (AFTTP) 3-1.IO, Information Operations Planning. Integration, and Employment Considerations, *and AFTTP 3-1,* Compass Call. *AFTTP 3-1 volumes are available online via SECRET Internet Protocol Router Network (SIPRNET) at http://www.nellis.af.smil.mil/units/561jts/.*

CHAPTER III
PLANNING JOINT ELECTRONIC WARFARE

"War plans cover every aspect of a war, and weave them all into a single operation that must have a single, ultimate objective in which all particular aims are reconciled."

Major General Carl von Clausewitz
***On War*, viii, 1832, tr. Howard and Paret**

1. Introduction

a. EW is a complex mission area that should be **fully integrated** with other aspects of joint operations in order to achieve its full potential. Such integration requires **careful planning.** EW planners must coordinate **their planned activities with other aspects of military operations that** use the EMS, as well as third party users that EW does not wish to disrupt. Coordination of military EMS use is done primarily by working with other staff sections (primarily the J-2 and J-6) and components (to include allies and coalition partners) that rely on the EMS to accomplish their mission. Coordination of EW activities, in the context of third party EMS use, is largely a matter of EMS management and adherence to established frequency usage regimens and protocols.

b. Joint EW is **centrally planned and directed and decentrally executed.** Service and functional component EW planners should be integrated into the joint planning process. The JFC may delegate control of EW operations to a component commander or other selected commanders; however, such delegation does not eliminate the requirement for joint and/or multinational coordination of EW operations. This chapter:

(1) Provides guidance on the joint EW planning process.

(2) Discusses some of the considerations for planning EW in support of military operations.

(3) Provides guidance on preparation of tab D (EW) to appendix 3 (Information Operations) to annex C (Operations) of the OPLAN and/or OPORD.

(4) Briefly discusses some of the automated decision aids that may be used to assist with planning joint EW.

c. EW and its divisions create effects throughout the OE to include the physical domains and the information environment (which includes cyberspace). The nature of EW means that effects have cross-domain implications. Fires must be integrated into joint planning and execution. EW planners must coordinate EW efforts at the JFC level in order to minimize unintended consequences, collateral damage, and collateral effects.

2. Electronic Warfare Planning Considerations

a. **EMS Management.** Since EW activity may create effects within and throughout the entire EMS, joint **EW planners must closely coordinate their efforts** with those members of the joint staff who are concerned with managing military EMS use. EMS management deconflicts military, national, and HN systems (e.g., EP, communication, sensors, space/PNT, and weapons) being used in the OE. EMS management primarily involves determining the specific activities that will take place in each part of the available EMS. This is accomplished by planning, coordinating, and managing EMS use through operational, engineering, and administrative procedures. Figure III-1 shows the steps involved in JFMO spectrum management responsibilities. For operations within a GCC's AOR, the subordinate JFCs follow this spectrum management guidance as amplified by the GCC. The JTF commander coordinates and negotiates modifications necessary for a specific JTF situation with the GCC's staff. Joint EW planners should establish and maintain a close working relationship with frequency management personnel. A critical management tool to enable effective use of the EMS during military operations is the EMS database. All frequencies need to be registered in the joint EMS database. Frequencies in the database that require extra protection from EA activities need to be listed on the JRFL. The JRFL is a list that operational, intelligence, and support elements use to identify the level of protection desired for various networks and frequencies and is limited to the minimum number of frequencies necessary for friendly forces to accomplish JTF objectives. The JRFL is based on inputs from the J-2, J-3, and J-6. It is usually published, distributed, and maintained by the J-6, typically through the JFMO/JSME. The J-3 is the release authority for the coordinated listing. It may be necessary to coordinate the protection of intelligence collection frequencies via the EA request process instead of the JRFL to meet the time-sensitive needs of collection activities.

For more information on frequency deconfliction procedures and generating the JRFL, refer to Appendix D, "Electronic Warfare Frequency Deconfliction Procedures." For more information on EMS management, refer to CJCSM 3320.01B, Joint Operations in the Electromagnetic Battlespace. For more information on the JSC, refer to Annex E, "Joint Spectrum Center," to Appendix B, "Organizations Supporting Joint Electronic Warfare."

b. **EW Support of SEAD.** SEAD is a specific type of mission intended to **neutralize, destroy, or temporarily degrade** surface-based adversary air defenses with destructive and/or disruptive means. Joint SEAD is a broad term that includes **all SEAD activities** provided by one component of the joint force in support of another. SEAD missions are of critical importance to the success of any joint operation when control of the air is contested by an adversary. SEAD relies on a variety of EW platforms to conduct ES and EA in its support, and EW planners should coordinate closely with joint and component air planners to ensure **EW support to SEAD missions is integrated into the overall EW plan.**

For more information on SEAD, refer to JP 3-01, Countering Air and Missile Threats.

c. **EW Support Against a Nontraditional Threat.** Contingency operations have shown the enemy's ability to use commercial EM communications in a number of nontraditional ways. These include early warning and coordinated attack communication,

Joint Frequency Management Office Spectrum Management Process

1   Develops the spectrum-use plan. This is particularly vital in support of command and control hand-overs that are highly dependent on radio systems.

2   In conjunction with the J-2, J-3, J-5, J-6, and combatant command joint frequency management office (JFMO), prepares a joint restricted frequency list (JRFL) for approval by the J-3.

3   Periodically updates and distributes the JRFL, as necessitated by changes in the task organization, geography, and joint communications-electronics operation instructions and by transition through operational phases.

4   Provides administrative and technical support for military spectrum use.

5   Exercises frequency allotment and assignment authority. This may be delegated to facilitate decentralization and to provide components with the maximum latitude and flexibility in support of combat operations.

6   Establishes and maintains the common database necessary for planning, coordinating, and controlling spectrum use. This database should contain spectrum-use information on all emitters and receivers (critical, friendly, military and civilian, available enemy, and neutral) as appropriate for the area of responsibility involved.

7   Analyzes and evaluates potential spectrum-use conflicts.

8   Assists and coordinates the resolution of spectrum-use conflicts.

9   In accordance with J-5 guidance, coordinates military spectrum use with the combatant command JFMO and the spectrum authorities of the United Nations or host nations involved.

10 Receives, reports on, analyzes, and attempts to resolve incidents of unacceptable electromagnetic interference; refers incidents that cannot be resolved to the next higher spectrum management authority.

Legend

J-2	intelligence directorate of a joint staff	J-5	plans directorate of a joint staff
J-3	operations directorate of a joint staff	J-6	communications system directorate of a joint staff

Figure III-1. Joint Frequency Management Office Spectrum Management Process

detonation means for improvised explosive devices (IEDs), and the denial of GPS information. The EW planner should be able to adapt to these new and creative uses and retain the flexibility to adjust to the adversary's next innovation.

d. **EW Reprogramming.** The purpose of EW reprogramming is **to maintain or enhance the effectiveness of EW and TSS equipment.** EW reprogramming includes

changes to self-defense systems, offensive weapons systems, ES, and intelligence collection systems. The reprogramming of EW and TSS equipment is the responsibility of each Service or organization through its respective EW reprogramming support programs. The swift identification and resolution of reprogramming efforts could become a matter of life and death in a rapidly evolving, congested, and contested EMOE. Service reprogramming efforts must include coordination from the JCEWS to ensure those reprogramming requirements are identified, processed, deconflicted, and implemented in a timely manner by all affected friendly forces.

For more information on EW reprogramming, refer to Appendix E, "Electronic Warfare Reprogramming."

e. **Electronic Masking**

(1) Electronic masking is the **controlled radiation of EM energy on friendly frequencies** in a manner to protect the emissions of friendly communications and electronic systems against adversary ES and SIGINT without significantly degrading the operation of friendly systems. Electronic masking is used to **disguise, distort, or manipulate friendly EM radiation data** to conceal military operations information and/or present false perceptions to adversary commanders. Electronic masking is an **important component to a variety of military functions** (e.g., MILDEC, OPSEC, and signals security) conducted wholly, or in part, within the EMS.

(2) Effective electronic masking of joint military operations involves the proactive management of all friendly radiated EM signatures of equipment being used in, or supporting, the operation. The **degree of masking required** in the management of these signatures is a function of the:

(a) Assessed adversary ES and SIGINT collection capability (or access to third party collection).

(b) Degree to which the EM signature of joint forces must be masked in order to accomplish the assigned mission.

(3) JFCs have **two primary responsibilities** with respect to electronic masking:

(a) Provide adequate electronic masking guidance to component commands through campaign plans, contingency plans, and OPORDs.

(b) Plan and implement appropriate electronic masking measures within the joint force HQ.

(4) To accomplish these responsibilities, the **following steps should be taken early** in the planning process:

(a) Assess adversary ES and SIGINT capabilities against friendly forces.

(b) Determine whether the mission assigned to joint forces may require electronic masking and, if so, to what degree.

(c) Request staff augmentation if necessary to acquire expertise in planning and implementing electronic masking TTP.

(d) Alert component commands at the earliest opportunity of the need to be prepared to implement electronic masking measures. This will afford them the necessary lead time to augment their forces with the necessary resources and expertise.

f. **Interoperability.** Interoperability is essential in order to use EW effectively as an element of joint military power. The major requirements of interoperability are to:

(1) **Establish standards and practice procedures** that allow for integrated planning and execution of EW operations.

(2) **Exchange EW information in a timely and routine fashion.** This exchange may be conducted in either non real time or near real time via common, secure, jam-resistant radios and data links. The ability to **exchange near-real-time data (such as targeting information) to enhance situational awareness and combat coordination** between various force elements is a critical combat requirement. This exchange of data relates to EA, EP, and ES, including friendly and adversary force data. Routine exchange of data among joint force components, the joint force and supporting commands and organizations, and, when possible, allies and coalition partners greatly facilitates all types of EW planning.

g. **Rules of Engagement.** EW activities frequently involve a unique set of complex issues. There are DOD directives and instructions, laws, rules, LOAC, and theater ROE that may affect EW activities. These laws, rules, and guidelines become especially critical during peacetime operations when international and domestic laws, treaty provisions, and political agreements may affect mission planning and execution. Commanders should seek legal review during all levels of EW planning and execution, to include development of theater ROE. This can best be accomplished by ensuring the legal advisor is available to EWC planners. While ROE should be considered during the planning process, they should not inhibit developing a plan that employs available capabilities to their maximum potential. If, during the planning process, an ROE-induced restriction is identified, planners should work with staff legal advisors to clarify the ROE or develop supplemental ROE applicable to EW.

h. **Unintended Consequences.** EW planners must coordinate EW efforts at the JFC level to minimize unintended consequences, collateral damage, and collateral effects. **Friendly EA could potentially deny essential services to a local population that, in turn, could result in loss of life and/or political ramifications.** The JFMO or JSME has an automated tool that can analyze the potential for interference of EW operations on friendly EMS-dependent systems. They should coordinate military EMS use with HN EMS authorities when conducting multinational operations or exercises. Due to the dual civil-military nature of GPS/GNSS and other PNT services, potential impacts from NAVWAR efforts on nonmilitary users and the civil/commercial critical infrastructure must be thoroughly analyzed during COA development and coordinated with HN EMS authorities.

The J-6 spectrum manager can provide this analysis to the JCEWS/joint EWC to better determine the impact of EW operations.

i. **Meteorological and Oceanographic Considerations.** EW planners must consider the effects of atmospherics and space weather on available EW systems, both friendly and adversary. The various types of atmospheric conditions and phenomena can positively or negatively affect EW systems. For example, atmospheric inversions can propagate radio transmissions; high humidity and rainy climates are detrimental to IR systems; and ionospheric scintillation can adversely affect GPS. Some atmospheric effects are well known and are categorized by season and location. Planners should consult with the combatant command METOC officer to determine the type of METOC support available for their operation.

j. **Chemical, Biological, Radiological, and Nuclear Considerations.** In a CBRN-threat environment, EW planners should consider the potential effects of a CBRN attack on sensitive EW equipment. Chemical contaminants and most decontamination solutions are corrosive and may damage sensitive equipment. Additionally, systems' operations may be impeded if operators are required to wear CBRN-protective ensembles. Redundancy, dispersal, protection, and decontamination of mission-critical EW equipment will help ensure mission continuation following CBRN attack.

For additional guidance, see JP 3-11, Operations in Chemical, Biological, Radiological, and Nuclear (CBRN) Environments.

3. Joint Electronic Warfare Planning Process

In order to be fully integrated into other aspects of a planned operation, the EWC conducts joint EW planning beginning as early as possible and coordinates it with other aspects of the plan throughout the joint operation planning process (JOPP). Figure III-2 shows the integration of EW into the JOPP. Thorough EW planning will minimize EMS conflicts and enhance EW effectiveness during execution. Proper EW planning requires understanding of the joint planning and decision-making processes; nature of time-constrained operations; potential contributions of EW; and employment of joint EW. During execution, EW planners must **monitor the plan's progress** and be prepared to make modifications to the plan as the dynamics of the operation evolve. Joint EW planners should take the following actions during the planning process to **integrate EW into the joint plan:**

a. Determine the type, expected length, geographic location, and level of hostility expected during the operation to be planned.

b. Review the scale of anticipated operations and the number and type of friendly forces (to include allied and coalition partners) expected to participate.

c. Review current ROE and existing authorities for EW activities and recommend any necessary modifications in accordance with current staff procedures. Coordinate with the staff judge advocate to ensure requirements of ROE, legal authorities, and LOAC are met.

Electronic Warfare Cell Actions and Outcomes as Part of Joint Planning

Planning Process Steps	Electronic Warfare (EW) Cell Planning Action	EW Cell Planning Outcome
Planning Initiation	• Monitor situation. • Review guidance and estimates. • Convene EW cell. • Ensure EW representation within information operations (IO) cell. • Gauge initial scope of the EW role. • Identify organizational coordination requirements. • Initiate identification of information required for mission analysis and course of action (COA) development. • Validate, initiate, and revise priority intelligence requirements (PIRs) and requests for information (RFIs). • Recommend EW strategies and conflict resolution.	Request taskings to collect required information.
Mission Analysis	• Identify specified, implied, and essential EW tasks. • Identify assumptions, constraints, and restraints relevant to EW. • Identify EW planning support requirements (including augmentation) and issue requests for support. • Initiate development of measures of effectiveness and measures of performance. • Analyze EW capabilities available and identify authority for deployment and employment. • Obtain relevant physical, informational, and cognitive properties of the information environment from the IO cell. • Refine proposed PIRs/RFIs. • Provide EW perspective in the development of restated mission for commander's approval. • Tailor augmentation requests to missions and tasks.	List of EW tasks. List of assumptions, constraints, and restraints. Planning guidance for EW. EW augmentation request. EW portion of the commander's restated mission statement.
COA Development	• Select EW supporting and related capabilities to accomplish EW tasks for each COA. • Revise EW portion of COA to develop staff estimate. • Provide results of risk analysis for each COA.	List of objectives to effects to EW tasks to EW capabilities for each COA.
COA Analysis and Wargaming	• Analyze each COA from an EW functional perspective. • Identify key EW decision points. • Recommend EW task organization adjustments. • Provide EW data for synchronization matrix. • Identify EW portions of branches and sequels. • Identify possible high-value targets related to EW. • Recommend EW commander's critical information requirements.	EW data for overall synchronization matrix. EW portion of branches and sequels. List of high-value targets related to EW.
COA Comparison	• Compare each COA based on mission and EW tasks. • Compare each COA in relation to EW requirements versus available EW resources. • Prioritize COAs from an EW perspective.	Prioritized COAs from an EW perspective with pros and cons for each COA.
COA Approval	• No significant EW staff actions during COA approval.	Not applicable.
Plan or Order	• Refine EW tasks from the approved COA. • Identify EW capability shortfalls and recommended solutions. • Update continually all supporting organizations regarding details of the EW portion of plan details (access permitting). • Advise supported combatant commander on EW issues and concerns during supporting plan review and approval. • Participate in time-phased force and deployment data (TPFDD) refinement to ensure the EW force flow supports the concept of operations.	Updated EW estimates based on selected COA. Draft EW appendices and tabs, supporting plans. EW requirements to TPFDD development. Synchronized and integrated EW portion of operation plan.

Figure III-2. Electronic Warfare Cell Actions and Outcomes as Part of Joint Planning

d. Review, with the NETOPS community, the contribution EW can make to protect the EMS for use by the DOD information networks. This should be done through the J-6 representative assigned to the JCEWS or EWC staff.

e. Review, with other planners, the contribution EW can make to efforts in other mission areas (e.g., military information support operations [MISO], MILDEC, and CNO) and determine the level of EW platform support they expect to need during the operation.

f. Review the role EW capabilities can play in creating NAVWAR effects and determine the level of EW platform support they expect to need during the operation.

g. Review, with intelligence planners, the type of ES platforms, capabilities, and products available to support the operation. IGL analysis of EW actions should start early and be frequently reviewed during the planning and execution phases of an operation.

h. Consult with Service, functional component, and multinational EW planners, wherever the most current and relevant expertise in the employment of EW capabilities resides, in order to understand and remain current on the full range of EW capabilities available for accomplishing operational objectives.

i. Work in concert with J-6 EMS managers to improve awareness and deconflict all military, civilian, and other systems (e.g., communication systems, sensors, and EMS-dependent weapon systems) that could impact the EMOE.

j. Determine the number and type of EW platforms that could reasonably be expected to be tasked to support the joint operation being planned. Consult automated force status reports (e.g., those provided through the Defense Readiness Reporting System for US forces) for this information. Service and functional components and multinational planners should be consulted to augment automated information.

k. Review, with component air planners, the requirement for EW support to the SEAD effort.

l. Recommend, to the EWC director (or other designated member of the J-3 or J-5 staff), the type and number of EW assets to be requested from component or supporting commands for the operation being planned.

m. Estimate the size and expertise of the EW staff required to plan and coordinate execution of the EW portion of the plan. Consult with Service, functional component, and multinational EW planners to refine these estimates.

n. Recommend how best to effectively prosecute EW operations to create NAVWAR effects and maintain a PNT advantage. Estimate the impact of NAVWAR effects on both military objectives and civil/commercial users.

o. Recommend staff augmentation in accordance with staff procedures from component, supporting, and multinational forces (MNFs) as necessary to assemble the staff required to conduct EW planning.

p. Coordinate with the combatant command JFMO or JSME early in the planning process to determine if JSC assistance is required.

q. During crisis action planning, evaluate each COA considered with respect to EW resources required and the EW opportunities and vulnerabilities inherent in the COA.

r. Integrate EW into joint targeting.

4. Electronic Warfare Planning Guidance

a. Planning guidance for EW is **included as tab D (EW) to appendix 3 (Information Operations) to annex C (Operations) of the OPLAN.**

Appendix A, "Electronic Warfare Guidance," shows the format of Joint Operation Planning and Execution System EW guidance as a tab to the IO guidance. For more information on OPLAN development, refer to CJCSM 3122.03C, Joint Operation Planning and Execution System, Volume II, Planning Formats.

b. **Planning Factors.** Development of the EW portion of the OPLAN requires consideration of a number of diverse factors about the proposed operations. These **planning factors** include, but are not limited to, the following:

(1) Identify the purpose and intent of performing EW operations, the immediate desired effects, and enabling characteristics for authorizing EW.

(2) Determination of status of EW capability of available forces relative to enemy capability, to determine if sufficient assets are available to perform the identified EW tasks. If in-place assets are insufficient, requests for support should be drafted.

(3) Determination of requirements for friendly communications nets, EM navigation systems, and radar. These requirements should be considered with respect to the anticipated operations, tactical threat expected, and EMI possibilities. Once identified, these requirements should be entered into the JRFL under appropriate categories (e.g., TABOO).

(4) Identification of measures necessary to deny OPSEC indicators to enemy passive-EM sensors.

(5) Determination of the coordination and processes that will be necessary when conducting EA in order to ensure continued effective ES. Development of the JRFL is a critical preliminary step to integrate EA and ES activities.

(6) Coordination and identification of specific resources required for interference resolution.

(7) Identification of commander's critical information requirements (CCIRs) that support EW operations. These CCIRs must be included as priority intelligence requirements in the intelligence annex (normally annex B) of the OPLAN to facilitate generation of ES.

(8) Coordination and establishment of procedures to ensure timely fulfillment of EW planning tasks, including tactical real-time dissemination.

(9) Review of ROE and applicable law to determine the authorities needed or the restrictions, if any, that apply to EW operations.

(10) Identification of EM target categories in order to guide collections priorities and support EM target development.

c. **EW plans should:**

(1) **Identify the desired EM profile** selected by the commander for the basic CONOPS and **provide EMCON guidance** to commanders so the desired EM profile is realized.

(2) Identify EW missions and tasks to Service or functional component commanders to enable them to plan for the resources required and conduct the pre-coordination necessary to deploy and employ those resources in foreign countries.

(3) **Evaluate adversary threats** to weapons systems, critical C2 communications, weapons control systems, target acquisition systems, surveillance systems, PNT systems, and computer networks. Specify EP guidance necessary to ensure effective operations.

(4) Reflect the guidance, policies, and EW employment authorities provided within instructions, regulations, or orders.

5. Electronic Warfare Planning Aids

There are a number of **automated planning tools** available to help joint EW planners carry out their responsibilities. These tools can be divided into three broad categories: **databases, planning process aids, and spatial and propagation modeling tools.**

a. **Databases.** Databases can assist EW planners by **providing easy access to a wide variety of platform-specific technical data** used in assessing the EW threat and planning appropriate friendly responses to that threat. However, planners should keep **several considerations** in mind when relying on automated data. There are two major categories for EW databases—intelligence and operational. Intelligence databases are repositories of intelligence information. They are not all-inclusive. They represent limited technical information on the capabilities, specifications, and parameters of known systems. Operational databases are complete databases required to operate models used in decision-making software such as mission planning systems. Operational databases must be complete so that operations can be conducted effectively. Engineer analysts use system knowledge, model requirements, and intent to ensure operational databases have all the necessary elements, in a form and function suitable, for operational use.

(1) There are a **large number of databases** available to military planners. The primary approved source for threat system data are DIA responsible producers: NASIC, Missile and Space Intelligence Center (MSIC), NGIC, and the 53rd Electronic Warfare Group (EWG). The Electronic Warfare Integrated Reprogramming Database is a DIA-managed database, maintained and distributed by NASIC as the executive agent. It is the primary DOD-approved source for technical parametric and performance data on non-

communications emitters and associated systems. Additionally, the ESAC at Fort Meade, MD, provides tactical and operational-level warfighters with fused, operational analysis of the various databases available. MSIC, NGIC, and the 53rd EWG are the source for early warning radars, surface-to-air missile systems, communication systems, and blue systems. These databases are maintained by the Services and other intelligence agencies. Information from other agencies, DOD organizations, allied organizations, and open sources used to prepare databases used for operations form the core intelligence databases. The compilation of accurate technical data into one place could be a lucrative target for hostile intelligence collection. For this reason, **access to friendly force data may be highly restricted** and harder for planners to obtain than threat data, which can be accessed through normal intelligence channels.

(2) The **level of detail, specific fields, and frequency of update** may vary widely across different databases dealing with the same data. The way data is organized into fields in a database and the level of detail (e.g., number of decimal places for certain technical data) depend on what the data is used for, the cost associated with data acquisition and compilation, and database maintenance.

(3) The sources of data being used for planning should be a topic of coordination among EW planners. The use of ESAC's Electromagnetic-Space (E-Space) portal as the common database source is recommended. Joint planners should understand the sources of **data being used for specific EW planning purposes and ensure those sources are current and relevant to the planned operation(s).** When planning specific operations, planners should coordinate with organizations that maintain important sources of EW data to ensure the data is current and suitable for the operation. Planners should be cautioned about using unofficial sources of data, particularly those available through the Internet that may be subject to manipulation by organizations hostile to US policies and objectives. However, **open-source intelligence** remains a viable and potentially important source of valuable information.

b. **Planning Process Aids.** There are **several automated aids** available that assist in the planning process, and others are under development. These include aids that **automate OPLAN development and automated frequency management tools.** Use of automated tools to consider disparate mission area requirements with respect to EW effects and capability employment will normally be determined by the EWC director and the director's planning staff. EW planners should ensure that any EW planning input developed separately from such systems is created in a format compatible with, and electronically transferable to, the designated planning tools. EW planning input from subordinate and supporting commands should follow the desired format.

c. **Spatial and Propagation Modeling Tools. Geographic information systems enable analysis and display of geographically referenced information. These spatial modeling tools can, for example, enhance targeting, awareness, and planning for GPS denied environments, and facilitate trends analysis.** The variables that affect the propagation of EM energy are known and **subject to mathematical predictability.** The use of propagation modeling tools **that graphically display transmission paths** of EM energy has become widespread in EW planning. However, the accuracy, speed, and flexibility of these tools depend greatly on the accuracy of the data provided to the tool and the sophistication of the software and hardware used to manipulate the data. These tools are essentially **models for EM propagation.** The accuracy and sophistication of the software and hardware being used may not be determined from the graphics display alone. **EW planners should have an understanding of how such modeling systems are computing the graphics being displayed.** Such an understanding, combined with operational experience, is the basis on which planners judge the strengths and weaknesses of different modeling tools and determine what is, and is not, an appropriate use of such systems.

For more information on EW models and their use, refer to Appendix F, "Electronic Warfare Modeling."

    d. **Reachback Resources.** If EW planners don't have the automated planning tools required on-site, reachback support is available. For joint EW planners, reachback support is available from organizations such as the ESAC; the USSTRATCOM/JEWC in San Antonio, Texas; and the JSC in Annapolis, Maryland. Support for NAVWAR and GPS is available from the Joint Navigation Warfare Center (JNWC) at Kirtland Air Force Base (AFB), New Mexico, and the Global Positioning System Operations Center (GPSOC) at Schriever AFB, Colorado, respectively. Additional resources include Army Reprogramming Analysis Team; NGIC in Charlottesville, Virginia; NSA-Electronic Intelligence; Joint Improvised Explosive Device Defeat Organization; Joint Warfare Analysis Center in Dahlgren, Virginia; and the IO Range.

For more information on the ESAC, GPSOC, JEWC, JNWC, JSC, and IO Range, refer to Appendix B, "Organizations Supporting Joint Electronic Warfare."

CHAPTER IV
COORDINATING JOINT ELECTRONIC WARFARE

"In the case of electronic warfare, as in any other kind of warfare, no weapon and no method is sufficient on its own."

Martin van Creveld
Technology and War, **1989**

1. Introduction

Once a plan has been approved and an operation has commenced, the preponderance of EW staff effort shifts to EMBM. **EMBM includes continuous monitoring of the EMOE, EMS management, and the dynamic reallocation of EW assets based on emerging operational issues.** Normally, this monitoring is performed by personnel on watch in the joint operations center (JOC). These watch personnel, stationed at a dedicated EW watch station, normally are tasked to alert other EW or staff personnel to carry out specific coordinating actions in response to emerging requirements. This chapter discusses the actions and concerns the EW staff personnel should focus on to accomplish such coordination.

2. Joint Electronic Warfare Coordination and Control

a. **Joint EW Organizational Coordination.** At combatant commands and subordinate unified commands, the J-3 is primarily responsible for the EW coordination function. The EW division of the J-3 staff should engage in the full range of EW functions to include deliberate planning; day-to-day planning and monitoring of routine theater EW activities in conjunction with the combatant command's theater campaign plan; and crisis action planning in preparation for EW as part of emergent joint operations. The EW division operates under the direction of the J-3 directorate and coordinates closely with other staff sections and JPGs, as required. In the very early stages of contingencies, the JCEWS should assess staffing requirements for planning and execution and should coordinate EW planning and COA development with the JFC's components. Subordinate and supporting commands should begin EW planning and activate their EWEs per CCDR or Service guidelines. When the scope of the contingency becomes clearer, the command EWO may request that the JFC stand up a joint EWC. The designated joint EWC would request additional augmentation from JFC components to form a representative and responsive EW planning and execution organization. To avoid confusion with the joint EWC (organizationally located with the JFC staff), component EW support cells are referred to as EWEs.

b. **Management of the Electromagnetic Spectrum**

(1) The J-6/J-2 pre-assessment of the EMOE—conducted during the planning phase—constitutes a best analysis based on information available at the time. Following deployment and buildup, overlaying joint force EM emissions on the existing EMOE will create a different environment. Further, this environment will constantly change as forces redeploy and C2, surveillance, weapon systems, and other spectrum-use applications realign.

Since EW is concerned with **attacking personnel, facilities, or equipment (EA); protecting capabilities and EMS access (EP); and monitoring, exploiting, and targeting use of the EMS (ES),** EW staff personnel have a role in the **dynamic management** of the EMS, via tools and processes, during operations. A **comprehensive and well-thought-out JRFL and EMCON plan** are two significant tools that **permit flexibility of EW actions** during an operation without compromising friendly EMS use. Some of the **coordination actions related to the EMS** that EW staff personnel should consider include:

(a) Monitoring compliance with the JRFL and EMCON plan by friendly EW assets, as well as remediating joint spectrum interference resolution (JSIR) events.

(b) Recommending changes to operations in the EMS based on emerging frequency deconfliction requirements.

(c) Establishing employment guidance consistent with standing ROE issued by the Chairman of the Joint Chiefs of Staff, theater-specific ROE issued by the GCC, and any mission-specific ROE issued by the Secretary of Defense (SecDef), CCDR, or JFC. Recommend supplemental ROE for EA employment as necessary.

(d) Coordinating a plan to ensure terrestrial and non-terrestrial communications net availability in the presence of EMI.

(e) Implementing a responsive plan for executing EWCA responsibilities in order to ensure operationally effective coordination, employment, targeting, and deconfliction of EA, ES, ISR, space, cyberspace, C2, and communications activities.

(f) Coordinating and deconflicting NAVWAR-related PNT EA/ES efforts. NAVWAR is a continuous effort within the EWC.

(g) Establishing and training staff on the EA request process to facilitate identification of spectrum use conflicts prior to execution of the EA.

For more information of EW frequency deconfliction, refer to Appendix D, "Electronic Warfare Frequency Deconfliction Procedures."

(2) **Electronic Warfare Control Authority.** The EWCA, the senior EA authority in the OA, develops guidance for performing EA on behalf of the JFC. EWCA can either be retained by the JFC or executed by the JFC's designated representative. Routine execution of EWCA responsibilities will normally be delegated to the staff EWO or EWC director (when an EWC is activated), and may be temporarily delegated to field units for the purpose of local/tactical mission refinement and CEASE BUZZER (an unclassified term to terminate EA activities, including the use of EW expendables) remediation. EWCA responsibilities include:

(a) Participating in JRFL development.

(b) Ensuring compliance with the approved JRFL.

(c) Gaining and maintaining situational awareness of all EA-capable systems in the OA.

(d) Acting as the JFC's executive agent for decisions on EW IGL recommendations.

(e) Coordinating introduction of new EMS-dependent systems in the OA.

(f) Coordinating with joint force components on EA requirements.

(g) Investigating and implementing corrective measures to unauthorized EA events.

(h) Contributing to the development of EA narratives in EW associated directives/guidance.

c. **Coordination Between the Divisions of EW.** There are a number of **coordinating actions that must occur** among the respective divisions of EW (EA, EP, and ES) during an operation. These actions include monitoring:

(1) The employment and effective integration of ES assets and the timely flow of ES information relevant to EA and EP to units responsible for those missions and coordinating corrective measures, as required. The deconfliction, coordination, integration, and synchronization of ES assets will normally require intensive, proactive action by the EWC director as some of these assets are controlled through SIGINT/ISR channels and organizations.

(2) Component input to the reprogramming process and coordinating urgent reprogramming actions based on recommendations from Service reprogramming centers.

(3) The interference resolution process for employment of EP, EA, and ES capabilities first requires that personnel operating an affected system recognize the problem as interference and begin the proper EP actions (e.g., WARM, reporting). If those actions cannot resolve the problem, they will need to request that EA assets cease EA activities that may be impacting their operations. If that does not resolve the problem, ES assets will need to determine the source of interference.

d. **Coordination with the IO Cell.** EW can support the IO LOO/LOE and enable or enhance other LOOs/LOEs. EW is viable in all military operations; therefore, integration of EW expertise in planning is important to creating synergistic effects to support the JFC's objectives.

(1) EA can create decisive, enhanced effects in the information environment and provide the JFC an operational advantage by gaining and maintaining information superiority. Information superiority is the operational advantage derived from the ability to collect, process, and disseminate an uninterrupted flow of information while exploiting or denying an adversary's ability to do the same.

(2) EW and its divisions enable operations in the air, land, maritime, and space physical domains and the information environment (which includes cyberspace). The nature of EW and its unique relationship to the EMS allow creation of effects that have implications throughout the OA and require planners to coordinate EW efforts in order to minimize unintended consequences, collateral damage, and collateral effects. When EW is employed as nonlethal fires, it often can be employed with little or no associated physical destruction. Fires must be deconflicted at the JFC level, through the JTCB or like body, to predict collateral damage and/or effects and incorporate risk mitigation strategies.

(3) One of the primary functions of the IO cell is to coordinate disparate military activities in order to produce optimized effects. Nearly all information-related capabilities depend on, use, or exploit the EMS for at least some of their functions. Deconfliction and coordination of EW in an operation is a continuous process and a constant consideration in IO planning efforts. Specific discussion on EW's relationship to other information-related capabilities is listed below.

For more information on IO, refer to JP 3-13, Information Operations.

(a) **Electronic Warfare and Military Information Support Operations.** MISO activities often use the EMS to broadcast their message to target audiences using platforms such as COMMANDO SOLO. EW activities support MISO by providing the means to deliver a message to a target audience via the EMS. EW planners must be aware of the potential to interfere with MISO efforts to convey information to adversaries or foreign target audiences. MISO supports EW by broadcasting products on target frequencies and by developing products for broadcast on other EW assets. MISO platforms and units depend on information gathered through ES to **warn them of potential threats and provide feedback about reaction** to MISO broadcasts and other activities. MISO units rely on effective EP efforts to prevent adversary EA activities or other inadvertent EMI from disrupting their efforts. Coordination of MISO and EW planned frequency use when developing the JRFL is the first step in deconflicting these two capabilities. During the execution phase of an operation, MISO and EW staff personnel should integrate their operations and frequency use on a regular basis.

For more information on MISO, refer to JP 3-13.2, Military Information Support Operations.

(b) **Electronic Warfare and Operations Security.** EA supports OPSEC by degrading adversary EM ISR operations against protected units and activities. ES can support the OPSEC effort by providing information about adversary capabilities and intent to collect intelligence **on friendly forces** through the EMS. ES can also be used to evaluate the effectiveness of friendly force EMCON measures and recommend modifications or improvements. An **effective and disciplined EMCON plan and other appropriate EP measures** are important aspects of good OPSEC. OPSEC supports EW by concealing EW units and systems to deny information on the extent of EW capabilities. During operations, OPSEC planners and EW staff personnel should frequently review the JFC's critical information requirements in light of the dynamics of the operation. Adjustments should be recommended to ES collection efforts, EMCON posture, and other EP measures as necessary to maintain effective OPSEC.

For more information on OPSEC, refer to JP 3-13.3, Operations Security.

          (c) **Electronic Warfare and Military Deception.** EW supports MILDEC by using EA/ES as deception measures; degrading adversary capabilities to see, report, and process competing observables; and providing the enemy with information received by electronic means that is prone to misinterpretation. Knowledge of MILDEC plans and actions is normally very restricted. Designated EW planners must work through the J-3 staff for deconfliction and EW support to MILDEC operations. MILDEC frequently relies on the EMS to convey the deception to adversary intelligence or tactical sensors. Forces assigned to the deception effort are often electronically "enhanced" to project a larger or different force structure to adversary sensors. Friendly EA assets may be an integral part of the deception effort by selectively jamming, interfering, or masking the EM profile of the main operational effort. Friendly assets can also be used to stimulate air defense systems (communications and radar) through either EM or physical means. Stimulation of an air defense system enables the ability to target or map the EOB, causes the adversary to commit assets (air or ground), as well as mission deception and saturation of the defense system. At the same time, coordination within the JTF staff must occur so EA activities do not interfere with frequencies being used to convey the EM aspects of the deception to adversary sensors. Disciplined EMCON and other appropriate EP efforts, by both deception assets and those of the main effort, are essential to preventing the adversary from distinguishing deception activities from the main effort. ES assets can provide immediate warning to deception forces about adversary forces reacting to their presence or actions. ES assets are also an important means to determine that the adversary is capable of receiving the EM aspects of a deception. Since deception forces are often positioned "off axis" from the main effort, ES platforms positioned with the deception effort may assist in location of adversary forces by assisting with triangulation in DF activities. Designated EW staff personnel should have the security clearances and access necessary to work with MILDEC planners during the planning and execution phases of an operation that involves deception. MILDEC supports EW by influencing an adversary to underestimate friendly EA/ES capabilities. EW planners should ensure that EM frequencies necessary to support deception plans are accounted for in EMS management databases and on the JRFL without disclosing that specific frequencies are related to deception. During the execution of an operation, EW staff personnel should monitor EW support to the deception effort and coordinate any changes or conflicts in a timely manner.

For more information on MILDEC, refer to JP 3-13.4, Military Deception.

          (d) **Electronic Warfare and Cyberspace Operations.** Cyberspace operations may be facilitated and enabled through EW, and vice versa. The increasing prevalence of wireless Internet and telephone networks in the OE has created a wide range of opportunities and vulnerabilities when EW and cyberspace operations TTP are used synergistically. While wired access to a particular computer network may be limited, EM access may prove the key to successful computer system penetrations. For example, use of an airborne weapons system to deliver malicious code into cyberspace via a wireless aperture would be characterized as "EW-delivered computer network attack (CNA)." The EMS can also be used as a vector for conveying an attack directly against the information technology infrastructures. For example, a computer server can be physically damaged or destroyed by

EM nonlethal fires (e.g., HPM or EMP weapons). EW operations (EA and ES) and attributes (EP) can assist in setting the conditions in cyberspace to ensure availability of the area requiring access, provide the ability to engage adversaries decisively, and conduct cyberspace operations to enable the creation of the desired effects in the physical domains (i.e., air, land, maritime, and space).

(e) **Electronic Warfare and Information Assurance (IA).** IA is concerned with measures that protect and defend information and information systems, and many of the measures involve the use of the EMS. EP equipment, attributes, and processes assist in assuring the availability and integrity of modulated data traversing the EMOE, whose usability and availability IA seeks to protect and defend. EA TTP assist in compromising those same qualities which adversary IA seeks to protect and defend. EMI resolution and EMS management procedures assist IA in overcoming the problem of EM fratricide.

(f) **Electronic Warfare and Physical Attack.** EW supports physical attack by providing target acquisition through ES and by destroying or degrading susceptible assets with EA. EP supports physical attack by protecting friendly targeting sensors, navigation, and communications in a contested environment. Physical attack supports EW by destroying adversary C2 targets and EMS-dependent systems. "Precision strike" is an increasingly important aspect of physical destruction actions in joint operations. EW is an important part of precision strike. Frequency management and deconfliction must account for frequencies used by various types of precision strike weapons. ES assets are an important part of efforts to dynamically map the EMOE for targeting and threat avoidance planning. Standoff munitions and anti-radiation ordnance are major assets in any operation and may, for example, be used to selectively destroy adversary emitters in support of MILDEC, SEAD, OPSEC, and MISO efforts. The employment of weapons must be carefully planned and deconflicted to prevent the engagement of unintended targets and potential fratricide. EA assets perform vital screening functions (including the use of standoff weapons) for friendly air strikes and other combat units on the ground and at sea. EA also plays an important role in defeating hostile air strikes and countering precision strike weapons. Disciplined EMCON and other EP measures are also an important part of protecting friendly air strikes and front line tactical units on the ground and at sea. EMCON and other EP measures also protect friendly forces handling or operating around live ordnance during combat operations by preventing inadvertent detonations due to hazards of EM radiation to ordnance. ES assets provide timely warning of adversary reaction to friendly air strike and other physical destruction actions that take friendly forces into hostile territory or contact with adversary combat forces. ES also performs an important combat assessment role by providing feedback about the results of friendly physical attack actions that can be obtained through SIGINT or changes in the EME. ES can also be used to evaluate the effectiveness of friendly force EMCON measures and recommend modifications or improvements. All of these factors require that joint EW staff personnel actively work with air planners, fire support personnel, and other staff personnel involved in coordinating physical destruction actions during combat operations.

For more information, refer to JP 3-09, Joint Fire Support, *and JP 3-60,* Joint Targeting.

(g) **Electronic Warfare and Physical Security.** EW supports physical security by using EP to safeguard communications used in protecting facilities. Additionally, EP features may guard personnel, facilities, and equipment from the broader effects (both intended and unintended) of EM energy. Physical security supports EW by safeguarding equipment used in EW. In an era when IEDs with radio-controlled electronic detonators have become ubiquitous, EW and physical security form one of the new, closely intertwined relationships in the EMS. EW capabilities can be used to preempt and disrupt threats that may be using part of the EMS to attack joint ground forces.

(h) **Electronic Warfare and Counterintelligence (CI).** There are many electronic aspects to CI. ES platforms, on occasion, might be called on to help monitor some aspect of CI operations in overseas locations. Frequencies used for CI operations in foreign locations should be coordinated through the JRFL. Close coordination through the J-3 EW and J-2 CI staff divisions should establish a battle rhythm and/or TTP to monitor and deconflict JRFL and other EW activities that either support or potentially jeopardize human intelligence activities.

(i) **Electronic Warfare and Combat Camera (COMCAM).** EW involves some of the most technologically sophisticated and innovative aspects of joint operations. Affording COMCAM the opportunity to capture photographs and film of EW units in action can help to convey, to domestic and foreign audiences, the technological sophistication and power of US forces, but may also divulge key operations characteristics, limitations, and vulnerabilities to adversaries, and thus should be carefully controlled.

(j) **Electronic Warfare and Public Affairs (PA).** The relationship of EW to PA is primarily one of deconfliction. News media personnel in the OA use a variety of electronic recording and transmitting devices to carry out their assignments. It is important that their equipment and operating frequencies are accounted for in the JRFL to enable deconfliction and identify potential fratricidal interference between news media equipment and friendly force military equipment.

For more information on PA, refer to JP 3-61, Public Affairs.

(k) **Electronic Warfare and Civil-Military Operations (CMO).** In support operations such as humanitarian operations, EW assets may be used to map the EMS and broadcast civil defense information similar to the way they have been used successfully to broadcast MISO messages. In all operations, CMO frequencies should be included on the JRFL to ensure deconfliction with EW assets' activities. As requirements for EW assets expand into peacetime contingency roles, it becomes more imperative that planners consider diplomatic clearance requirements of HNs as early as possible.

For more information on CMO, refer to JP 3-57, Civil-Military Operations.

(l) **Electronic Warfare and Defense Support to Public Diplomacy (DSPD).** EW support and deconfliction with DSPD parallels EW support and deconfliction with MISO.

e. **Electronic Warfare and Legal Support.** Legal review is required to ensure EW operations are in compliance with existing DOD directives and instructions, ROE, and applicable domestic and international law, including LOAC.

For more information, refer to JP 1-04, Legal Support to Military Operations.

f. **Exploitation of Captured Equipment and Personnel.** Exploitation of adversary equipment can verify adversary electronic equipment capabilities, to include WARM. This information can lead to the testing or verification of friendly EW equipment or begin the process of EW reprogramming to counter new adversary capabilities. Exploitation of captured adversary personnel can lead to discoveries of adversary capabilities, tactics, and procedures against friendly EW capabilities. Information gleaned through the interrogation of captured personnel may help EW planners **evaluate the effectiveness of friendly EW actions.** This information can also aid in **after-action report reconstruction** of EW. The joint captured materiel exploitation center and joint interrogation and debriefing center conduct exploitation of captured material and interrogation of captured personnel, respectively. The EW staff should establish EW exploitation and interrogation requirements, through the J-2, to take advantage of the opportunities that may be realized through exploitation of captured equipment and interrogation of captured personnel.

For more information, refer to JP 2-01, Joint and National Intelligence Support to Military Operations.

3. Service Component Coordination Procedures

a. Components requiring EW support from another component should be encouraged to **directly coordinate that support** when possible, informing joint EW planners of the results of such coordination, as appropriate. However, at the joint force level, EW planners should be familiar with how this coordination occurs across Service and functional component lines in order to be **prepared to assist and facilitate coordination** when necessary, or when requested. An overview of component EW coordination factors and procedures are provided in this section. When the JFC has chosen to conduct operations through functional components, the functional component commanders will determine how their components are organized and what procedures are used. EW planners should coordinate with the functional component EWEs to determine how they are organized and what procedures are being used by functional component forces.

b. **Army.** The Army Service component command (ASCC) or G-3 plans, coordinates, and integrates EW requirements in support of the JFC's objectives. At corps level, coordination with the G-3, the fire support coordination center or fire support element (FSE), and the communications systems staff officer is required. These requirements are translated into EW support requests and, where possible, are coordinated directly with the appropriate staff elements having EW staff responsibility within other component HQ. Conversely, other components requiring Army EW support initially coordinate those support requirements with the EW officer at the Army forces HQ or tactical operations center. This coordination is normally done in person or through operational channels when planning joint EW operations. However, the Global Command and Control System (GCCS) or Global

Command and Control System-Army (GCCS-A) may be used to **coordinate immediate requests for Army EW support.** In this case, other components will communicate their EW support requests via the GCCS or GCCS-A to the FSE and EW officer or to the EW section at ASCC, corps, or division level. Air Force and Army coordination will normally **flow through the battlefield coordination detachment** at the AOC. EW staffs at higher echelons monitor the EW requests and resolve conflicts, when necessary. The G-3 also:

(1) Provides an assessment of Army EW capabilities to the other component operation centers.

(2) Coordinates preplanned EW operations with other Service components.

(3) Updates preplanned EW operations in coordination with other components, as required.

(4) Coordinates with the intelligence staff officer to ensure an IGL analysis is conducted for potential EW targets.

(5) Coordinates and integrates cyberspace and EM activities.

c. **Marine Corps.** The MAGTF HQ **EWCC,** if established, or the MAGTF EWO, if there is no EWCC, is responsible for **coordination of the joint aspects of MAGTF EW requirements.** Requirements for other component EW support are established by the operations staff, in coordination with the aviation combat element, the ground combat element, and the combat logistics element of the MAGTF. These requirements are translated by the EWCC or EWO into tasks and coordinated with the other component EW staffs. In addition, the EWCC or EWO:

(1) Provides an assessment of Marine Corps forces' EW capabilities to other component operation centers to be used in planning MAGTF EW support to air, ground, and naval operations.

(2) Coordinates preplanned EW operations with appropriate component operation centers.

(3) Updates EW operations based on coordination with other component EW agencies.

(4) Coordinates with the intelligence staff officer to ensure that an IGL analysis is conducted for potential EW targets.

d. **Navy.** The Navy component commander is normally a numbered fleet commander within a theater. The Navy operations directorate is responsible for all Navy EW efforts and provides coordination and tasking to task forces assigned. The IWC at the carrier strike group or amphibious ready group-Marine expeditionary unit provides for execution at the tactical level. When naval task forces are operating as a component of a joint force, the IWC:

(1) Provides an assessment of Navy EW capabilities to the other component operation centers.

(2) Coordinates preplanned EW operations with appropriate component EW agencies.

See NTTP 3-51.1, Navy Electronic Warfare, *for a full list of IWC responsibilities to EW.*

NOTE: When employed in a strike support role, airborne EA and ES assets (e.g., EA-6B Prowler and EA-18G Growler) will be the responsibility of the strike warfare commander. The strike warfare commander is responsible for coordinating integration of air wing assets into the ATO with the JFACC.

e. **Air Force.** Air Force requirements for other component EW support are established through close coordination between the JFC's EWC and the **COMAFFOR's A-3** (or equivalent operations directorate) **or A-5** (or equivalent plans directorate), in coordination with the Director for Intelligence, A-2. Ideally, this coordination will involve the COMAFFOR's AOC and JFC's JOC. The JFC's EWC and A-3 or A-5 staff translate requirements for other component EW support into tasks and coordinate those tasks, through the EWC, with the component EWE. In addition, the A-3 or A-5 staff officer:

(1) Provides an assessment of Air Force capabilities to the joint EWC.

(2) Updates EW operations based on coordination with the joint EWC.

f. **Special Operations Forces.** The joint force special operations component commander will establish a JOC to serve as the task integration and planning center for joint force special operations. Requirements from special operations units for EW support will be transmitted to the joint force special operations component command JOC for coordination with the joint force special operations component command IO cell.

For more information, refer to JP 3-05, Special Operations.

g. **United States Coast Guard (USCG).** In peacetime, the USCG operates as part of the Department of Homeland Security (DHS). Upon the declaration of war or when the President directs, the USCG will operate as part of the DOD. During both peacetime and war, joint operations may include USCG assets that possess EW capabilities. Coordination with USCG assets should be through assigned USCG liaison personnel or operational procedures specified in the OPLAN or OPORD.

4. Electronic Warfare and Intelligence, Surveillance, and Reconnaissance Coordination

Detailed coordination is essential between the EW activities and the intelligence activities supporting an operation. A major portion of the intelligence effort, prior to and during an operation, relies on collection activities targeted against various parts of the EMS. ES depends on the **timely collection, processing, and reporting of various intelligence and combat information** to alert EW operators and other military activities about important intelligence collected in the EMS. It is vital that all prudent measures are taken to **ensure EMS activities are closely and continuously deconflicted with ES** and intelligence collection activities. The J-2 must ensure that EW collection priorities and ES sensors are integrated into a **complete intelligence collection plan.** This plan ensures that use of scarce intelligence and ES collection assets is maximized in order to support all aspects of the JFC's objectives.

For more information, refer to JP 2-01, Joint and National Intelligence Support to Military Operations, *and its classified supplement.*

5. Electronic Warfare and Interagency Coordination

Although OPLANs and commander's intent are limited to military contexts, the desired effects, coordination required, and agencies affected within the EMOE extend beyond those contexts. The increasingly prolific and congested EMS will require a better understanding of which government, nongovernmental organization (NGO), and commercial entities affect segments of the EMS required for effective military operations (e.g., Department of State [DOS] contractors in the OA and Federal Communications Commission sale/migration of frequencies that impact DOD systems). Although there may not be intentional targeting of the EMS, inadvertent and unintentional interference may wreak havoc on the systems being used to support the execution of interagency operations. As such, constant and detailed coordination is essential between EW activities and relevant interagency organizations (e.g., DOS, DHS, CIA, and NSA). While EW operations are handled by the JCEWS or EWC, interagency coordination should be accomplished through the JSME, in concert with the JCEWS or EWC chief, to help provide separation from the more sensitive nature of EW operations. The JSME maintains a database of military EMS usage and frequency assignments and has the ability to coordinate with agency partners and collect, analyze, and deconflict frequency assignments without direct linkage to possible EW COAs or operations. In the event planning efforts are not successful in preventing EMS conflicts during the execution of interagency operations, the JSME has the capability to provide EMI and electronic countermeasures analysis and actively pursue both, as required.

Other books we publish on Amazon.com

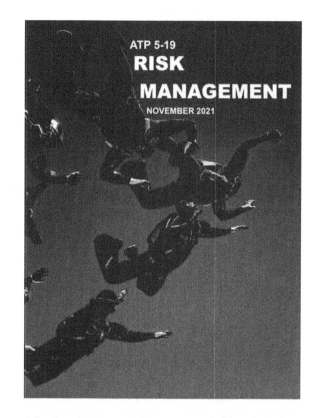

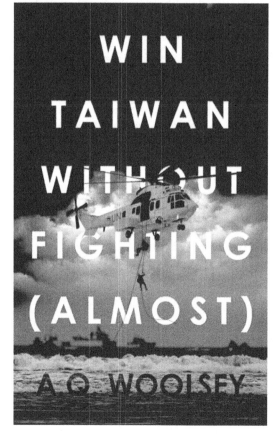

CHAPTER V
MULTINATIONAL ASPECTS OF ELECTRONIC WARFARE

"The foundation of United States, regional, and global security will remain America's relations with our allies, and our commitment to their security is unshakable."

The National Security Strategy of the
United States of America 2010

1. Introduction

Operations since 2001 have reinforced the benefits of integrating US joint operations with those of our multinational partners. US planners should integrate US and partner nations' EW capabilities into an overall EW plan, provide partner nations with information concerning US EW capabilities, and provide EW support to partner nations. As in joint operations, **EW is an integral part of multinational operations.** However, the planning of MNF EW is made more difficult because of **security issues, different cryptographic equipment, differences in the level of training** of involved forces, and **language barriers.** These problems are well understood throughout North Atlantic Treaty Organization (NATO) commands and are normally addressed by **adherence to NATO standardization agreements.** Therefore, it makes sense for US forces, as participants in NATO, to adopt these procedures when working with NATO or other MNFs such as may be drawn from members of the American, British, Canadian, Australian Armies Program (ABCA) and the Air and Space Interoperability Council (ASIC) made up of the ABCA members plus New Zealand. NATO and the ABCA have developed documents to deal with MNF EW mission support. However, with the exception of Australia, Britain, and Canada (who are on the official distribution list of this publication), allied and coalition EW officers may not understand the terminology or procedures being used. A fundamental task for the EWO of a US-led MNF is to **recognize and resolve terminology and procedural issues** at the outset. This can be achieved by comparing multinational doctrine to this publication. GCCs should provide guidance to the multinational force commander (MNFC) (if the MNFC is a US Service member), within their joint OPLANs, on the release of classified material to MNFs. However, the MNFC must determine the need to know and release information essential to accomplishing the mission at the earliest stages of planning. To do this, US EW planners must be intimately aware of both sides of the issue—national security as well as mission accomplishment—in order to advise the MNFC. Intelligence components must ensure they plan sufficiently ahead for necessary approvals. See DIA Instruction 2000.001, *International Military Intelligence Relationships*, for additional information.

2. Multinational Force Electronic Warfare Organization and Command and Control

a. **MNFC.** The MNFC **provides guidance for planning and conducting EW operations to the MNF** through the operations directorate's combined EWCC. It should be recognized that the EWCC assumes responsibilities set forth in Chapter II, "Organizing for Joint Electronic Warfare."

NOTE: NATO/multinational terminology still references the EWCC. Therefore, EWCC, not EWC, will be used when discussing NATO/multinational operations.

b. **Multinational Staff.** The MNFC should assign responsibilities for management of EW resources in multinational operations among the staff for the following:

(1) **Operations Officer.** The multinational staff's operations directorate has primary responsibility for planning and integrating EW operations with other mission areas.

(2) **Staff EW Officer.** The staff EWO's primary responsibility should be to ensure the MNFC is provided the same EW support that a US JFC would expect. In addition to the duties outlined in Chapter II, "Organizing for Joint Electronic Warfare," the EWO should be responsible for the following:

(a) Ensure all component commanders of the MNF **provide qualified EWOs** as members of the MNFC EW staff. The chain of command should be established by the director for operations. The rationale for augmentee status is that partner nation officers must be full members of the multinational EW planning cell and responsible to the chain of command. They should not be subjected to the possibility of split loyalties to a lower command within the force, as could be the case if they adopted the traditional liaison role.

(b) Determine the need for placing US EW LNOs with multinational commands to ensure that the MNFC's EW **plans and procedures are correctly interpreted.**

(c) **Integrate partner nation EWO augmentees** at the initial planning stage, delegating to them duties and responsibilities similar to those given to equivalent US officers.

(d) **Coordinate the necessary EW communications connectivity** for assigned forces. Particular emphasis should be given to equipment, encryption devices and keying material, and procedural compatibility when integrating MNFs.

(e) Ensure constant liaison with the multinational staff's intelligence directorate and CSG in order to provide the most adaptive and effective intelligence support to EW efforts. Ensure planned EW targeting efforts have minimal impact on friendly C2 collection efforts.

(f) Integrate partner nation communications system directorate processes into EW planning and oversight. Integrate EW C2 requirements into the JRFL. Coordinate with the multinational staff's communications system directorate to ensure tracking and remediation of JSIR events.

(g) Provide, at the earliest possible stage, MNFs with current US EW doctrine and planning guidelines.

(3) **Partner Nation EW Officers.** Partner nation commanders should assign qualified EWOs to the MNF EW planning cell. These officers should:

(a) Have an in-depth knowledge of their own forces' operational SIGINT and EW requirements, organization, capabilities, national support facilities, and C2 structure.

(b) Possess national clearances equivalent with the level of classified US military information they are eligible to receive in accordance with US national disclosure policy. These requirements may mean the individuals concerned will be a senior O-3 or O-4 pay grade level or equivalent. As a result, they may be augmentees drawn from national sources other than the unit(s) involved in the MNF.

3. Multinational Electronic Warfare Coordination Cell with Allies and Other Friendly Forces

a. Although NATO EW policy contained in Military Committee (MC) 64/10, *NATO Electronic Warfare Policy,* is consistent with much of US EW policy, the **perspective and procedures of an MNF EWCC will be new to most.** MC 515, *Concept for the NATO SIGINT and EW Operations Centre (SEWOC),* provides the operational requirements and the operational procedures for an interoperable SEWOC to support the full range of possible NATO and NATO-led operations in a combined and joint environment. It also provides a standard of operations between agencies, services, organizations, and nodes. In addition, it outlines the basic principles, relationships, establishments, and specific details required to manage SIGINT and EW in support of NATO operations and to exercise the capability in peacetime. MC 486, *Concept for NATO Joint Electronic Warfare Core Staff (JEWCS),* describes the functions of the JEWCS. The primary functions of the JEWCS would be to provide a core staff to augment EWCCs, serve as the primary EWCC element for the NATO response force, and provide an operational planning capability for NATO operations and exercises. EWCCs and the primary EWCC element for the NATO response force are to be augmented by those nations contributing to the operation with assets using EW. The JEWCS provides EW training for NATO forces and Alliance members and provide EW support for, and analysis of, NATO and Alliance member EW systems and capabilities. At best, participants may have worked joint issues and served in adjacent forces who have exchanged EW LNOs. However, precedent exists; maritime forces have, for many years, worked multinational issues with little difficulty. Allied Tactical Publication (ATP)-08(B), *Doctrine for Amphibious Operations,* now contains a supplement on EW. This includes procedures necessary to exchange SIGINT information. In addition, Allied Joint Publication (AJP)-01(C), *Allied Joint Doctrine,* includes a chapter on EW and the EWCC. NATO members invariably base their national EW doctrine on that agreed within NATO MC 64/10. However, there is a need to ensure the most recent, releasable, US EW publications are provided to supporting MNFs. NATO has also established a NATO Emitter Database to exchange information about member countries' and nonmember countries' EM emissions and facilitate the coordination of EW.

b. Strong ties are maintained with traditional allied forces from Great Britain, Canada, and Australia. This is true particularly within the field of EW and SIGINT. **Much information is exchanged at the national level,** and this publication has been released to these nations. One example of the close ties is the Quadripartite Working Group on EW, the ABCA EW forum. Although Australia is not a party to NATO agreements, it is aware of the current status of NATO's EW policy contained in MC 64/10. Quadripartite Standardization

Agreement (QSTAG) 593, *Doctrine on Mutual Support Between EW Units,* reflects current NATO policy and meets Australia's needs. This document contains standard operating procedures for an EWCC. ASIC Working Parties (WPs) 45 (Air Operations) and 70 (Mission Avionics) both deal with EW issues. WP 45 looks at the operational employment of the MNF's EW assets, while WP 70 investigates the possibility of standardizing EW systems.

c. The principles expressed above are equally applicable to other MNFs. The MNFC should include EWOs from supporting MNFs within the EWCC. Should this not be practical for security reasons or availability, the MNFC should, based on the mission, be prepared to provide EW support and the appropriate LNOs to the multinational units.

4. Electronic Warfare Mutual Support

a. **Exchange of SIGINT information** in support of EW operations should be conducted in accordance with standard NATO, ABCA, and ASIC procedures, as appropriate. The information data elements, identified at tabs 1 and 2 and annex C, also are contained in appropriate allied publications—notably, NATO's supplement to ATP-8(A), *EW in Amphibious Operations;* ATP-44(C), *Electronic Warfare (EW) in Air Operations;* ATP-51(A), *Electronic Warfare in the Land Battle;* MC 101/12, *NATO Signals Intelligence Policy and Directive;* and ABCA's QSTAG 593, *Doctrine on Mutual Support Between EW Units.* Care should be taken not to violate SIGINT security rules when exercising EW mutual-support procedures.

b. **Exchange of Electronic Order of Battle.** In peacetime, this type of exchange is normally achieved under **bilateral agreement.** NATO has procedures in place within the major NATO commanders' precautionary system that can be put into effect during times of tension. They include the requirement to **exchange information on WARM.** The procedures also determine at what stage allied forces change to the use of WARM; however, in low-level conflict, they are unlikely to be activated. Therefore, the EWCC chief, through the EW intelligence support organization and the theater joint analysis center or theater JIOC, should ensure maintenance of an up-to-date EOB. Multinational staff officers should be included and should ensure their national commands provide appropriate updates to theater joint analysis in discussions on EOB. These staff officers should ensure their national commands provide appropriate updates to theater joint automated communication-electronics operating instructions system (JACS) and JIOCs. MC 521, *Concept for Resources and Methods to Support an Operational NATO EWCC/SEWOC,* describes a NATO EOB and who is responsible for its development and upkeep.

c. **Reprogramming.** Reprogramming of EW equipment is a **national responsibility.** However, the EWCC chief should be aware of reprogramming efforts being conducted within the MNF. The EWCC chief should keep the MNFC aware of limitations that could result in fratricide and, when necessary, seek the MNFC's assistance in attaining a solution. To do this, national and multinational commands should provide the EWCC chief with information on the following on request:

(1) Capabilities and limitations of MNF allied and/or coalition EW equipment.

(2) EW reprogramming support available within MNF allied and/or coalition units.

(3) Country-specific letters of agreement on reprogramming support for allied and/or coalition units employing US EW equipment, to include any agreement on flagging support.

(4) Country-specific letters of agreement on exchange of EW reprogramming information with those nations not employing US EW equipment.

(5) Reports from friendly units experiencing reprogramming difficulties, to include information on efforts being made to rectify the problem.

(6) Immediate reports on incidents that could have resulted in fratricide.

(7) Operational change requests sent to US reprogramming organizations that identify deficiencies in the partner nation's EW equipment and their request for reprogramming support. In turn, the EWCC chief should ensure that multinational units in the MNF receive the most recent data held within the theater tactical EOB database and, as appropriate, the associated parametric information. This should allow multinational units within the MNF to address the operational change requests, **judge the reliability of their current reprogramming data,** and, if necessary, **identify problems** to the MNF EWCC and national support agencies. Without this level of EW mutual support, fratricide may occur.

For more information on EW reprogramming, refer to Appendix E, "Electronic Warfare Reprogramming."

d. **US EW Planning Aids.** Significant improvements have been made within the US in the automation of EW planning aids. These improvements allow US EW planners to **extract information from theater and national databases and depict it in graphic format** for planning and briefing purposes. Supporting allied and/or coalition forces are unlikely to have an equal level of automation. Working with the allied and/or coalition officers, the EWCC chief should determine what EW information would assist the MNF at the planning and unit level and ensure that they get it. To do this, EWCC personnel should understand security issues that preclude the release of some data and its source but do not necessarily preclude the release of EW mission planning tools.

5. Releasability of Electronic Warfare Information to Multinational Forces

The integration of multinational EWOs into US-led MNF activities is often perceived by US staff officers as too difficult due to the complexity of national disclosure policy. As a result, this integration often occurs late in the planning process. A clear, easily understood policy on the disclosure of EW information requested by multinational partners should be developed by the commander's foreign disclosure officer as early as possible.

Don't have time to read the book? Get these **AUDIOBOOKs** on Amazon.com

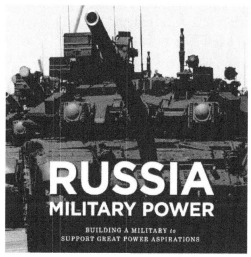

APPENDIX A
ELECTRONIC WARFARE GUIDANCE

The guidance in this appendix relates to the development of tab D (Electronic Warfare) of appendix 3 (Information Operations) to annex C (Operations) of the format found in CJCSM 3122.03C, *Joint Operation Planning and Execution System, Volume II, Planning Formats,* for campaign plans, applicable contingency plans, and OPORDs. **This is guidance to supplement the format in CJCSM 3122.03.**

1. Situation

a. Enemy

(1) What are the capabilities, limitations, and vulnerabilities of enemy EMS-dependent (e.g., command, control, communications, computers, ISR; non-emitting; PNT service; and EW) systems?

(2) What is the enemy capability to interfere with EMS control (i.e., EW mission accomplishment and EMS management)?

(3) What are the capabilities, limitations, and vulnerabilities of enemy EMS-dependent (e.g., command, control, communications, computers, ISR; non-emitting; PNT service; and EW) systems resulting from third party support?

b. Friendly

(1) Is a JFC EWC currently in place? If so, is the manning adequate to address the anticipated scope of operations?

(2) What friendly EW facilities, resources, and organizations may affect or support EW planning by operational commanders?

(3) Who are the friendly forces with which operational commanders may operate?

(4) What are the capabilities, limitations, and vulnerabilities of friendly EMS-dependent (e.g., command, control, communications, computers, ISR; non-emitting; PNT service; and EW) systems?

(5) What are the impacts of civilian/commercial EM systems/networks on the EMOE?

c. **Assumptions.** What are the assumptions concerning friendly or enemy capabilities and COAs that significantly influence the planning of EW operations?

2. Mission

What is the joint force's mission (who, what, when, where, why)?

3. Execution

a. Concept of Operations

(1) What is the role of EW in the commander's strategy?

(2) What is the scope of EW operations?

(3) What methods and resources will be employed? Include organic and nonorganic capabilities.

(4) How will EW support other IO capabilities?

(5) What legal requirements exist that may affect EW operations?

b. **Tasks.** What are the individual EW tasks and responsibilities for each component or subdivision of the force? Include all instructions unique to that component or subdivision.

c. Coordinating Instructions

(1) What instructions, if any, are applicable to two or more components or divisions of EW?

(2) What are the requirements, if any, for the coordination of EW actions between subordinate elements?

(3) What is the guidance on the employment of each activity, special measure, or procedure that is to be used but is not covered elsewhere in this tab?

(4) What is the EMCON control guidance? Place detailed or lengthy guidance in an exhibit to this tab.

(5) What coordination between the J-2, J-3, and J-6 is required to plan, approve, and publish the JRFL?

4. Administration and Logistics

a. Administration

(1) What, if any, administrative guidance is required?

(2) What, if any, reports are required? Include example(s).

b. **Logistics.** What, if any, are the special instructions on logistic support for EW operations?

5. Command and Control

a. Command Relationships

(1) **Feedback**

      (a) What is the CONOPS for monitoring the effectiveness of EW operations during execution?

      (b) What are the specific intelligence requirements for feedback?

(2) **After-Action Reports.** What are the requirements for after-action reporting?

b. **Communications Systems.** What, if any, are the special or unusual EW-related communications requirements?

Other books we publish on Amazon.com

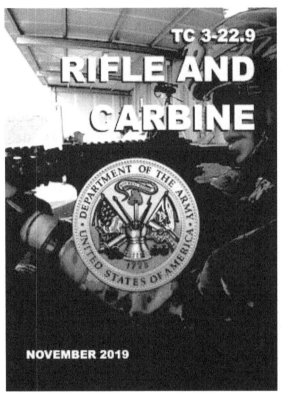

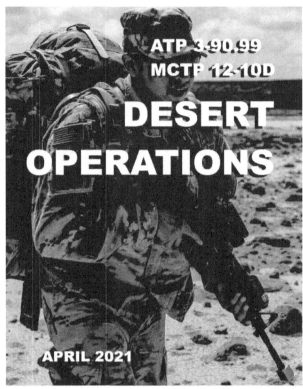

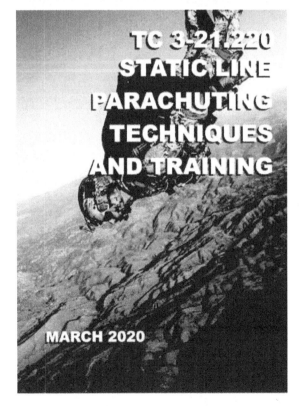

Includes info on REAL-TIME ELECTRONIC
SPECTRUM SITUATIONAL AWARENESS

APPENDIX B
ORGANIZATIONS SUPPORTING JOINT ELECTRONIC WARFARE

Other books we publish on Amazon.com

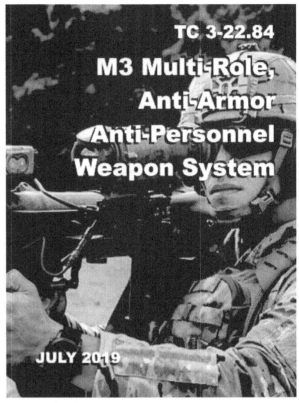

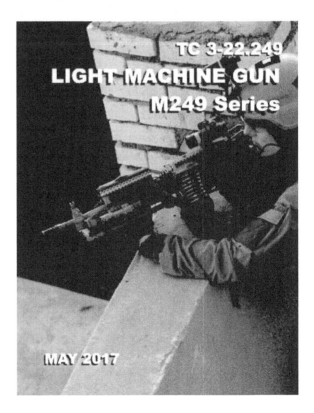

ANNEX A TO APPENDIX B
ELECTROMAGNETIC-SPACE ANALYSIS CENTER

1. General

a. As a DOD focal point, the E-Space program is chartered by the Under Secretary of Defense for Intelligence to provide combatant commands and their component commands with intelligence support for EW operations.

b. The increased operations tempo of the 1990s, beginning with Operation DESERT SHIELD/STORM, highlighted the growing requirement for intelligence support to IO planning, with a focus on EW.

c. The NSA is designated as the Executive Agent for the program. Organizationally, the E-Space Program Office (S1E) is part of the Customer Relationships Directorate within the NSA SIGINT Directorate.

d. Self-service data source portals are established on SIPRNET and Joint Worldwide Intelligence Communications System (JWICS) to provide access to intelligence data from across DOD and the IC. This capability, combined with the all-source analytic center, provides direct support to EW consumers across the DOD intelligence, operations, planning, and communication communities. Direct support is also afforded the IC.

2. Mission

a. Deliver full EMS views of an adversary's EM space to enable CCDRs to develop operational COAs.

b. Serve operational users' needs by providing tailored support and technical analytic expertise to operational planners, tactical warfighters, EW system developers, and the modeling and simulation communities.

c. Ensure access to all-source, targetable, and operationally actionable intelligence information relating to EM capabilities and potential means of access to those targets using collaborative tools, databases, and analysis.

d. Provide holdings of information that will assist in preparation of the OE and electronic mapping of targets.

3. Electromagnetic-Space Support to Electronic Warfare

a. There are two entities within E-Space. The first is the acquisition of secure Web portals for both SIPRNET and JWICS. The second is the daily operations of an all-source intelligence analysis center with resident expertise capable of providing tailored support to US military forces conducting EW missions.

b. The E-Space secure Web portals provide users with a single point of access to a variety of data sources. They also provide an analytic environment to retrieve, assess, and display or format data for use in external analytic tools. These portals are designed to provide those involved in EW operations with "self-service" rapid access to critical, decision quality intelligence.

c. The ESAC provides tailored all-source analysis to EW customers based on specific requests for intelligence. This joint center gathers intelligence from across DOD and the IC to produce tailored intelligence summaries for its customers. ESAC analysts leverage access to other experts, data sources, and analytic tools to provide warfighters with decision quality intelligence.

4. Mailing Address

E-Space

9800 Savage Road, Suite 6295

Fort George G. Meade, MD 20755-6295

5. Telephone Numbers

Defense Switched Network (DSN): 689-9910 (Portal)

DSN: 689-5811/9991 (ESAC)

COMMERCIAL: 443-479-5811 (ESAC)

6. E-Mail

SIPRNET: ESpace_Helpdesk@nsa.smil.mil (Portal)

JWICS: ESpace_Helpdesk@nsa.ic.gov (Portal)

SIPRNET: ESpaceAC@nsa.smil.mil (ESAC)

JWICS: ESpaceAC@nsa.ic.gov (ESAC)

7. URLs

SIPRNET: www.nsa.smil.mil/producer/other/espace/index.shtml

JWICS: www.nsa.ic.gov/producer/other/espace/index.shtml

ANNEX B TO APPENDIX B
GLOBAL POSITIONING SYSTEM OPERATIONS CENTER

1. General

The GPSOC provides a single center of excellence for user support and GPS constellation operations. The GPSOC, located at Schriever AFB, Colorado, provides DOD and allied GPS users worldwide with anomaly reports and other information 24 hours a day, seven days a week. USSTRATCOM's Joint Functional Component Command for Space (JFCC SPACE) has operational control of the GPSOC that is exercised through the Joint Space Operations Center (JSPOC).

2. Mission

a. The mission of the GPSOC is to operate, maintain, and employ GPS to produce a desired effect in support of military, civil, and allied operations. Key aspects of this mission are:

(1) Optimized constellation operations fully synchronized and supportive of CCDRs' needs and operational priorities.

(2) Robust, real-time performance monitoring and reporting to ensure a common operational picture and full situational awareness across all echelons of command. This is done through operational coordination with other PNT services.

(3) Full integration, coordination, and deconfliction of GPS NAVWAR operations with routine military and civil GPS operations for maximized impact and minimal collateral effects.

(4) Direct and immediate access to time-critical GPS products and services designed to leverage the effectiveness of operations reliant on GPS services.

(5) Rapid identification, isolation, and resolution of user reported outages or interference.

b. The GPSOC brings together the expertise, data fusion, and visualization capabilities, security controls, and performance information required to operate, maintain, and employ GPS to produce the desired effects to support military operations.

3. Global Positioning System Operations Center Support to Electronic Warfare

a. The GPSOC maintains databases and provides data about friendly force GPS system technical characteristics for use in planning EP measures. These databases provide EW planners with information covering GPS receivers and augmentations operated by DOD, other government departments and agencies, and private businesses or organizations. Information from these databases is available on a quick reaction basis in a variety of formats and media to support EW planners and spectrum managers.

b. The GPSOC assists GPS users across DOD with predicted GPS performance impacts to operations; post performance analysis of GPS constellation accuracy; DOD user reports of interference or jamming; user problems or questions regarding GPS; tactical support for planning; and assessing military missions involving GPS use. For EW planners, the GPSOC can assist with COA development for the EP of GPS frequencies and access to GPS information for authorized users. Additionally, the GPSOC can assist with ES through its monitoring of the GPS Jammer Location System hosted by NGA and the integration of Global Positioning System Interference and Navigation Tool (GIANT) to predict GPS jamming effects on GPS receivers. With additional information, GIANT can be used to model and predict the effects of blue force jamming on friendly systems and the use of blue force EA to prevent enemy use of GPS frequencies.

c. The GPSOC assists in the resolution of operational interference and jamming incidents through the use of the GPS Jammer Location System and the request for information or request for anomaly analysis process. The GPSOC also maintains a historical database of interference and jamming incident reports and solutions to assist in trend analysis and correction of recurring problems. Combatant commands, subordinate unified commands, JTFs, and their components can request assistance in resolving suspected GPS interference, jamming, and anomalous behavior.

4. Mailing Address

2nd Space Operations Squadron

300 O'Malley Avenue, Suite 41

Schriever AFB, CO 80912

5. Telephone Numbers

DSN: 560-2541/5081 (UNCLASSIFIED)

COMMERCIAL: 719-567-2541/5081

6. E-Mail

Nonsecure Internet Protocol Router Network (NIPRNET): gps_support@ schriever.af.mil

SIPRNET: gpsv3@afspc.af.smil.mil

ANNEX C TO APPENDIX B
US STRATEGIC COMMAND JOINT ELECTRONIC WARFARE CENTER

1. General

The JEWC integrates joint EW capabilities and employment in support of worldwide military operations and USSTRATCOM's Unified Command Plan EW responsibilities. The JEWC is USSTRATCOM's EW organization.

2. Mission

The mission of the JEWC is to integrate joint EW capabilities by providing adaptive operational solutions and advocating for the coherent evolution of capabilities and processes in order to control the EMS during military operations.

3. Joint Electronic Warfare Center

a. Serves as the central DOD repository for joint EW-related subject matter expertise supporting SecDef, Joint Staff, CCDRs, JFCs, and partner nations.

b. Advocates joint EW doctrinal, organizational, training, material, leadership and education, and personnel advancements in pursuit of EMS control.

c. Serves as office of the Deputy Under Secretary of Defense's single point of contact for EW vulnerabilities inherent in joint capability technology demonstration systems and technologies.

d. Provides advanced EW analysis support to JFC operations, tests, and exercises. In addition to short-suspense, crisis-action EW analysis and mission development, this support includes providing RF propagation and three-dimensional terrain modeling and simulation for airborne, ground-based, and shipboard EMS-dependent systems.

e. Maintains an EW rapid deployment team (the Joint EW Support Element) capable of supporting JFCs with a surge capability for initiating theater contingency operations.

f. Maintains, as the DOD lead for joint EW training oversight, the Joint EW Theater Operations Course. As a certified and required course for joint EWOs, it transforms Service EW experts into theater EW staff officers capable of shaping the EME for JFCs.

g. Monitors and evaluates the impact of current US and adversary EW technologies, systems, and TTP employed within the EMS. It also maintains an EM opposing force (OPFOR). The EM OPFOR (red team) replicates a coherent, realistic EME capable of mirroring adversary and civilian infrastructure in order to train and enhance DOD/United States Government (USG) EM capabilities, processes, and TTP proficiency. The red team is vital in providing blue forces the keys to developing a joint culture of robust, survivable EM processes via a contested/congested EME. For EM OPFOR applications, they provide a scalable real-world target set (primarily commercial off-the-shelf equipment such as wireless networks/computers, cellular infrastructure, SATCOM, and push-to-talk) for operators to train against. Other capabilities include, but are not limited to, radio DF and communications intercept, RF vulnerability assessments, STO validation, and EW effects validation. The red team also supports TTP development for ground, sea, and air EW asset integration across the OE.

h. Collaborates with laboratories, joint and Service analysis centers, weapons schools, battle labs, centers of excellence, US and Allied operational EW communities, and academia to explore innovative EW employment options and concepts for capabilities against existing and emerging EM targets throughout the OE.

i. Provides oversight and advocacy for evolving EW capabilities and joint force requirements by identifying emerging capability gaps and technology trends employed within the EMS in order to advocate short-term mitigation possibilities and long-term solutions to the Services, combatant commands, and other agencies able to fund, or otherwise address, these shortfalls.

j. Assists commanders, as the executive agent for exercising JCEWR, with identification, confirmation, and dissemination of electronic threat changes; coordinates compatibility; and facilitates the joint EW reprogramming data exchange among the IC, Services, and combatant commands per CJCSI 3210.04, *Joint Electronic Warfare Reprogramming Policy.*

k. Manages, as the Joint Staff's Executive Agent and technical advisor, US participation in the NATO Emitter Database and performs management and coordination functions of the US Electromagnetic Systems Database in accordance with Memorandum Joint Chiefs of Staff 187-84 and CJCSI 3210.03C, *Joint Electronic Warfare Policy.*

4. Mailing Address

JEWC

2 Hall Boulevard, Suite 217

San Antonio, TX 78243-7074

5. Telephone Numbers

DSN: 969-5967 (UNCLASSIFIED)

COMMERCIAL: 210- 977-5967

DSN 969-2507 (Duty Officer)

COMMERCIAL 210-977-2507 (Duty Officer)

Facsimile (FAX): DSN 969-4233 (UNCLASSIFIED)

FAX: DSN 969-2507 (CLASSIFIED)

6. E-Mail

NIPRNET: ew_ewos@jiowc.osis.gov

SIPRNET: ew_ewos@jiowc.smil.mil

JWICS: ew_ewos@jiowc.ic.gov

Other books we publish on Amazon.com

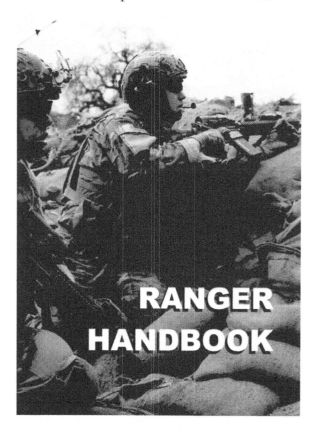

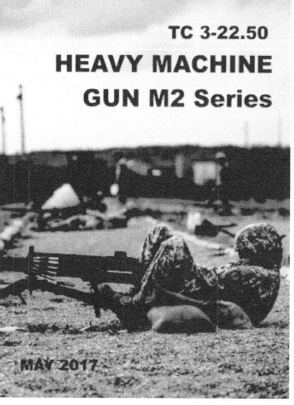

ANNEX D TO APPENDIX B
JOINT NAVIGATION WARFARE CENTER

1. General

The JNWC was established in 2004 under the Assistant Secretary of Defense/Networks and Information Integration. It was assigned to USSTRATCOM's JFCC SPACE in October 2007.

2. Mission

The JNWC's primary mission is to provide operation-level joint warfighter support and serve as the center of excellence for all NAVWAR-related issues. In addition, the JNWC integrates and coordinates PNT capabilities across DOD; provides a core interagency framework to coordinate, conduct, and report on NAVWAR testing and integration and identify mitigation strategies and TTP for PNT-based vulnerabilities (to include all terrestrial and space-based user equipment and platforms and their augmentation); and advises decision makers on significant NAVWAR issues.

3. Joint Navigation Warfare Center Support to Electronic Warfare

a. Develops and maintains current information on NAVWAR matters of interest to the warfighter and JFCs. These include assessments of adversary capabilities, assessments of coalition capabilities and limitations, and EW topics of special interest. The JNWC actively disseminates NAVWAR information to warfighters and JFCs, as well as joint and Service training organizations.

b. Analyzes and tests ES system capabilities, EA system TTP and EP vulnerabilities in relation to NAVWAR and submits recommendations to the Joint Staff, warfighter, trainers, and weapon system developers.

c. Provides a capability for independent field testing of EA/EP/ES against rapidly emerging NAVWAR threats.

d. Integrates NAVWAR PNT capabilities across ISR, IO, and space control.

4. Joint Navigation Warfare Center Navigation Warfare Support Cell

The Joint Navigation Warfare Center Navigation Warfare Support Cell (JNSC) provides a 24/7/365 operational reachback capability to the warfighter to address NAVWAR concerns during planning and current operations. The JNSC functions as the JNWC's operating staff and implements decisions, on behalf of the JNWC Director, and provides assistance to higher HQ and combatant commands as authorized in applicable orders. The JNSC develops operational-level support recommendations for Commander, JFCC SPACE; coordinates appropriate command responses to requests for information; responds to higher HQ tasking; assists with EMI event information collection and analysis; and assists operational planners in developing integrated NAVWAR plans. The JNWC reachback capabilities include GPS jamming modeling and simulation, access to the NAVWAR capabilities and vulnerabilities database repository, current country-specific NAVWAR threat briefs, and consultation with operational planners.

5. Mailing Address

JNWC/J-3

2050A 2nd Street SE

Kirtland AFB, NM 87117-5669

6. Telephone Numbers

STE DSN: 312-246-6792

COMMERCIAL: 505-206-7594 (JNWC Duty Officer, available 24/7)

COMMERCIAL: 505-846-6846 (JNWC office, available during normal working hours)

DSN: 246-6846 (JNWC office, available during normal working hours)

7. E-Mail

NIPRNET: JNWC@kirtland.af.mil

SIPRNET: jnwcadmin@afmc.af.smil.mil

JWICS: ~wccas_jnwccdodiis.ic.gov

ANNEX E TO APPENDIX B
JOINT SPECTRUM CENTER

1. General

The JSC is a field activity of the Defense Information Systems Agency.

2. Mission

The mission of the JSC is to ensure DOD's effective use of the EMS in support of national security and military objectives. The JSC serves as the DOD center of excellence for EMS management matters in support of the combatant commands, Military Departments, and DOD agencies in planning, acquisition, training, and operations. Since EW is a principal use of the spectrum within the IO effort, JSC support extends to the EW aspects of joint military operations.

3. Joint Spectrum Center Support to Electronic Warfare

a. Maintains multiple databases that provide technical data about friendly force C2 system locational and nominal characteristics for use in planning EP measures. Databases maintained by the JSC provide EW planners with information covering communications, radar, navigation aids, broadcast, identification, and EW systems operated by DOD, other USG departments and agencies, and private businesses or organizations. Information from these databases is available through searchable Web portals or on a quick reaction basis in a variety of formats and media to support EW planners and spectrum managers.

b. Assists spectrum managers, the JCEWS/EWC, the IO cell, and EWOs in the development and management of the JRFL. The JSC maintains a worldwide DOD spectrum assignment database that is accessible through SPECTRUM XXI (SXXI), a spectrum management tool that has the capability to create, edit, and manage the JRFL. The JSC also has combatant command support teams consisting of trained JTF spectrum managers from each selected Service along with contractor support that can be deployed to assist combatant commands, subordinate unified commands, JTFs, or their components, when requested. These teams provide training and assistance in JRFL preparation and also serve as on-site advisors, assistants, and liaisons for EMS management operations and EW deconfliction, as required.

c. Assists in the resolution of operational interference and jamming incidents through the auspices of the JSIR program. The objective of the JSIR program is to resolve problems at the lowest possible level in the chain of command. The JSC maintains a rapid deployment team that is able to quickly locate and identify interference sources. This team recommends technical and operational fixes to resolve identified interference sources. The JSC also maintains a historical database of interference and jamming incident reports and solutions to assist in trend analysis and correction of recurring problems. Combatant commands, subordinate unified commands, JTFs, or their components should contact the JSC to request assistance in resolving suspected spectrum interference problems.

d. Provides foreign communications frequency and location data. Databases containing this data are developed primarily from open sources.

e. Provides unclassified communications area studies about the communications infrastructure of over 150 countries. These area studies are developed entirely from open-source material. Information in these studies includes an overview of telecommunications systems and EM frequencies registered for use within the geographic boundaries of each country and civilian, military, and radio and television broadcast frequencies. Frequency data is provided in automated form to facilitate direct input into automated spectrum management tools like SXXI.

4. Mailing Address

JSC/J-3

2004 Turbot Landing

Annapolis, MD 21402-5064

5. Telephone Numbers

DSN: 281-4357 (help desk)/9802/9850

COMMERCIAL: 410-293-4357 (help desk)/9850/9802

FAX: DSN 281-3763 (UNCLASSIFIED)

FAX: DSN 281-5309 (CLASSIFIED)

6. E-Mail

NIPRNET: operations@jsc.mil

SIPRNET: jscoperations@disa.smil.mil

JWICS: operations@jsc.ic.gov

ANNEX F TO APPENDIX B
INFORMATION OPERATIONS RANGE

1. General

The IO Range was established in 2006 to fill a requirement outlined in the 2003 IO Roadmap that called for the establishment of an IO Range to assess IO technologies and tactics in a representative OE against realistic targets.

2. Mission

The IO Range mission is to create a flexible, seamless, and persistent environment that allows CCDRs to gain confidence and experience in employing IO weapons with the same level of confidence that they have with other weapons.

3. Information Operations Range Support to Electronic Warfare

a. The IO Range supports operations through training, testing, and experimentation of nonlethal capabilities, to include EW. The range provides the ability to conduct secure operations and communications at multiple independent levels of security (Secret to Top Secret sensitive compartmented information/special access requirement). This provides users with an opportunity to conduct EW operations in both cooperative and segmented environments. The range provides a standing infrastructure that is always available and a closed loop network that ensures protection of EW operations, resources, and intellectual capital.

b. The IO Range provides an operationally realistic environment that allows EW forces to war game; conduct proficiency training; test COAs and TTP; and experiment with new and evolving EW capabilities utilizing targets and threat systems similar to those found in real-world areas of interest. Integration of EW onto the IO Range has added traditional RF-spectrum operations; nontraditional (e.g., wireless telephony networks) capabilities; and the ability to explore the use of DE, including HPM programs.

c. The integration of EW capability into the IO Range is based on several key concepts:

(1) A common federation of independent ranges that cross-leverage each other's EW capabilities.

(2) The ability to integrate fixed sites, mobile platforms, and transient targets.

(3) The execution of operations combining more than one capability, using full-spectrum EW against targets. Impacted targets would include traditional (e.g., RF), irregular (e.g. wireless), catastrophic (e.g., EMP), and disruptive (e.g., DE).

(4) The visualization of effects created in a multiple independent levels of security environment that allows interaction of EW range events simultaneously at the proper levels of security.

d. Cross-linking and sharing of EW capabilities maximizes use of low density/high demand assets. By linking sites, the IO Range architecture provides the right EW capabilities and targets necessary to conduct, for example, combined EW/CNA operations and generate effects. The IO Range gives its users access to a one-of-a-kind capability and difficult to obtain, perishable targets.

e. By linking multiple ranges, platforms, and targets with different EW and CNA capabilities, IO Range users can test, train, and develop technology and operational capabilities. Also, combined EW/CNA capabilities can be phased in over time, with additional classification levels, to more accurately reflect the EME representative of a larger campaign plan or tactical-level engagement. The IO Range provides opportunities for improved visualization of both EW and combined EW/CNA events for event controllers and test managers. This visualization improves operational execution, enhances situational awareness as events transpire, and provides ground truth for key individuals or organizations (e.g., the exercise/event white cell).

f. EW integrated onto the architecture of the IO Range enables, through virtual simulations, high-fidelity emulations, and actual threat systems, the following activities:

(1) Examination of the potential synergies of EW-enabled wireless CNA and computer network exploitation. The growing trend toward wireless networks, in both civil and military applications, increases the importance of leveraging existing capabilities or developing new EW capabilities to exploit these networks.

(2) Testing and training with EW capabilities for US forces. For example, to attack an integrated air defense system (IADS), US forces could employ a mix of capabilities (e.g., low-observable, standoff jamming, escort jamming, stand-in jamming, and self-protection TTP) against the tracking, targeting, and engagement radar systems, as well as CNA against the radars' C2 network. The IO Range could facilitate this type of engagement by supporting an integration of live, virtual, and constructive entities from geographically distributed sites. These sites could be physical ranges, labs, anechoic chambers, and other EW-related sites and organizations.

(3) Testing and training against an adversary's EW capabilities. A modern IADS consists of a mix of target acquisition and target tracking radar systems plus a layered system of man-portable, vehicle mounted, and fixed surface-to-air missile systems. While a few of the more capable US ranges might be able to support a subset of these systems, the IO Range allows pooling of the resources and capabilities of multiple ranges to create a more realistic representation of the threat(s). The IO Range also enhances the ability of US forces to train against a red OPFOR, which improves the abilities of US forces and hones their TTP.

g. The IO Range has personnel who serve as event coordinators. Event coordinators include EW subject matter experts, some of whom reside at the JEWC. They work as a team to identify sites with capabilities that can support the customer's mission objectives and are available for an event. The IO Range has additional personnel who serve as "technical event support." These individuals travel to approved IO Range sites to conduct site surveys and ensure the required infrastructure is in place. Once infrastructure concerns have been addressed, technical event support team members again travel to the event site(s) to install necessary IO Range hardware, software, etc. The IO Range Network Operations Support Center ensures event synchronization, distribution of information, and, if desired, a common operational picture.

4. Mailing Address

Joint Staff, J-7, Deputy Director, Joint and Coalition Warfighting

ATTN: Joint IO Range

9712 Virginia Avenue, Building X-132

Norfolk, VA 23511-3212

5. Telephone Numbers

DSN: 836-9787 (UNCLASSIFIED)

COMMERCIAL: 757-836-9787

FAX: COMMERCIAL: 757-836-8911 (UNCLASSIFIED)

6. E-Mail

NIPRNET: IOR-Ops@hr.js.mil

7. Portal

https://us.jfcom.mil/sites/J7/IO_JMO/Range/default.aspx

Other books we publish on Amazon.com

Customer reviews
★★★☆☆ 3 out of 5

THE SOVIET ARMY
SPECIALIZED WARFARE AND REAR AREA SUPPORT

Customer reviews
★★★☆☆ 3.5 out of 5

THE SOVIET ARMY
OPERATIONS AND TACTICS

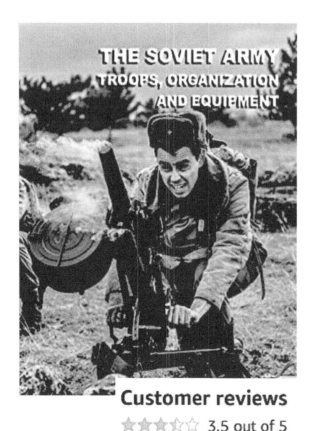

THE SOVIET ARMY
TROOPS, ORGANIZATION AND EQUIPMENT

Customer reviews
★★★☆☆ 3.5 out of 5

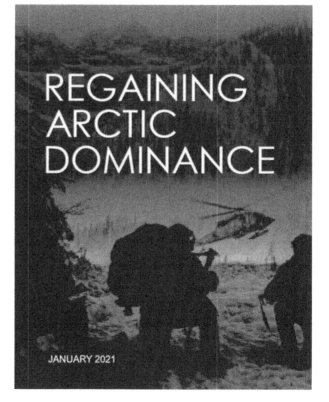

REGAINING ARCTIC DOMINANCE

JANUARY 2021

PODCAST: https://regaining-arctic-dominance.castos.com

APPENDIX C
ELECTRONIC WARFARE JOINT MUNITIONS EFFECTIVENESS
MANUAL PLANNING

1. General

a. The modern warfighter requires the ability to engage an adversary with a combination of lethal and nonlethal capabilities. Effective employment of these capabilities requires a planning mechanism capable of comparing lethal and nonlethal effectiveness and risks to determine the best mix of capabilities for the mission. While the planning process for lethal effects is easily quantifiable (e.g., 80 percent probability of destruction) and well established, the process for nonlethal effects is subjective (e.g., "good," "fair," "poor") and requires new analysis tools.

b. Communications and Radar Electronic Attack Planning Effectiveness Reference (CREAPER) is designed to improve both the EW community's application of EA capabilities as well as offer the opportunity to compare effectiveness predictions among nonlethal EA and lethal weapon options.

c. CREAPER is a computer application that uses the Improved Many-On-Many Engineer modeling algorithms to determine jammer and threat power levels, then references test and analysis data from the jamming weapons manager to display the relative effectiveness of EA weapons against specific targets. It is designed to be used by EWC operational planners to provide weapon-to-target pairing recommendations for task order generation. In short, it is a tool to be used in the capabilities analysis phase (phase 3) of the joint targeting cycle.

2. Current Applications

a. **Radar "Quick Look."** Provides a list of all EA weapons with published capabilities against the selected threat and includes a radial depicting the level of effectiveness relative to range. Figure C-1 provides an example of this application. It is used to determine weapons-target pairing versus radar systems and requires the following input: selected threat, protected entity identified, and penetration altitude.

b. **Communications "Quick Look."** Displays a list of published EA weapons that are available against the receiver in question and includes a range bar depicting the effectiveness relative to range of the receiver from the transmitter. It is used to determine weapons–target pairing for communications systems and requires the following input: threat transmitter and receiver (target).

c. **Radar Geospatial.** A radar analysis that aids the user in highlighting employment options and desired effects. The user can select a targeted threat radar from an order of battle display in a "quick look," selecting a protected entity and EA weapon (from the published list) that can then be located on the map and oriented to the threat. Subsequent analysis will display effectiveness (including terrain and meteorological effects) for the given EA weapon and protected entity approaching the threat from inbound radials color coded with the

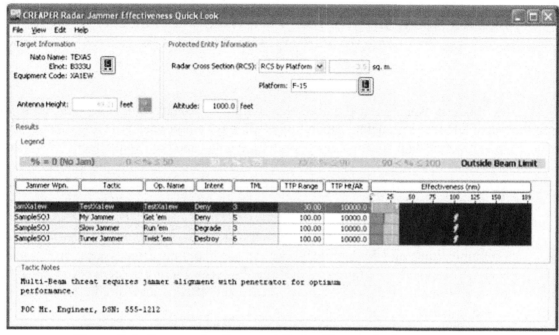

Figure C-1. Communications and Radar Electronic Attack Planning Effectiveness Reference Radar Jammer Effectiveness Quick Look

effectiveness. It is used to determine weapons–target employment and requires the following input: threat, threat location from EOB, and manual insert or live feed.

d. **Communications Geospatial.** A communication analysis that allows the user to select a transmitter and location, and a targeted receiver. By using the "quick look" against the receiver pair, the operator can select an appropriate EA weapon (from a published list), locate it on a map, and orient it to the threat. The subsequent analyses will display the effectiveness (including terrain and meteorological effects) for the given EA weapon against the receiver on any of the radials from the transmitter. It is used to determine weapons–target employment and requires the following input: transmitter geolocation and EA weapon location and orientation on the map.

e. **Ad Hoc Network.** An analysis tool used to display the portion of a designated area of operations in which communications is denied by a selected level, using percent maximum range or desired range beyond which communication is denied. Figure C-2 provides an example of this application. The Ad Hoc Network is a specialized communications jamming effectiveness tool for determining weapons-target employment and requires the following input: operating area of targeted receiver system, transmitter and receiver being targeted, desired range beyond which communications is denied, and location and orientation of the EA weapon. The resultant display shows effectiveness of the EW weapon in achieving the desired level of communications denial in the designated area of operations.

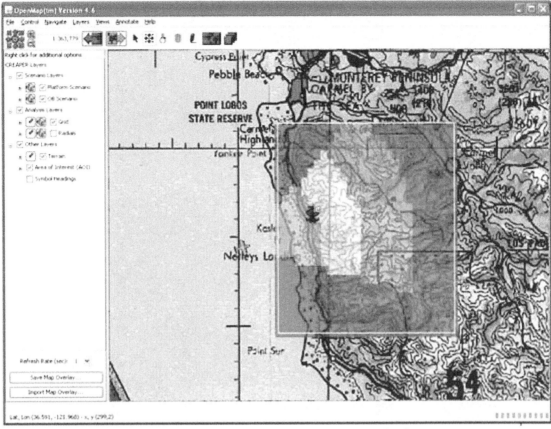

Figure C-2. Ad Hoc Network Analysis Tool

3. Applicability

a. CREAPER is designed to facilitate the selection of EA weapons by comparing systems operating in accordance with their TTP and displaying the effects against a designated threat radar or communications asset. The decision maker can then select a suitable asset to achieve his mission objectives, even if his primary expertise may be on a different platform. To further assist the decision maker, the program includes a section provided by the weapons manager for additional information, notes, warnings and cautions, as well as implementation guidance and limitations.

b. Should issues of air space allocation or potential interference from terrain and geolocation have potential impact on employment, the user can use the Radar Geospatial and Ad Hoc Network tools to perform a first order spatial analysis. This process assists the operator in both examining the impact and producing graphical displays that can be used to brief decision makers on the employment impact. For example, limiting the jammer orbit area to flight level 200 and south of the mountain range may prevent the jammer from reaching a target. However, moving the orbit area east and allowing operations at flight level 250 would provide coverage.

Other books we publish on Amazon.com

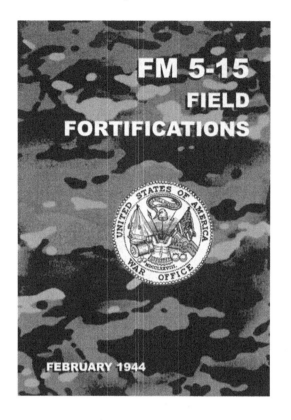

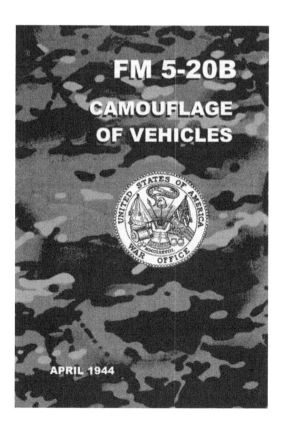

APPENDIX D
ELECTRONIC WARFARE FREQUENCY DECONFLICTION PROCEDURES

1. General

Friendly, adversary, and third party operations that use or affect the EMS (e.g., communications, noncommunications, EA) have the potential to interfere with joint force communications and other EM-dependent systems. To counter this, the US military has established EMS management and EW frequency deconfliction procedures. Spectrum management is composed of an entire range of technical and nontechnical processes designed to quantify, plan, coordinate, and control the EMS to satisfy EMS-use requirements while minimizing unacceptable interference. EW frequency deconfliction is a systematic management procedure to coordinate the use of the EMS for operations, communications, and intelligence functions. While systematic, the increasingly dynamic nature of the EMOE requires that frequency deconfliction be accomplished on timescales as short as real time, depending on mission requirements. This appendix provides guidance for developing joint EW frequency deconfliction procedures. To facilitate the development process, procedures and specific staff responsibilities are discussed. To the extent possible, these procedures should be followed during joint, multinational, and single-Service operations and exercises.

2. Electronic Warfare Deconfliction Procedures

a. The steps involved in the EW frequency deconfliction process are as follows. While these steps are listed sequentially, the process is continuous and steps can occur concurrently.

b. **Define the Operations Concept and Critical Functions.** The J-3 defines the CONOPS to include each discrete phase. For each phase, the J-3 defines the critical mission functions that require uninterrupted communications connectivity or noncommunications operations. For example, communications with long-range reconnaissance elements or close air support assets could be crucial to preparing for transition from defense to offense. At the same time, noncommunications equipment such as identification, friend or foe, systems and fire-control radars also need protection. The J-3 provides this guidance to the joint force staff and subordinate commanders for planning. The J-3 also identifies these channels to the JSME for inclusion in the JRFL as either PROTECTED or TABOO.

c. **Develop the Intelligence Assessment.** Based on the CONOPS, the J-2 determines intelligence support requirements and identifies adversary EM-dependent system targets for each phase of the operation (including the critical adversary functions) and associated EM-dependent system nodes that must be guarded. For example, during the friendly attack, adversary communications and noncommunications associated with C2 of counterattack forces could be crucial to friendly forces in determining the timing and location of the counterattack. Therefore, those critical nodes should be protected from EA. To achieve that protection, the J-2 must identify to the JSME those adversary channels to be included in the JRFL as GUARDED. An IGL analysis should identify the value of the data being exploited to enable the JFC to make a decision to strike adversary C2 despite its value to intelligence.

In a dynamic situation such as troops in contact, the J-2 should work closely with the J-3 to make IGL recommendations in real time.

d. **Manage the Electromagnetic Spectrum.** The J-6 is responsible for the administrative and technical management of the EMS within the EMOE. This includes maintaining, in conjunction with the J-2 and J-3, the necessary database that contains information on all friendly, available adversary, and selected neutral or civil EM emitters or receivers. With the aid of the database, the J-6 assigns frequencies, analyzes and evaluates potential conflicts, resolves internal conflicts, recommends alternatives, and participates in EMS-use conflict resolution. The assignment of frequencies is based on the CONOPS, frequency availability, unit geographic dispersion, EM propagation, equipment technical parameters, and criticality of unit functions. Operating on assigned frequencies could spell the difference between operational success and failure.

e. **Define and Prioritize Candidate Nodes and Nets.** The joint force staff and subordinate commanders should define functions, and identify specific nodes and equipment critical to friendly and adversary operations. Candidate nodes and nets are submitted for EA protection to the JCEWS/EWC. (The submission should follow the standard JRFL format listed in paragraph 7, "Standardized Joint Restricted Frequency List Format.") Friendly and neutral EOB information is provided by the J-6 and adversary EOB information is provided by the J-2. Standard OPSEC measures should be taken when making JRFL inputs.

f. **Generate the JRFL.** The JRFL is a time- and geographic-oriented listing of TABOO, PROTECTED, and GUARDED functions, nets, and frequencies. The JRFL should be limited to the minimum number of frequencies necessary for friendly forces to accomplish objectives. The J-6 compiles the JRFL based on the coordinated inputs from the operations, intelligence, and communications staffs within the command and affected subordinate commands. An example of these inputs is the J-3 providing the J-6 with potential EA load sets for self-protection systems such as counter radio-controlled IED EW and aircraft EA in order to build coordinated communications/self-protection EA load sets. The J-6 should ensure the frequency assignments of unit nets designated for inclusion as PROTECTED or TABOO are submitted to the J-3 for final approval prior to dissemination. The restrictions imposed by the JRFL may only be removed, by direction of the J-3, if the J-3 determines the benefit of EA on a restricted frequency surpasses the immediate criticality of exploited or required information to friendly forces. Operations and intelligence functions should be consulted before this decision. However, the self-protection of friendly forces has priority over all controls. GUARDED, PROTECTED, and TABOO frequencies are as follows.

(1) **GUARDED.** GUARDED frequencies are adversary frequencies that are currently being exploited for combat information and intelligence. A GUARDED frequency is time-oriented in that the list changes as the adversary assumes different combat postures. These frequencies may be jammed after the commander has weighed the potential operational gain against the loss of the technical information.

(2) **PROTECTED.** PROTECTED frequencies are friendly frequencies used for a particular operation, identified and protected to prevent them from being inadvertently

jammed by friendly forces while active EW operations are directed against hostile forces. These frequencies are of such critical importance that jamming should be restricted unless absolutely necessary or until coordination with the using unit is made. They are generally time-oriented, may change with the tactical situation, and should be updated periodically.

(3) **TABOO.** TABOO frequencies are friendly frequencies of such importance that they must never be deliberately jammed or interfered with by friendly forces. Normally these include international distress, safety, and controller frequencies. They are generally long-standing frequencies. However, they may be time-oriented in that, as the combat or exercise situation changes, the restrictions may be removed. Specifically, during crisis or hostilities, short duration EA may be authorized on TABOO frequencies for self-protection to provide coverage from unknown threats or threats operating outside their known frequency ranges, or for other reasons.

g. **Disseminate the JRFL.** The JRFL is maintained and disseminated by the J-6.

h. **Update the JRFL.** The JRFL is reviewed by all joint force staff sections and subordinate commands. The J-2 might need additions, deletions, or qualified frequencies based on possible SIGINT and ES targets. The J-3 and JCEWS/EWC monitor the JRFL with respect to changes in operations, timing, dates, and TABOO frequencies. The J-6 ensures TABOO and PROTECTED frequencies are congruent with assigned frequencies. The J-6 also amends the JRFL based on J-2 and J-3 input. Supporting EW units should check the JRFL because this is the source of "no jam" frequencies. A review of the JRFL is required to identify potential conflicts between frequencies afforded protection by the JRFL and those designated for EW activities. If conflicts are identified, they should be brought to the attention of the JSME. If the JSME can't resolve the conflict, they should advise the JCEWS/EWC for final resolution. The resolution will take the form of either "override" of the JRFL protection or alter/cancel the EW activity. The decision ultimately rests with the JFC, or his designated representative, and is based on the value of the EW mission versus the gains from JRFL protection.

3. Joint Spectrum Interference Resolution Program

a. The interference reporting procedures and format are outlined in CJCSM 3320.02C, *Joint Spectrum Interference Resolution (JSIR) Procedures*. The program is coordinated and managed by the JSC and addresses all interference incidents, whether resolved or not, at the unified, subordinate unified, JTF, and component levels. The JSIR program also satisfies the requirements of the Joint Staff and the stated needs of the CCDRs for a joint-level agency to coordinate resolution of EMI incidents.

b. JSC has a 24-hour capability for receiving interference reports.

(1) The primary means for reporting EMI is through the online JSIR reporting tool that can be accessed through www.intelink.sgov.gov/sites/jsir (SIPRNET).

(2) A secondary means for submitting a JSIR report is to e-mail the report to the JSC at operations@jsc.smil.mil (SIPRNET). Enclosure C of CJCSM 3320.02C, *Joint*

Spectrum Interference Resolution (JSIR) Procedures, lists the recipients for these reports, and enclosure B contains the report format.

  (3) Telephone: DSN: 281-4357, COMMERCIAL: 410-293-4357.

  (4) Sensitive compartmented information traffic is serviced directly through secure FAX and Intelink in the JSC SCIF.

  c. When experiencing a suspected EMI incident, resolution should be attempted at the lowest level possible in the operational chain of command. Whether a resolution is reached or not, a JSIR report should be submitted to the JSC JSIR Online Portal. If the EMI incident is resolved before the initial report is submitted, an "opening/closing" report should be submitted. If an initial report is made and the incident is resolved locally, a "closing" report should be done. These reports are necessary since the JSC JSIR team maintains a historical database in order to assist with the resolution of future problems of a similar nature. Submission of a JSIR report will not automatically generate a response or assistance from the JSC JSIR team. A response is requested in the JSIR report, including the type of assistance required.

  d. Upon receipt of either a JSIR report requesting assistance or EMI support request, the JSC JSIR team performs an analysis using JSC models and databases to determine the source and works with the appropriate field activity and frequency manager to resolve interference problems. In accordance with CJCSM 3320.02C, *Joint Spectrum Interference Resolution (JSIR) Procedures,* the JSC JSIR team can deploy to the location of the victim organization to resolve interference problems. The organization requesting JSIR services is provided a report containing JSIR analysis results, and appropriate information is incorporated into the JSIR database. This database supports trend analysis and future interference analysis.

  e. USSTRATCOM has overall responsibility for managing spectrum interference resolution to SATCOM systems, satellite anomaly resolutions, and global SATCOM systems for the operation and defense of the DOD information networks. Space system interference reporting and resolution is similar to the terrestrial reporting and resolution process except that the interference report is sent directly to USSTRATCOM's JSPOC from the space system manager affected. The space system includes both the space-based and earth segments. The JSPOC forwards the incident report to the appropriate lead agency for investigation and resolution. Lead agencies are the Global SATCOM Support Center for SATCOM interference and the GPSOC for GPS interference. Each lead agency coordinates with the JSC for analytical support.

4. Responsibilities

  a. The responsibilities of the respective staff sections and commands in EW frequency deconfliction are noted below.

b. **J-3**

(1) Determine and define critical friendly functions (TABOO and PROTECTED) to be protected from EA and electronic deception based on the CONOPS and in coordination with components.

(2) Approve the initial JRFL and subsequent changes.

(3) Provide guidance in plans and orders as to when EA takes precedence over intelligence collection and vice versa.

(4) Resolve problems with the use of EA and electronic deception in tactical operations when conflicts arise.

(5) Weigh continually the operational advantages of employing EW against the advantages of intelligence collection.

(6) Develop and promulgate specific employment guidance and request supplemental ROE for EA and electronic deception in support of joint combat operations. Coordinate ROE and the approval process with the command staff judge advocate.

c. **J-2**

(1) In coordination with the national SIGINT authority, NSA, determine and define critical adversary functions and frequencies (GUARDED) and intelligence system processing and dissemination frequencies (PROTECTED) to be protected from friendly EA, and provide them to the J-3 (through the JCEWS/EWC) for approval.

(2) Assist in prioritizing the JRFL before J-3 approval.

(3) Develop and maintain map of nonmilitary operations in, or near, the area being jammed. Evaluate probable collateral effect on nonmilitary users.

(4) Nominate changes to the JRFL.

(5) Assist JSC in resolving reported disruption resulting from EMI.

d. **J-6**

(1) Attempt to resolve all reported non-EA-related interference.

(2) Manage all frequency assignments associated with the joint force.

(3) Conduct EW deconfliction analysis as required to support EW objectives and assist in minimizing adverse impact of friendly EA on critical networks by providing alternative frequency assignments. Compile, consolidate, coordinate, and disseminate the JRFL and provide the JCEWS/EWC with the frequency assignments for those PROTECTED or TABOO unit nets that are designated for inclusion in the JRFL.

(4) Nominate changes to the JRFL.

(5) Assist in minimizing adverse impact of friendly EA on critical networks by providing alternative communications.

e. **JCEWS/EWC**

(1) Attempt to resolve all reported EA-related interference.

(2) Coordinate and provide input to the JRFL.

(3) Recommend a joint force EW target list.

(4) Identify and resolve, if possible, conflicts that might occur between planned EA operations and the JRFL.

(5) Coordinate with J-6 and J-2 on reported interference to determine if friendly EA actions could be responsible.

(6) Establish and implement an EA request process that will identify spectrum conflicts resulting from requested EA activities.

f. **JTF Spectrum Management Element**

(1) Prepare and combine J-2, J-3, J-6, EWC, and component inputs to develop a JRFL for approval by the J-3.

(2) Update and distribute the JRFL, as required.

(3) Maintain the common EMS-use database necessary for planning and coordinating EMS control. This database contains EMS use information on all available friendly military and civilian, adversary, and neutral forces.

g. **Joint force subordinate commands and components** should, where applicable, establish a unit staff element to perform the frequency deconfliction process. This staff element should be patterned after the JCEWS/EWC and should be the focal point for frequency deconfliction for the subordinate command and component forces it represents. The responsibilities of this frequency deconfliction staff element are as follows.

(1) Submit, to the J-6, candidate nodes and nets (both friendly and adversary) with associated frequencies (if known), for inclusion in the JRFL using the format in paragraph 7, "Standardized Joint Restricted Frequency List Format." Units should specifically designate only those functions critical to current operations for inclusion in the JRFL. Overprotection of nonessential assets complicates the EA support process and significantly lengthens the time required to evaluate mission impact resulting from EMS protection. Normally, candidate nodes and nets should be submitted either through intelligence channels and consolidated by the J-2 or through operations channels and consolidated by the J-3.

(2) Identify conflicts between JRFL and friendly EA operations and request changes, as necessary, to resolve the conflicts.

(3) Report unresolved EMS disruption incidents as they occur in accordance with this publication and current interference reporting instructions.

(4) Keep the JCEWS/EWC apprised of issues that potentially impact EW planning and operations.

(5) Execute the EA request process directed by the JCEWS or EWC.

h. **JSC.** The JSC manages the DOD JSIR program as described in paragraph 3 above.

5. Frequency Deconfliction Analysis

a. Personnel analyzing frequency conflicts must consider frequency, location geometry, and time.

b. **Frequency.** The potential for interference exists whenever emitters operate at, or close to, the same frequency range. Interference can also occur through frequency harmonics, throughout the EMS, during EA operations. The JRFL limits the frequencies that require immediate review by the JCEWS/EWC. When possible, automated decision aids (e.g., SXXI, Coalition Joint Spectrum Management Planning Tool [CJSMPT]) should be used to conduct this comparison.

c. **Location Geometry.** Because of the fluid nature of the OE (mobility), the locations of friendly emitters constantly change. Locations of friendly emitters should be analyzed by the J-6 in order to predict possible interference. Analysis results depend highly on the accuracy of data and the analytical technique used.

d. **Time.** Time analysis attempts to protect critical network equipment from friendly interference during friendly EA missions. This subjective judgment is one that should be made by the J-3 or JTF commander since they must weigh the trade-off between critical EA operations and protection of vital C2 resources.

6. Automated Spectrum Management Tools

a. Commands are also encouraged to use automated spectrum management tools that will assist in developing and managing a constantly changing JRFL. To support a time and geographically oriented JRFL, automated systems must possess an engineering module that considers such factors as broadcast power, reception sensitivity, terrain, locations, distances, and time. The capability for direct computer data exchange between echelons for JRFL nominations and approval is recommended.

b. **SPECTRUM XXI.** SXXI is the DOD standard automated spectrum management tool that supports operational planning, as well as near-real-time management of the RF spectrum, with emphasis on assigning compatible frequencies and performing spectrum engineering tasks. During peacetime, SXXI is used by a joint staff at its permanent headquarters to facilitate the complex task of EMS management during the planning and execution phases of exercises, as well as performing routine spectrum management functions. In the combat environment, SXXI is used by joint staffs to assist with joint spectrum management. It is capable of implementing any variations between peacetime and wartime operations, such as OA, frequency assignments, terrain data, equipment characteristics, and tactical constraints.

For more information on the DOD standard automated spectrum management tool, refer to Appendix G, "SPECTRUM XXI."

7. Standardized Joint Restricted Frequency List Format

The following JRFL format (see Figure D-1) is a sample listing of information for developing a JRFL. This JRFL format is unclassified but, when actually accomplished, should show the proper classification of each paragraph. The actual requirements will be determined by the JCEWS/EWC and be published in the data call for JRFL submissions.

Sample Joint Restricted Frequency List Format		
1.	CLASSIFICATION	One character (U=Unclassified, C=Confidential, S=Secret).
2.	DECLASSIFICATION	The declassification date for the frequencies to be protected.
3.	UNIT	Sixteen characters (net name as identified in the communications-electronics operating instructions). Disregard for GUARDED nominations.
4.	FREQUENCY	Twenty-four characters (K=kilohertz, M=megahertz, G=gigahertz, T=terahertz); identifies a frequency or band (e.g., M13.250-15.700).
5.	STATUS	Four characters (T=TABOO, P=PROTECTED, G=GUARDED, and a slash followed by priority A–Z and 1–9 (e.g., T/A1).
6.	START DATE	Eight characters (MM/DD/YYYY) indicate start date when protection is required, if known.
7.	END DATE	Eight characters (MM/DD/YYYY) indicate end date when protection is no longer required, if known.
8.	START HOUR	Four characters in 24-hour format (HHMM) indicate start time when protection is required, if known.
9.	END HOUR	Four characters in 24-hour format (HHMM) indicate end time when protection is no longer required, if known.
10.	TRANSMITTER COORDINATES	Fifteen characters (latitude [dd(N or S) mmss]/longitude [ddd(E or W) mmss]) provide the location to the transmitter or system, if known.
11.	RECEIVER COORDINATES	Fifteen characters (latitude [dd(N or S) mmss]/longitude [ddd(E or W) mmss]) provide the location of the receiver or system to be protected, if known.
12.	AGENCY SERIAL NUMBER	All joint restricted frequency list entries must have a frequency record in the electromagnetic spectrum database to be protected from other sources of interference. This number can be obtained from the unit frequency manager in the joint frequency management office or joint spectrum management element.
13.	POWER	Nine characters (W=watts, K=kilowatts, M=megawatts, G=gigawatts) and a maximum of five decimal places, (e.g., W10.01234), if known.
14.	EMISSION	Eleven characters (the emission designator contains the necessary bandwidth and the emission classification symbols [e.g., 3KOOJ3E]), if known.
15.	EQUIPMENT NOMENCLATURE	Eighteen characters (e.g., AN/GRC-103), if known.
16.	COMMENTS	Forty characters (provided for user remarks); optional entry.
17.	CEOI NAME	24/7 point of contact for the element operating the net that would need to be notified in the event their frequency will be targeted by planned electronic attack activities.

Figure D-1. Sample Joint Restricted Frequency List Format

Other books we publish on Amazon.com

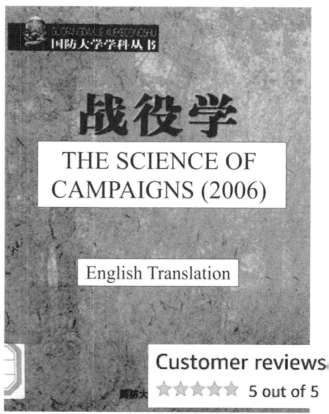

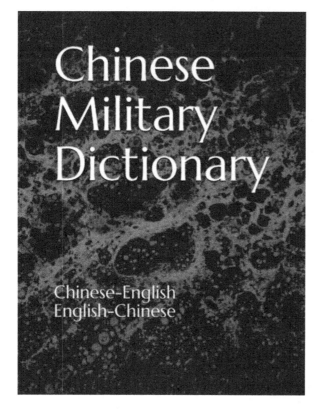

APPENDIX E
ELECTRONIC WARFARE REPROGRAMMING

1. Electronic Warfare Reprogramming

a. **Purpose.** The purpose of EW reprogramming is to maintain or enhance the effectiveness of EW and TSS equipment maintained by field and fleet units. EW reprogramming includes changes to self-defense systems, offensive weapons systems, and intelligence collection systems. The reprogramming of EW and TSS equipment is the responsibility of each Service through its respective EW reprogramming support programs.

b. **Types of Changes.** Several types of changes constitute EW reprogramming. These fall into three major categories: tactics, software, and hardware.

(1) **Tactics.** Tactics changes include changes in procedures, equipment settings, or EW systems mission-planning data. These changes are usually created at the Service level by tactics developers and implemented at the unit level using organic equipment and personnel.

(2) **Software.** Software changes include actual changes to the programming of computer-based EW and TSS equipment. This type of change requires the support of a software support activity to alter programmed look-up tables, threat libraries, or signal-sorting routines.

(3) **Hardware.** Hardware changes and/or long-term system development is necessary when tactics or software changes cannot correct equipment deficiencies. These changes usually occur when the complex nature of a change leads to a system modification.

c. **EW Reprogramming Actions.** During crisis action planning or actual hostilities, EW reprogramming provides operational commanders with a timely capability to respond to changes in adversary threat systems, correct EW and TSS equipment deficiencies, and tailor equipment to meet unique theater or mission requirements.

(1) **Threat Changes.** Service EW reprogramming support programs are primarily designed to respond to adversary threat changes affecting the combat effectiveness of EW and TSS equipment. A threat change may be any change in the operation or EM signature of an adversary threat system.

(2) **Geographic Tailoring.** Geographic tailoring is the reprogramming of EW and TSS equipment for operations in a specific area or region of the world. Geographic tailoring usually reduces the number of threats in system memory. This results in decreased processing time and a reduction in system display ambiguities.

(3) **Mission Tailoring.** Mission tailoring is the reprogramming of EW and TSS equipment for the mission of the host platform. Mission tailoring may be desirable to improve system response to the priority threat(s) to the host platform.

d. **General Reprogramming Process.** The reprogramming process for EW and TSS equipment can be divided into four phases. Although the last three phases of the reprogramming process are unique by Service, each Service follows the general process described below and in FM 3-13.10, Marine Corps Reference Publication 3-40.5A, NTTP 3-51.2, AFTTP 3-2.27, *Multi-Service Tactics, Techniques, and Procedures for the Reprogramming of Electronic Warfare Systems.*

(1) **Determine the Threat.** The first phase of reprogramming is to develop and maintain an accurate description of the equipment's OE, specifically enemy threat systems and tactics. Since EW and TSS equipment is programmed to identify and respond to particular threat or target signature data, intelligence requirements must be identified to ensure an accurate description of the EME is maintained at all times. Maintaining an accurate description of the environment requires fusion of known EM data with the collection, analysis, and validation of enemy "threat" signature changes. This first phase of the reprogramming process can be divided into the following three steps.

(a) **Collect Data.** Threat signature data collection (e.g., collection of threat system parametric information) is the responsibility of combatant and component command collection managers. Signature data may be collected as a matter of routine intelligence collection against targeted systems, while other data collection may occur as the result of urgent intelligence production requests. Regardless of the means of collection, signature data is disseminated to appropriate intelligence production centers and Service equipment support and flagging activities for analysis.

(b) **Identify Changes.** At Service equipment support and flagging activities, collected signature data is analyzed for EW and TSS equipment compatibility. Incompatible data is "flagged" for further analysis and system impact assessment. At the intelligence production centers, collected data is processed and analyzed to identify threat signature changes in the EME. Identified changes are further analyzed to ensure collector bias (i.e., collector contamination or manipulation of signature data attributed to the collector or its reporting architecture) was addressed during the analysis process.

(c) **Validate Changes.** The most important step of this initial phase of reprogramming is to validate threat signature changes. Therefore, once an identified signature change is correlated to a threat system and analyzed to ensure the reported parameters are correct and not a collector anomaly, it is further analyzed to "validate" it as an actual system capability change or identify it as a probable malfunction. Information on threat system engineering and tactical employment is critical to this validation process. Technical analysis and validation of threat changes is normally provided by one of three Service scientific and technical intelligence production centers or the DIA. During times of crisis, the combatant command must ensure this phase of the reprogramming process provides for the expeditious identification, technical analysis, and dissemination of threat change validation messages to component commands and Service reprogramming centers.

(2) **Determine the Response.** During this second phase of reprogramming, validated threat change information is used to assess its impact upon friendly EW and TSS equipment and a decision to initiate a reprogramming change is determined. If the

equipment fails to provide appropriate indications and warning or countermeasures in response to a threat change, a decision must be made to change tactics, software, or hardware to correct the deficiency. To support this decision-making process, the Service reprogramming analysis or flagging activities normally generate a system impact message (SIM) to inform combatant and component command staffs of the operational impact of the threat change to EW and TSS equipment performance. The SIM often recommends appropriate responses for each identified threat change. The Service component employing the affected equipment is ultimately responsible for determining the appropriate response to validated threat changes.

(3) **Create the Change.** The third phase of the reprogramming process is to develop tactics, software, or hardware changes to regain or improve equipment performance and combat effectiveness. A change in tactics (e.g., avoiding the threat) is usually the first option considered because software and hardware changes take time. Often, a combination of changes (e.g., tactics and software) is prescribed to provide an immediate and long-term fix to equipment deficiencies. Regardless of the type of change created, reprogramming support activities will verify equipment combat effectiveness through modeling and simulation, bench tests, or test range employments simulating operational conditions. Following the verification of effectiveness, the reprogramming change and implementation instructions are made available to appropriate field and fleet units worldwide.

(4) **Implement the Change.** The final phase of the reprogramming process is to actually implement the change to ensure unit combat effectiveness is regained or enhanced by the tactics, software, or hardware change(s). To accomplish this task, component commands ensure tactics changes are incorporated into mission pre-briefs, and software and hardware changes are electronically or mechanically installed in host platform EW and TSS equipment.

2. Joint Coordination of Electronic Warfare Reprogramming

a. **General.** Coordination of EW reprogramming is critical because threat signature changes and equipment reprogramming changes will affect the EME and, therefore, communications and all three divisions of joint EW operations conducted by US forces, MNFs, NGOs, and intergovernmental organizations. Combatant commands must ensure JCEWR policy and procedures are developed and exercised during all major training events and real-world operations.

b. **Policy.** The Joint Staff is responsible for JCEWR policy. Each Service is responsible for its individual EW reprogramming policies and procedures. The establishment and execution of JCEWR procedures is the responsibility of the combatant commands, component commands, and subordinate joint force commands. CJCSI 3210.04, *Joint Electronic Warfare Reprogramming Policy,* outlines policy and the responsibilities of the Joint Staff, Services, combatant commands, Service components, NSA, and the DIA regarding the JCEWR process. The instruction also sets forth joint procedures, guidelines, and criteria governing joint intelligence support to EW reprogramming.

Other books we publish on Amazon.com

APPENDIX F
ELECTRONIC WARFARE MODELING

1. General

Modeling and simulation tools are essential for the evaluation of EW capabilities and vulnerabilities. These tools must cover the full EW analytical spectrum from the basic engineering/physics level through the aggregate effects at tactical, operational, and strategic applications levels. Simulations are critical because of the high cost associated with system development, field testing, and training exercises. Additionally, it is often impossible to replicate the scenarios required to test or exercise the multitude of variables, conditions, and interactions that occur at various levels of combat operations.

2. Application

a. **Operational Test Support.** Laboratory and range agencies use simulations to assist in test planning, scenario development, test equipment configuration, and data reduction and verification, as well as for extrapolating or expanding the use of test results.

b. **Analysis Support.** Combat developers and other analysis activities use simulations to conduct cost and operational effectiveness studies, assist in defining requirements, perform force mix and trade-off analyses, and develop TTP.

c. **Operational Support.** Operational commands use simulations to provide training from the individual to theater staff levels, serve as tactical decision aids, develop and evaluate OPLANs, and conduct detailed mission planning.

d. **Weapon System Development.** Materiel developers use simulations to support engineering development and design, capability/vulnerability and survivability analyses, and value-added assessments.

e. **Intelligence Support.** Intelligence agencies use simulations to evaluate raw intelligence, reverse engineer developing threats, develop threat projections, analyze threat design options, and evaluate threat tactics and employment options.

3. Modeling Agencies

a. There are numerous government agencies and contractors involved in EW modeling. The Joint Staff Director for Force Structure, Resource, and Assessment periodically publishes the *Catalog of Wargaming and Military Simulation Models*. This is the most comprehensive catalog of models available and identifies most agencies involved in EW modeling. Listed below are some of the joint and Service organizations involved with EW modeling and simulation.

b. **Joint.** Defense Modeling and Simulation Office, JIOWC, Joint Warfighting Analysis Center, Joint Training and Simulation Center, JSC, Warrior Preparation Center, and Joint Warfighting Center.

c. **Army.** Aviation and Missile Command, NGIC, Air Defense Center and School, Intelligence Center and School, US Army Training and Doctrine Command Analysis Center, 1st Information Operations Command (Land), Electronic Proving Ground, Communications Electronics Command, Army Material Systems Analysis Agency, Test and Evaluation Command, Signal Center and School, and National Simulation Center.

d. **Navy.** Navy Information Operation Commands, Naval Command and Control and Ocean Surveillance Center, Naval Air Warfare Center, Naval Research Laboratory, Navy Modeling and Simulation Office, Naval Strike Air Warfare Center, Naval Oceanographic Office, Center for Naval Analyses, Naval Space Command, Space and Naval Warfare Systems Command, and Naval Surface Warfare Center.

e. **Air Force.** Air Force Agency for Modeling and Simulation, Air Force Research Laboratory, NASIC, 53rd EWG, Air Force Operational Test and Evaluation Center, Air Force A9, Aeronautical Systems Center, Survivability and Vulnerability Information Analysis Center, Air Armaments Center, Air and Space C2 Agency, Aeronautical Systems Center Simulation and Analysis Facility, and Air Force Wargaming Centers.

f. **Marine Corps.** Commandant's Warfighting Lab, Marine Corps Combat Development Command's Wargaming and Combat Simulated Division, and MAGTF Staff Training Program's Modeling and Simulation Branch.

4. Fidelity Requirements

Fidelity is the degree of accuracy and detail to which the environment, physical entities, and their interactions are represented. Fidelity requirements vary widely depending on the particular purpose and application. Considerations in determining the proper fidelity should be based on scope (e.g., individual versus corps staff, engineering versus operational), consequences of inaccurate results (e.g., strike planning and execution), time available (minutes/hours to weeks/months), computer resources available (processing speed and memory/storage), accuracy and availability of data (level of detail, confidence level, and form/format), and allowable tolerance of results. Regardless of the fidelity required, a consistent methodology is required to define and guide the process. This typically entails problem definition (scope and objective), research (data gathering), analytical methodology development (how the data is used or applied), and the results/reporting format (satisfy objective/answer question). High-fidelity tools often are needed to generate data that can be used to aggregate realistic effects at higher order simulation levels (e.g., mission/campaign level wargaming). In such cases, audit trails should be available in analyst manuals or other documentation to document data sources, thereby simplifying assumptions, limitations, and aggregation techniques. In general, the setup time, input data requirements, run time, computer resources, and user knowledge/expertise increase proportionally with the model scope, fidelity, and flexibility of the modeling and simulation tools.

5. Model Design

a. **User Interface, Preprocessors, and Postprocessors.** These requirements will vary widely depending on the particular application. For example, a radar design engineer will need much more flexibility and detail for input data than a targeting analyst would need in a tactical decision aid. Other than purpose, setup, and analysis, time requirements and user expertise are key considerations in designing preprocessors and postprocessors and the user interface. In general, maximum use should be made of standard graphic user interfaces.

b. **Electronic Warfare Functions.** Depending on the analytical level, any one EW function, or various combinations of functions, may need to be replicated in the model. EW model functions and capabilities must address areas such as RF and EO-IR wavelength propagation, radar line of sight, terrain masking, self-protect jamming, standoff jamming (communications and noncommunications), ES systems, expendables (chaff and flares), decoys (active and passive), SEAD targeting, acquisition and tracking sensors (radar, EO-IR), clutter (land/sea/atmospheric), satellite coverage (polar/geosynchronous), link analysis, missile guidance and flyout, evasive maneuvers, communications processes, EP, communications targeting, and doctrinal issues.

c. **Software Architecture.** The design of an EW model or system of models should be modular and object oriented. Existing standards and commonly used commercial software packages should be used where appropriate. Standards include those from the Institute of Electrical and Electronics Engineers (IEEE), American National Standards Institute), Federal Information Processing Standards, Military Standard-498, *Military Standard: Software Development and Documentation,* Open Software Foundation, and NSA/CSS. Military Standard-498 standards should be tailored to meet the user requirements for documentation. Standards are particularly important with regard to interfaces. The primary objective of standardization is to make the simulation as machine independent as possible. To this end, the operating system environment should conform to IEEE Portable Operating System Interface for Computer Environments standards. Additionally, communications protocols and interfaces should conform to the Government Open Systems Interconnection Profile, which is the DOD implementation of international Open Systems Interconnect standards.

6. Verification and Validation

a. **Verification.** Model verification is related to the logic and mathematical accuracy of a model. Verification is accomplished through such processes as design reviews, structured walk-throughs, and numerous test runs of the model. Test runs are conducted to debug the model as well as determine the sensitivity of output to the full range of input variables. Included in verification is a review of input data for consistency, accuracy, and source. Ultimately, verification determines if the model functions as designed and advertised. Verification is rather straightforward but time-consuming.

b. **Validation.** Model validation relates to the correlation of the model with reality. In general, as the scope of a simulation increases, validation becomes more difficult. At the engineering level for a limited scope problem, it is often possible to design a laboratory experiment or field test to replicate reality. At the force level, it is not possible to replicate all the variables in the OE and their interaction. It may be possible to validate individual functional modules by comparison with test data, or previously validated engineering-level or high- to medium-resolution models. No model totally represents reality. This disparity and the number of assumptions and limitations increase as the model scope increases. At the force level, models tend to be stochastically driven but can provide relative answers, insights, and trends so alternatives may be rank ordered. Model users must thoroughly understand the capabilities, limitations, and assumptions built into the tool and integrate results with off-line or manual methods, as necessary, to compensate for these shortfalls. Although the above methods may be used for the validation of individual modules in a force level model, three techniques are used for validating the bottom-line output of force-on-force simulations: benchmarking with an accepted simulation, comparing with historical data, and using sound military judgment. As rapidly moving technological advances are incorporated in modern force structures, availability of useful historical data becomes less prevalent for predicting outcomes in future mid- to high-intensity conflicts. The use of forecasts and assumptions becomes necessary, but such efforts tend to be less reliable the further into the future one tries to project. Benchmarking against widely accepted simulations provides a straightforward and less biased method of validation. However, problems are caused by differences in input data structures, assumptions, and output formats between the models. To the extent possible, careful review, analysis, and data manipulation must be applied to minimize the potential of creating apparent discrepancies that can result from attempts to "compare apples to oranges."

7. Databases

Numerous databases are available to support EW modeling. Data include doctrinal, order of battle, parametric, signature, antenna pattern, communications networks, and topographic. One of the most comprehensive database catalogs available is the directory of DOD-sponsored research and development databases produced by the Defense Technical Information Center. Some sources of data for EW modeling include the following:

a. **Doctrinal or Scenario Order of Battle and Communications Networks.** DIA, NSA, Joint Training and Simulation Center, Combined Arms Center, NGIC, NASIC, 688th Information Operations Wing, Naval Air Warfare Center Weapons Division, Naval Maritime Intelligence Center, Marine Corps Intelligence Activity, and Air Force Air Warfare Center.

b. **Parametric, Signature, and Antenna Pattern.** NSA, DIA, NGIC, Naval Maritime Intelligence Center, MSIC, Office of Naval Intelligence, nuclear weapons reconnaissance list, Navy Information Operations Command, NASIC, JSC, Air Force Research Lab, Army Research Lab, Navy Research Lab, and 688th Information Operations Wing.

c. **Topographic.** NGA, CIA, US Geological Survey, Army Geospatial Center, and Waterways Experiment Station.

APPENDIX G
SPECTRUM XXI

1. General

SXXI is the standard tool used by frequency managers within DOD for managing EMS use of all known emitters. Spectrum databases are maintained worldwide through SXXI connectivity to five regional servers via SIPRNET. SXXI can be operated in stand-alone capacity when SIPRNET connectivity is not available.

2. Capabilities

a. **SXXI consists of 12 modules.** Each module and one of the module's features is listed below:

b. **Frequency Assignment.** Store, retrieve, and output databases for frequency records in both standard frequency action format (SFAF) and government master file views.

c. **Data Exchange.** Perform an automated exchange of frequency records between the client computer and the SXXI server(s).

d. **System Manager.** Purge the frequency assignment database.

e. **Topoman.** Create new topographic data files from NGA source level 1 digital terrain elevation data.

f. **Interference Analysis.** Determine the potential source of unintended interference through database analysis of current frequency assignments.

g. **Interference Report.** Create and output new interference reports.

h. **Engineering Tools.** Perform a point-to-point (path profile) link analysis.

i. **Spectrum Certification System.** Contains two tools:

    (1) **Data Maintenance and Retrieval.** Create, edit, query, and output spectrum certification records (DD-1494).

    (2) **Analysis Tools.** Perform engineering checks for spectrum certification records to ensure equipment parameters are within the band limitations and constraints.

j. **JRFL Editor.** Create, edit, import, and export a JRFL.

k. **EW Deconfliction.** Predict and analyze frequency conflicts from the effects of EW jamming.

l. **Allotment Plan Generator.** Create, edit, export, import, output, and delete allotment (or channel) plans.

m. **Compliance.** Run validation and allocation table checks on frequency records.

3. Interfaces

a. SXXI interfaces with other spectrum management/communications planning software through the use of the SFAF. SFAF is the Military Communications-Electronics Board Pub 7 directed format to be used for all actions concerning spectrum frequency assignments, to include spectrum database storage. SXXI interfaces with the following software/systems:

b. **Joint Automated Communication-Electronics Operating Instructions System Software.** JACS is the standard tool within DOD for management of the joint communications-electronics operating instructions and allows for the seamless transfer of data between spectrum managers and communication planners.

c. **CJSMPT** provides an integrated spectrum management, modeling and simulation, and planning capability. It enables spectrum managers and communications planners to automate and accelerate spectrum planning, thereby making it easier for personnel to communicate while avoiding interference from EM jamming operations. CJSMPT enables better management of the EMS by displaying a real-time, three-dimensional view of frequency use in the OE for land, air, and space emitters. A key feature of CJSMPT is its faster-than-real-time simulation capability that can predict and visualize potential interference from maneuver forces. This allows planners to study alternatives. In addition, by coordinating all emitters and knowing their locations in an area of operations, spectrum planners can increase their reuse of specific frequencies and significantly increase communication bandwidth to MNFs.

4. SPECTRUM XXI-Online

SXXI will be replaced by SPECTRUM XXI-Online (SXXI-O). SXXI-O will utilize the spectrum management allied data exchange format as a replacement for SFAF. Spectrum management allied data exchange format will be an extensible markup language based data format that will be the standard format used by NATO members when conducting spectrum management tasks. SXXI-O will have similar software interfaces to SXXI, as those software programs also convert to, or are replaced by, programs that produce/utilize extensible markup language based data. SXXI-O will improve on SXXI by:

a. Enhancing the frequency assignment algorithms to increase spectral efficiency.

b. Migrating to a Web-based system with a simplified user interface.

c. Developing a real-time frequency scheduling capability to enable more efficient assignment of frequencies.

d. Developing an automated capability to support the Services in the acquisition of replacement systems.

APPENDIX H
REFERENCES

The development of JP 3-13.1 is based upon the following primary references.

1. Department of Defense

a. Department of Defense Directive (DODD) 3000.3, *Policy for Non-Lethal Weapons.*

b. DODD 3222.3, *DOD Electromagnetic Environmental Effects (E3) Program.*

c. DODD 5101.14, *DOD Executive Agent and Single Manager for Military Ground-Based Counter Radio-Controlled Improvised Explosive Device Electronic Warfare (CREW) Technology.*

d. DOD Instruction 4650.01, *Policy and Procedures for Management and Use of the Electromagnetic Spectrum.*

2. Chairman of the Joint Chiefs of Staff

a. CJCSI 3121.01B, *Standing Rules of Engagement/Standing Rules for the Use of Force for US Forces.*

b. CJCSI 3150.25D, *Joint Lessons Learned Program.*

c. CJCSI 3210.03C, *Joint Electronic Warfare Policy.*

d. CJCSI 3210.04, *Joint Electronic Warfare Reprogramming Policy.*

e. CJCSI 3320.01C, *Electromagnetic Spectrum Use in Joint Military Operations.*

f. CJCSI 3320-02D-1, *Classified Supplement to the Joint Spectrum Interference Resolution (JSIR).*

g. CJCSI 6510.01F, *Information Assurance (IA) and Computer Network Defense (CND).*

h. CJCSM 3122.03C, *Joint Operation Planning and Execution System, Volume II, Planning Formats.*

i. CJCSM 3212.02C, *Performing Electronic Attack in the United States and Canada for Tests, Training, and Exercises.*

j. CJCSM 3320.01B, *Joint Operations in the Electromagnetic Battlespace.*

k. CJCSM 3320.02C, *Joint Spectrum Interference Resolution (JSIR) Procedures.*

l. CJCSM 3500.04F, *Universal Joint Task Manual.*

m. JP 1-02, *Department of Defense Dictionary of Military and Associated Terms.*

n. JP 1-04, *Legal Support to Military Operations.*

o. JP 2-0, *Joint Intelligence.*

p. JP 2-01, *Joint and National Intelligence Support to Military Operations.*

q. JP 3-0, *Joint Operations.*

r. JP 3-05, *Special Operations.*

s. JP 3-09, *Joint Fire Support.*

t. JP 3-11, *Operations in Chemical, Biological, Radiological, and Nuclear (CBRN) Environments.*

u. JP 3-13, *Information Operations.*

v. JP 3-13.2, *Military Information Support Operations.*

w. JP 3-13.3, *Operations Security.*

x. JP 3-13.4, *Military Deception.*

y. JP 3-14, *Space Operations.*

z. JP 3-41, *Chemical, Biological, Radiological, Nuclear, and High-Yield Explosives Consequence Management.*

aa. JP 3-57, *Civil-Military Operations.*

bb. JP 3-60, *Joint Targeting.*

cc. JP 3-61, *Public Affairs.*

dd. JP 5-0, *Joint Operation Planning.*

ee. JP 6-0, *Joint Communications System.*

ff. JP 6-01, *Joint Electromagnetic Spectrum Management Operations.*

3. Service

a. Air Force Doctrine Document (AFDD) 3-13, *Information Operations.*

b. AFDD 3-51, *Electronic Warfare.*

c. Air Force Instruction 10-703, *Electronic Warfare Integrated Reprogramming.*

d. Army Regulation 525-22, *US Army Electronic Warfare.*

e. FM 2-0, *Intelligence.*

f. FM 3-0, *Operations.*

g. FM 3-05.120, *Army Special Operations Forces Intelligence.*

h. FM 3-36, *Electronic Warfare in Operations.*

i. NTTP 3-13.2, *Navy Information Operation Warfare Commander's Manual.*

j. NTTP 3-51.1, *Navy Electronic Warfare.*

4. Multi-Service

a. FM 3-11.4/MCWP 3-37.2/NTTP 3-11.27/AFTTP(I) 3-2.46, *Multiservice Tactics, Techniques, and Procedures for Nuclear, Biological, and Chemical Protection.*

b. FM 3-13.10, MCRP 3-40.5A, NTTP 3-51.2, AFTTP 3-2.7, *Multi-Service Tactics, Techniques, and Procedures for the Reprogramming of Electronic Warfare Systems.*

5. Multinational

a. MC 64/10 NATO, *Electronic Warfare Policy.*

b. MC 101/10 NATO, *SIGINT Policy and Directive.*

c. MC 486 NATO, *Concept for NATO Joint Electronic Warfare Core Staff (JEWCS).*

d. MC 515, *Concept for the NATO SIGINT & Electronic Warfare Operations Centre (SEWOC).*

e. MC 521, *Concept for Resources and Methods to Support an Operational NATO EW Coordination Cell/SIGINT & EW Operations Centre (EWCC/SEWOC).*

f. Air STD 45/14, *Electronic Warfare.*

g. Air STD 45/3B, *Joint Air Operations Doctrine.*

h. AJP-01(C), *Allied Joint Doctrine.*

i. AJP-2, *Allied Joint Intelligence, Counter Intelligence and Security Doctrine.*

j. AJP-3.6(A), *Allied Joint Electronic Warfare Doctrine.*

k. ATP-8(B), *Doctrine for Amphibious Operations.*

l. ATP-44(C), *Electronic Warfare (EW) in Air Operations.*

m. ATP-51(A), *Electronic Warfare in the Land Battle.*

n. QSTAG 593, *Doctrine on Mutual Support Between EW Units.*

o. QSTAG 1022, *Electronic Warfare in the Land Battle.*

APPENDIX J
ADMINISTRATIVE INSTRUCTIONS

1. User Comments

Users in the field are highly encouraged to submit comments on this publication to: Joint Staff J-7, Deputy Director, Joint and Coalition Warfighting, Joint and Coalition Warfighting Center, ATTN: Joint Doctrine Support Division, 116 Lake View Parkway, Suffolk, VA 23435-2697. These comments should address content (accuracy, usefulness, consistency, and organization), writing, and appearance.

2. Authorship

The lead agent for this publication is Joint Staff, J-7, Deputy Director, Joint and Coalition Warfighting. The Joint Staff doctrine sponsor for this publication is the Director for Operations (J-3).

3. Supersession

This publication supersedes JP 3-13.1, 25 January 2007, *Electronic Warfare*.

4. Change Recommendations

    a. Recommendations for urgent changes to this publication should be submitted:

        TO: JOINT STAFF WASHINGTON DC//J-3-DDGO//

        INFO: JOINT STAFF WASHINGTON DC//J-7-JEDD//

    b. Routine changes should be submitted electronically to the Deputy Director, Joint and Coalition Warfighting, Joint and Coalition Warfighting Center, Joint Doctrine Support Division, and info the lead agent and the Director for Joint Force Development J-7/JEDD.

    c. When a Joint Staff directorate submits a proposal to the CJCS that would change source document information reflected in this publication, that directorate will include a proposed change to this publication as an enclosure to its proposal. The Services and other organizations are requested to notify the Joint Staff J-7 when changes to source documents reflected in this publication are initiated.

5. Distribution of Printed Publications

Local reproduction is authorized, and access to unclassified JPs is unrestricted. However, access to and reproduction authorization for classified JPs must be in accordance with DOD 5200.1-R, *Information Security Program*.

6. Distribution of Electronic Publications

a. Joint Staff J-7 will not print copies of JPs for distribution. Electronic versions are available on JDEIS at https://jdeis.js.mil (NIPRNET) and https://jdeis.js.smil.mil (SIPRNET), and on the JEL at http://www.dtic.mil/doctrine (NIPRNET).

b. Only approved JPs and joint test publications are releasable outside the combatant commands, Services, and Joint Staff. Release of any classified JP to foreign governments or foreign nationals must be requested through the local embassy (Defense Attaché Office) to DIA, Defense Foreign Liaison/IE-3, 200 MacDill Blvd., Joint Base Anacostia-Bolling, Washington, DC 20340-5100.

c. CD-ROM. Upon request of a JDDC member, the Joint Staff J-7 will produce and deliver one CD-ROM with current JPs.

GLOSSARY
PART I—ABBREVIATIONS AND ACRONYMS

A-3	operations directorate (COMAFFOR staff)
A-5	plans directorate (COMAFFOR staff)
ABCA	American, British, Canadian, Australian Armies Program
AFB	Air Force base
AFDD	Air Force doctrine document
AFTTP	Air Force tactics, techniques, and procedures
AFTTP(I)	Air Force tactics, techniques, and procedures (instruction)
AJP	allied joint publication
AOC	air and space operations center (USAF)
AOR	area of responsibility
ASCC	Army Service component command
ASIC	Air and Space Interoperability Council
ATO	air tasking order
ATP	allied tactical publication
C2	command and control
CBRN	chemical, biological, radiological, and nuclear
CCDR	combatant commander
CCIR	commander's critical information requirement
CI	counterintelligence
CIA	Central Intelligence Agency
CJCSI	Chairman of the Joint Chiefs of Staff instruction
CJCSM	Chairman of the Joint Chiefs of Staff manual
CJSMPT	Coalition Joint Spectrum Management Planning Tool
CMO	civil-military operations
CNA	computer network attack
CNO	computer network operations
COA	course of action
COMAFFOR	commander, Air Force forces
COMCAM	combat camera
CONOPS	concept of operations
CONPLAN	concept plan
CREAPER	Communications and Radar Electronic Attack Planning Effectiveness Reference
CSG	Cryptologic Support Group
CSS	central security service
DCCC	defense collection coordination center
DE	directed energy
DEW	directed-energy warfare
DF	direction finding
DHS	Department of Homeland Security
DIA	Defense Intelligence Agency

DOD	Department of Defense
DODD	Department of Defense directive
DOS	Department of State
DSN	Defense Switched Network
DSPD	defense support to public diplomacy
E3	electromagnetic environmental effects
EA	electronic attack
ELINT	electronic intelligence
EM	electromagnetic
EMBM	electromagnetic battle management
EMC	electromagnetic compatibility
EMCON	emission control
EME	electromagnetic environment
EMI	electromagnetic interference
EMOE	electromagnetic operational environment
EMP	electromagnetic pulse
EMS	electromagnetic spectrum
EOB	electronic order of battle
EO-IR	electro-optical-infrared
EO-IR CM	electro-optical-infrared countermeasure
EP	electronic protection
ES	electronic warfare support
ESAC	Electromagnetic-Space Analysis Center (NSA)
E-Space	Electromagnetic-Space
EW	electronic warfare
EWC	electronic warfare cell
EWCA	electronic warfare control authority
EWCC	electronic warfare coordination cell
EWE	electronic warfare element
EWG	electronic warfare group
EWO	electronic warfare officer
EWWG	electronic warfare working group
FAX	facsimile
FM	field manual (Army)
FSE	fire support element
G-2	Army or Marine Corps component intelligence staff officer
G-3	Army or Marine Corps component operations staff officer
G-6	Army or Marine Corps component command, control, communications, and computer systems staff officer
G-7	Army component information operations staff officer
GCC	geographic combatant commander
GCCS	Global Command and Control System

GCCS-A	Global Command and Control System-Army
GIANT	Global Positioning System Interference and Navigation Tool
GNSS	global navigation satellite system
GPS	Global Positioning System
GPSOC	Global Positioning System Operations Center
HEMP	high-altitude electromagnetic pulse
HN	host nation
HPM	high-power microwave
HQ	headquarters
IA	information assurance
IADS	integrated air defense system
IC	intelligence community
IED	improvised explosive device
IEEE	Institute of Electrical and Electronics Engineers
IGL	intelligence gain/loss
IO	information operations
IR	infrared
ISR	intelligence, surveillance, and reconnaissance
IW	irregular warfare
IWC	information operations warfare commander
J-2	intelligence directorate of a joint staff
J-3	operations directorate of a joint staff
J-5	plans directorate of a joint staff
J-6	communications system directorate of a joint staff
JACS	joint automated communication-electronics operating instructions system
JCEWR	joint coordination of electronic warfare reprogramming
JCEWS	joint force commander's electronic warfare staff
JEMSMO	joint electromagnetic spectrum management operations
JEMSO	joint electromagnetic spectrum operations
JEWC	Joint Electronic Warfare Center (USSTRATCOM)
JEWCS	Joint Electronic Warfare Core Staff (NATO)
JFACC	joint force air component commander
JFC	joint force commander
JFCC SPACE	Joint Functional Component Command for Space
JFMO	joint frequency management office
JIOC	joint intelligence operations center
JISE	joint intelligence support element
JNSC	Joint Navigation Warfare Center Navigation Warfare Support Cell
JNWC	Joint Navigation Warfare Center
JOC	joint operations center

JOPP	joint operation planning process
JP	joint publication
JPG	joint planning group
JRFL	joint restricted frequency list
JSC	Joint Spectrum Center
JSIR	joint spectrum interference resolution
JSME	joint spectrum management element
JSPOC	Joint Space Operations Center
JTCB	joint targeting coordination board
JTF	joint task force
JWICS	Joint Worldwide Intelligence Communications System
L-EWE	land-electronic warfare element
LNO	liaison officer
LOAC	law of armed conflict
LOE	line of effort
LOO	line of operation
MAGTF	Marine air-ground task force
MC	Military Committee (NATO)
MCWP	Marine Corps warfighting publication
METOC	meteorological and oceanographic
MILDEC	military deception
MISO	military information support operations
MNF	multinational force
MNFC	multinational force commander
MOC	maritime operations center
MSIC	Missile and Space Intelligence Center
NASIC	National Air and Space Intelligence Center
NATO	North Atlantic Treaty Organization
NAVWAR	navigation warfare
NETOPS	network operations
NGA	National Geospatial-Intelligence Agency
NGIC	National Ground Intelligence Center
NGO	nongovernmental organization
NIPRNET	Nonsecure Internet Protocol Router Network
NSA	National Security Agency
NTTP	Navy tactics, techniques, and procedures
OA	operational area
OE	operational environment
OPFOR	opposing force
OPLAN	operation plan
OPORD	operation order
OPSEC	operations security

PA	public affairs
PNT	positioning, navigation, and timing
QSTAG	quadripartite standardization agreement
RADBN	radio battalion
RF	radio frequency
ROE	rules of engagement
S-2	battalion or brigade intelligence staff office (Army battalion or regiment)
S-6	battalion or brigade communications staff office (Army battalion or regiment)
SATCOM	satellite communications
SCIF	sensitive compartmented information facility
SEAD	suppression of enemy air defenses
SecDef	Secretary of Defense
SEWOC	signals intelligence/electronic warfare operations centre (NATO)
SFAF	standard frequency action format
SIGINT	signals intelligence
SIM	system impact message
SIPRNET	SECRET Internet Protocol Router Network
STO	special technical operations
SXXI	SPECTRUM XXI
SXXI-O	SPECTRUM XXI-Online
TNCC	theater network operations control center
TSS	target sensing system
TTP	tactics, techniques, and procedures
USCG	United States Coast Guard
USCYBERCOM	United States Cyber Command
USG	United States Government
USSTRATCOM	United States Strategic Command
VMAQ	Marine tactical electronic warfare squadron
WARM	wartime reserve mode
WP	working party

PART II—TERMS AND DEFINITIONS

acoustical surveillance. None. (Approved for removal from JP 1-02.)

acoustic jamming. None. (Approved for removal from JP 1-02.)

barrage jamming. None. (Approved for removal from JP 1-02.)

chaff. Radar confusion reflectors, consisting of thin, narrow metallic strips of various lengths and frequency responses, which are used to reflect echoes for confusion purposes. (Approved for incorporation into JP 1-02.)

control of electromagnetic radiation. None. (Approved for removal from JP 1-02.)

countermeasures. That form of military science that, by the employment of devices and/or techniques, has as its objective the impairment of the operational effectiveness of enemy activity. (Approved for incorporation into JP 1-02 with JP 3-13.1 as the source JP.)

directed energy. An umbrella term covering technologies that relate to the production of a beam of concentrated electromagnetic energy or atomic or subatomic particles. Also called **DE.** (Approved for incorporation into JP 1-02 with JP 3-13.1 as the source JP.)

directed-energy device. A system using directed energy primarily for a purpose other than as a weapon. (Approved for incorporation into JP 1-02.)

directed-energy protective measures. None. (Approved for removal from JP 1-02.)

directed-energy warfare. Military action involving the use of directed-energy weapons, devices, and countermeasures. Also called **DEW.** (Approved for incorporation into JP 1-02.)

directed-energy weapon. A weapon or system that uses directed energy to incapacitate, damage, or destroy enemy equipment, facilities, and/or personnel. (Approved for incorporation into JP 1-02.)

direction finding. A procedure for obtaining bearings of radio frequency emitters by using a highly directional antenna and a display unit on an intercept receiver or ancillary equipment. Also called **DF.** (Approved for incorporation into JP 1-02.)

electromagnetic battle management. The dynamic monitoring, assessing, planning, and directing of joint electromagnetic spectrum operations in support of the commander's scheme of maneuver. Also called **EMBM.** (Approved for inclusion in JP 1-02.)

electromagnetic compatibility. The ability of systems, equipment, and devices that use the electromagnetic spectrum to operate in their intended environments without causing or suffering unacceptable or unintentional degradation because of electromagnetic radiation or response. Also called **EMC.** (Approved for incorporation into JP 1-02.)

electromagnetic environment. The resulting product of the power and time distribution, in various frequency ranges, of the radiated or conducted electromagnetic emission levels encountered by a military force, system, or platform when performing its assigned mission in its intended operational environment. Also called **EME.** (Approved for incorporation into JP 1-02.)

electromagnetic environmental effects. The impact of the electromagnetic environment upon the operational capability of military forces, equipment, systems, and platforms. Also called **E3.** (Approved for incorporation into JP 1-02.)

electromagnetic hardening. Action taken to protect personnel, facilities, and/or equipment by blanking, filtering, attenuating, grounding, bonding, and/or shielding against undesirable effects of electromagnetic energy. (Approved for incorporation into JP 1-02.)

electromagnetic interference. Any electromagnetic disturbance, induced intentionally or unintentionally, that interrupts, obstructs, or otherwise degrades or limits the effective performance of electronics and electrical equipment. Also called **EMI.** (Approved for incorporation into JP 1-02.)

electromagnetic intrusion. The intentional insertion of electromagnetic energy into transmission paths in any manner, with the objective of deceiving operators or of causing confusion. (JP 1-02. SOURCE: JP 3-13.1)

electromagnetic jamming. The deliberate radiation, reradiation, or reflection of electromagnetic energy for the purpose of preventing or reducing an enemy's effective use of the electromagnetic spectrum, and with the intent of degrading or neutralizing the enemy's combat capability. (JP 1-02. SOURCE: JP 3-13.1)

electromagnetic pulse. The electromagnetic radiation from a strong electronic pulse, most commonly caused by a nuclear explosion that may couple with electrical or electronic systems to produce damaging current and voltage surges. Also called **EMP.** (JP 1-02. SOURCE: JP 3-13.1)

electromagnetic radiation hazard. Transmitter or antenna installation that generates or increases electromagnetic radiation in the vicinity of ordnance, personnel, or fueling operations in excess of established safe levels. Also called **EMR hazard** or **RADHAZ.** (Approved for incorporation into JP 1-02.)

electromagnetic spectrum. The range of frequencies of electromagnetic radiation from zero to infinity. It is divided into 26 alphabetically designated bands. (JP 1-02. SOURCE: JP 3-13.1)

electromagnetic spectrum control. The coordinated execution of joint electromagnetic spectrum operations with other lethal and nonlethal operations that enable freedom of action in the electromagnetic operational environment. Also called **EMSC.** (Approved for inclusion in JP 1-02.)

electromagnetic vulnerability. The characteristics of a system that cause it to suffer a definite degradation (incapability to perform the designated mission) as a result of having been subjected to a certain level of electromagnetic environmental effects. Also called **EMV.** (JP 1-02. SOURCE: JP 3-13.1)

electronic attack. Division of electronic warfare involving the use of electromagnetic energy, directed energy, or antiradiation weapons to attack personnel, facilities, or equipment with the intent of degrading, neutralizing, or destroying enemy combat capability and is considered a form of fires. Also called **EA.** (JP 1-02. SOURCE: JP 3-13.1)

electronic intelligence. Technical and geolocation intelligence derived from foreign noncommunications electromagnetic radiations emanating from other than nuclear detonations or radioactive sources. Also called **ELINT.** (JP 1-02. SOURCE: JP 3-13.1)

electronic masking. The controlled radiation of electromagnetic energy on friendly frequencies in a manner to protect the emissions of friendly communications and electronic systems against enemy electronic warfare support measures/signals intelligence without significantly degrading the operation of friendly systems. (JP 1-02. SOURCE: JP 3-13.1)

electronic probing. Intentional radiation designed to be introduced into the devices or systems of potential enemies for the purpose of learning the functions and operational capabilities of the devices or systems. (JP 1-02. SOURCE: JP 3-13.1)

electronic protection. Division of electronic warfare involving actions taken to protect personnel, facilities, and equipment from any effects of friendly or enemy use of the electromagnetic spectrum that degrade, neutralize, or destroy friendly combat capability. Also called **EP.** (JP 1-02. SOURCE: JP 3-13.1)

electronic reconnaissance. The detection, location, identification, and evaluation of foreign electromagnetic radiations. (JP 1-02. SOURCE: JP 3-13.1)

electronics security. The protection resulting from all measures designed to deny unauthorized persons information of value that might be derived from their interception and study of noncommunications electromagnetic radiations, e.g., radar. (JP 1-02. SOURCE: JP 3-13.1)

electronic warfare. Military action involving the use of electromagnetic and directed energy to control the electromagnetic spectrum or to attack the enemy. Also called **EW.** (Approved for incorporation into JP 1-02.)

electronic warfare frequency deconfliction. Actions taken to integrate those frequencies used by electronic warfare systems into the overall frequency deconfliction process. (JP 1-02. SOURCE: JP 3-13.1)

electronic warfare reprogramming. The deliberate alteration or modification of electronic warfare or target sensing systems, or the tactics and procedures that employ them, in response to validated changes in equipment, tactics, or the electromagnetic environment. (Approved for incorporation into JP 1-02.)

electronic warfare support. Division of electronic warfare involving actions tasked by, or under direct control of, an operational commander to search for, intercept, identify, and locate or localize sources of intentional and unintentional radiated electromagnetic energy for the purpose of immediate threat recognition, targeting, planning and conduct of future operations. Also called **ES.** (JP 1-02. SOURCE: JP 3-13.1)

electro-optical-infrared countermeasure. A device or technique employing electro-optical-infrared materials or technology that is intended to impair the effectiveness of enemy activity, particularly with respect to precision guided weapons and sensor systems. Also called **EO-IR CM.** (Approved for incorporation into JP 1-02.)

emission control. The selective and controlled use of electromagnetic, acoustic, or other emitters to optimize command and control capabilities while minimizing, for operations security: a. detection by enemy sensors; b. mutual interference among friendly systems; and/or c. enemy interference with the ability to execute a military deception plan. Also called **EMCON.** (JP 1-02. SOURCE: JP 3-13.1)

emission control orders. None. (Approved for removal from JP 1-02.)

ferret. None. (Approved for removal from JP 1-02.)

frequency deconfliction. A systematic management procedure to coordinate the use of the electromagnetic spectrum for operations, communications, and intelligence functions. Frequency deconfliction is one element of electromagnetic spectrum management. (JP 1-02. SOURCE: JP 3-13.1)

guarded frequencies. A list of time-oriented, enemy frequencies that are currently being exploited for combat information and intelligence or jammed after the commander has weighed the potential operational gain against the loss of the technical information. (Approved for incorporation into JP 1-02.)

imitative communications deception. None. (Approved for removal from JP 1-02.)

information. None. (Approved for removal from JP 1-02.)

jamming. None. (Approved for removal from JP 1-02.)

joint restricted frequency list. A time and geographically oriented listing of TABOO, PROTECTED, and GUARDED functions, nets, and frequencies and limited to the minimum number of frequencies necessary for friendly forces to accomplish objectives. Also called **JRFL.** (Approved for incorporation into JP 1-02.)

meaconing. None. (Approved for removal from JP 1-02.)

nondestructive electronic warfare. None. (Upon approval of this revised publication, this term and its definition will be removed from JP 1-02.)

precipitation static. Charged precipitation particles that strike antennas and gradually charge the antenna, which ultimately discharges across the insulator, causing a burst of static. Also called **P-STATIC.** (JP 1-02. SOURCE: JP 3-13.1)

protected frequencies. Friendly, generally time-oriented, frequencies used for a particular operation, identified and protected to prevent them from being inadvertently jammed by friendly forces while active electronic warfare operations are directed against hostile forces. (Approved for incorporation into JP 1-02.)

pulse duration. None. (Approved for removal from JP 1-02.)

radar spoking. None. (Approved for removal from JP 1-02.)

radio frequency countermeasures. Any device or technique employing radio frequency materials or technology that is intended to impair the effectiveness of enemy activity, particularly with respect to precision guided weapons and sensor systems. Also called **RF CM.** (JP 1-02. SOURCE: JP 3-13.1)

scan. None. (Approved for removal from JP 1-02.)

scan period. None. (Approved for removal from JP 1-02.)

scan type. None. (Approved for removal from JP 1-02.)

TABOO frequencies. Any friendly frequency of such importance that it must never be deliberately jammed or interfered with by friendly forces including international distress, safety, and controller frequencies. (Approved for incorporation into JP 1-02.)

verification. 1. In arms control, any action, including inspection, detection, and identification, taken to ascertain compliance with agreed measures. (JP 3-41) 2. In computer modeling and simulation, the process of determining that a model or simulation implementation accurately represents the developer's conceptual description and specifications. (JP 3-13.1) (Approved for incorporation into JP 1-02 with JP 3-41 and JP 3-13.1 as the source JPs.

wartime reserve modes. Characteristics and operating procedures of sensor, communications, navigation aids, threat recognition, weapons, and countermeasures systems that will contribute to military effectiveness if unknown to or misunderstood by opposing commanders before they are used, but could be exploited or neutralized if known in advance. Also called **WARM.** (Approved for incorporation into JP 1-02.)

JOINT DOCTRINE PUBLICATIONS HIERARCHY

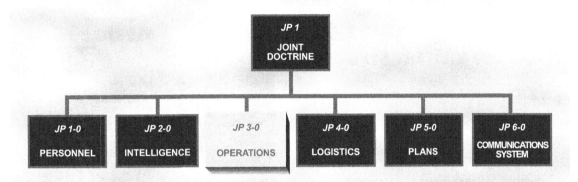

All joint publications are organized into a comprehensive hierarchy as shown in the chart above. **Joint Publication (JP) 3-13.1** is in the **Operations** series of joint doctrine publications. The diagram below illustrates an overview of the development process:

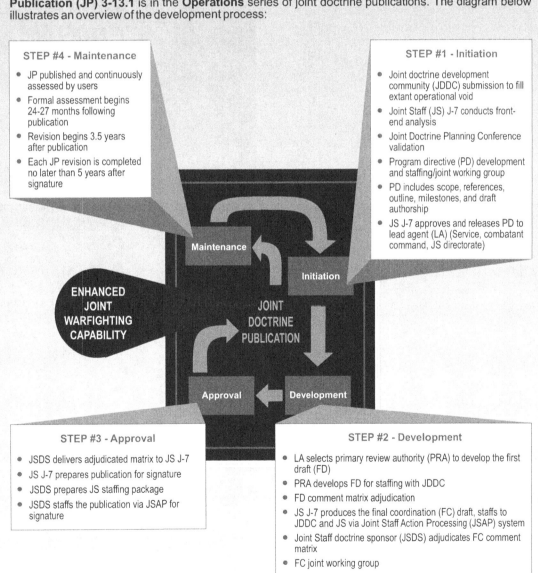

STEP #4 - Maintenance

- JP published and continuously assessed by users
- Formal assessment begins 24-27 months following publication
- Revision begins 3.5 years after publication
- Each JP revision is completed no later than 5 years after signature

STEP #1 - Initiation

- Joint doctrine development community (JDDC) submission to fill extant operational void
- Joint Staff (JS) J-7 conducts front-end analysis
- Joint Doctrine Planning Conference validation
- Program directive (PD) development and staffing/joint working group
- PD includes scope, references, outline, milestones, and draft authorship
- JS J-7 approves and releases PD to lead agent (LA) (Service, combatant command, JS directorate)

STEP #3 - Approval

- JSDS delivers adjudicated matrix to JS J-7
- JS J-7 prepares publication for signature
- JSDS prepares JS staffing package
- JSDS staffs the publication via JSAP for signature

STEP #2 - Development

- LA selects primary review authority (PRA) to develop the first draft (FD)
- PRA develops FD for staffing with JDDC
- FD comment matrix adjudication
- JS J-7 produces the final coordination (FC) draft, staffs to JDDC and JS via Joint Staff Action Processing (JSAP) system
- Joint Staff doctrine sponsor (JSDS) adjudicates FC comment matrix
- FC joint working group

Other titles we publish on Amazon.com:

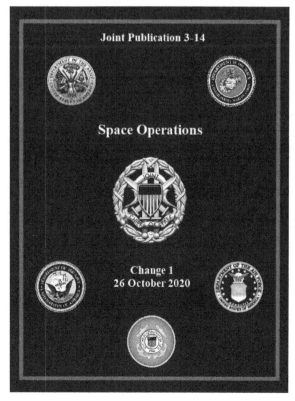

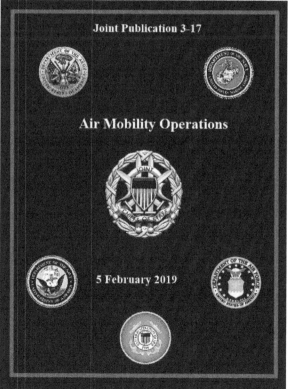

Joint Publication 3-13.2

Military Information Support Operations

07 January 2010
Incorporating Change 1
20 December 2011

EXECUTIVE SUMMARY
COMMANDER'S OVERVIEW

- **Provides an Overview of Military Information Support Operations**

- **Addresses Roles, Responsibilities, and Relationships**

- **Discusses Military Information Support Operations Command and Control**

- **Explains Military Information Support Operations Planning**

- **Presents the Joint Military Information Support Operations Process**

- **Discusses Military Information Support Operations Employment**

- **Highlights Military Information Support Operations Enablers**

Overview

The informational, cultural, social, moral, political, and physical aspects of the operational environment are as critical to operational success as the traditional orientation on adversary military capabilities has been in the past.

Today's global information environment is complex, rapidly changing, and requires integrated and synchronized application of the instruments of national power to ensure responsiveness to national goals and objectives. In the current operational environment, effective influence is gained by unity of effort in what we say and do, and how well we understand the conditions, target audiences (TAs), and operational environment. Within the military and informational instruments of national power, the Department of Defense (DOD) is a key component of a broader United States Government (USG) communications strategy. To be effective, all DOD communications efforts must inherently support the credibility, veracity, and legitimacy of USG activities.

The Department of Defense communications strategy and the separate and unique capabilities of military information support operations (MISO), public affairs (to include visual information), and defense support to public diplomacy address a

Military information support operations (MISO) play an important role in DOD communications efforts through the planned use of directed programs specifically designed to support USG and DOD activities and policies. MISO are planned operations to convey selected information and indicators to foreign audiences to influence their emotions, motives, objective reasoning, and ultimately the behavior of foreign governments, organizations, groups, and individuals in a manner favorable to the originator's objectives. Military information support (MIS) professionals follow a deliberate process that aligns

variety of communication roles and specific audiences as permitted by operational parameters and policy.

commander's objectives with an analysis of the environment; select relevant TAs; develop focused, culturally, and environmentally attuned messages and actions; employ sophisticated media delivery means; and produce observable, measurable behavioral responses.

Legal Framework and Authorities

The employment of MIS units is governed by explicit legal authorities that direct and determine how their capability is utilized. This legal foundation establishes MISO as a communications means and allows their integration with those strategies that apply the instruments of national power. Leaders and planners interpret relevant laws and policies to conduct MISO in any situation or environment, internationally and domestically.

Levels of War

Joint MISO support policy and commanders' objectives from strategic to tactical levels. Although military leadership and local key communicators are examples of TA engaged at the operational and tactical levels that are capable of affecting the accomplishment of a strategic objective.

The Purpose of MISO

MISO are used to establish and reinforce foreign perceptions of US military, political, and economic power and resolve. In conflict, MISO as a force multiplier can degrade the enemy's relative combat power, reduce civilian interference, minimize collateral damage, and maximize the local populace's support for operations.

Key Considerations for Effective MISO

Key considerations for effective MISO include: early planning and sustained employment; integration of MISO with the communication strategies of the USG and multinational partners; the use of indigenous assets; command emphasis and resourcing; a responsive MISO approval process; and a quantifiable and timely assessment criteria.

Roles, Responsibilities, and Relationships

Guidance for Combatant Commanders

The *Unified Command Plan* (UCP) and *Joint Strategic Capabilities Plan* (JSCP) provide direction and guidance to combatant commanders (CCDRs) concerning joint operation planning and their respective responsibilities.

Roles and Responsibilities

The **Secretary of Defense (SecDef)** provides strategic MISO advice to USG departments and agencies and multinational partners and approves all MISO programs submitted as part of a CCDR's operation plan (OPLAN).

The **Under Secretary of Defense for Policy** approves all MISO programs not submitted as part of a CCDR's OPLAN.

Assistant Secretary of Defense for Special Operations and Low-Intensity Conflict and Interdependent Capabilities develops, coordinates, and oversees the implementation of DOD policy for MISO activities and reviews, evaluates, coordinates, and oversees MISO plans, programs, and resources to ensure adherence to approved policy and planning guidance.

General Counsel, DOD, conducts legal reviews of all proposed MISO plans and programs for consistency with US public law, regulations, and internationally recognized legal standards as applicable.

CCDRs (to include Commander, United States Special Operations Command [CDRUSSOCOM], when designated the supported commander for MISO) plan, support, and conduct MISO in support of theater military missions and US national and regional objectives and integrate MISO into the preparation and review of joint OPLANs to ensure appropriate collaboration and deconfliction of information operations (IO), public affairs (PA), and civil-military operations.

CDRUSSOCOM is the designated joint proponent for MISO, which includes leading the collaborative development, coordination, and integration of the MISO capability across DOD. CDRUSSOCOM has the following responsibilities in addition to those detailed in the JSCP: prepares and provides assigned MIS forces to the other CCDRs and USG lead agencies, when directed by SecDef; coordinates and synchronizes transregional MISO when directed by SecDef or Chairman of the Joint Chiefs of Staff (CJCS); and coordinates with the Service Chiefs for planning and providing sustainment of MIS forces assigned to the other CCDRs for conduct of MISO.

The **Joint Staff** supports transregional MISO programs and activities as well as the programs and plans of geographic combatant commanders (GCCs) with integration and coordination of applicable strategic IO capabilities assigned to the Joint Staff under the UCP.

Military Departments and Services provide capabilities organic to Service forces to execute MISO actions and develop such dedicated MIS forces and equipment as directed by SecDef and CJCS.

Relationships

DOD information activities include IO, MISO, PA (to include visual information), and defense support to public diplomacy (DSPD).

MISO and Strategic Communication

Strategic communication (SC) integrates various instruments of national power with other activities across the USG to synchronize crucial themes, messages, images, and actions. MISO are a key capability that supports SC by influencing foreign audiences in support of US objectives.

MISO and Information Operations

MISO play a central role in the achievement of the joint force commander's (JFC's) information objectives through their ability to induce or reinforce adversary attitudes and behavior favorable to these objectives. In order to ensure all aspects of IO are properly integrated and synchronized into the combatant command planning process, an IO cell chief is chosen. This cell chief convenes meetings of the IO cell periodically in order to facilitate the integration of information-related capabilities. Within the IO cell, the MISO representative integrates, coordinates, deconflicts, and synchronizes the use of MISO with other IO capabilities.

MISO and Computer Network Operations

Computer network operations support MIS forces with dissemination assets (including interactive Internet activities) and the capabilities to deny or degrade an adversary's ability to access, report, process, or disseminate information.

MISO and Military Deception

MISO create and reinforce actions that are executed to deliberately mislead adversary military decision makers about US military capabilities, intentions, and operations. Military deception operations that integrate MIS unit's targeting input provide the JFC with the ability to influence the adversary to take specific actions (or inactions), giving the joint force an advantage.

MISO and Operations Security

It is essential that MISO plans and messages are protected prior to execution through the proper use of information security, information assurance, physical security, and operations security.

MISO and Electronic Warfare

Electronic warfare (EW) platforms provide a means of disseminating MISO messages and shaping the information environment through the electronic dissemination of MISO products. EW validates the assessment of MISO effectiveness by providing information on threat responses to broadcasts.

MISO and Public Affairs

PA and MISO activities are separate and distinct, but they must support and reinforce each other, which requires coordination, synchronization, and occasionally deconfliction. JFCs must ensure that appropriate coordination between MISO and PA activities are consistent with the DOD Principles of Information, policy or statutory limitation, and security.

Command and Control

US Special Operations Command, Services, and Combatant Commands

In accordance with SecDef and *Forces for Unified Commands Assignment Tables,* CDRUSSOCOM exercises combatant command (command authority) over all assigned Active Component MIS forces. Designated Reserve Component MIS forces and other MIS functions tasked to the Services remain under the control of the parent Service during training and mobilization. When directed by SecDef, the losing commander transfers MIS forces to the supported geographic or functional combatant commander. When these forces are transferred, the command relationship of the gaining and losing commanders over those forces must be specified. In most cases, the gaining unit commander will have operational control (OPCON). Commanders centralize operational MISO planning at the combatant command due to its importance to the commander's strategic concept. When a CCDR establishes a subordinate joint force they include MISO staff positions on the JFC's staff. The requested MIS force size and planned disposition may exceed the command and control capabilities of the joint force components. In these cases, the CCDR may identify the requirement to establish a joint military information support task force (JMISTF) or military information support task force (MISTF) as a component of the joint force. MIS forces may be organized as large as a JMISTF or as small as a MIS team that provides a planning capability. The JFC may delegate OPCON of all MIS forces to the JMISTF commander or may exercise OPCON of specified MIS forces through the commander of the units or components to which they are assigned.

The Joint Military Information Support Task Force

The JMISTF is responsible for providing MISO support to joint or multinational operations at the tactical and operational levels. The JMISTF is also responsible for deconflicting all MISO that occur under the joint task force and other commands as designated by the establishing authority.

Organizing Military Information Support Forces

If the JFC determines that MISO planning and execution requires control by a component command with that mission as its sole purpose, then the JFC requests establishment of a JMISTF or MISTF. **Control should favor centralized planning and direction and decentralized execution.** Considerations for MISO may dictate that control be at high national levels.

Planning

Joint Operation Planning and Phasing

Guidance for Employment of the Force and the JSCP set priorities for activities undertaken in the near term—usually the period covered by budget execution (present through two years). These plans define how a GCC will conduct all DOD activities within their area of responsibility. Joint planning integrates US military actions with other instruments of national power and multinational partners to achieve specified end states. CCDRs translate national and theater strategy into strategic and operational concepts through the development of security cooperation strategies and implementation plans, and operation and campaign plans. MISO have significant impact on the JFC objectives as they involve the need to mobilize the civilian population, while simultaneously isolating the adversary, taking away its ability to muster popular support.

Phasing

Phasing helps JFCs and staffs to visualize and think through the entire operation or campaign and to define requirements in terms of forces, resources, time, space, and purpose.

Planning Considerations

To plan for the effective employment of MISO, JFCs and their staffs must possess a thorough knowledge of national security policy and objectives, as well as national and theater military objectives. They must ensure planning is consistent with IO, PA, and DSPD planning as well as overall USG objectives. In addition, they must ensure all MISO are closely coordinated and synchronized to ensure that consistent themes and messages are communicated to TAs.

Requesting Forces

CCDRs clearly articulate MIS requirements in terms of the required capabilities. CCDRs submit requests for MIS forces to the Joint Staff. The Joint Staff is responsible for validating MIS force requests and will assign the appropriate joint force provider, depending on the activity, type of forces necessary, and availability.

Military Engagement, Security Cooperation, and Deterrence

Actions that can be applied to meet military engagement, security cooperation, and deterrence objectives and can be supported by joint MISO include foreign internal defense, security assistance, humanitarian and civic assistance, antiterrorism, DOD support to counterdrug operations, show of force operations, and arms control.

Crisis Response and Limited Contingencies

In military operations involving the use or threat of force, MISO offer SecDef options for engagement that potentially avoid the employment of additional combat forces, reduce the period of confrontation, and enhance the diplomatic, informational, military, and economic instruments.

Major Operations and Campaigns

CCDR activities executed during the shape phase assist in determining the character of future operations. MISO can be employed to gather information, undermine a potential opponent's will or capacity to wage war, and enhance the capabilities of multinational forces.

Interagency and Multinational Coordination

Coordination of DOD MISO with other USG departments and agencies facilitates the communication of the objectives of each organization and synchronization of effort. The **joint interagency coordination group** at the combatant command headquarters is an interagency staff group that establishes regular, timely, and collaborative working relationships between civilian and military operational planners. The Department of State's (DOS's) Bureau of International Information Programs engages audiences on issues of foreign policy, society, and values to help create an environment receptive to US national interests. In addition to DOS, MISO should be coordinated with other USG departments and agencies, including, but not limited to, the Central Intelligence Agency; International Broadcasting Bureau; Broadcasting Board of

Governors; Departments of Commerce, Homeland Security, Transportation, Energy, and Justice; Drug Enforcement Administration; and the US Coast Guard. When MISO are planned during multinational operations, planners must coordinate with multinational partners to ensure the attainment of US and multinational security objectives.

Support of Irregular Warfare

Irregular warfare (IW) is defined as a violent struggle among state and non-state actors for legitimacy and influence over the relevant populations. When MISO occur in IW, their role usually is much greater than during major operations and campaigns. MISO are key supporting operations to each contextual application of indirect approaches to executing IW. The ideological and political factors associated with IW create a fertile field for MISO.

Joint Military Information Support Operations Process

US MISO are developed and executed through a multiphase approach.

The joint MISO process is a standard framework by which MISO assets and critical enablers plan, execute, and evaluate MISO with proficiency and consistency throughout major campaigns, operations, and peacetime engagements. The joint MISO process consists of seven phases: planning; target audience analysis (TAA); series development; product development and design; approval; production, distribution, dissemination; and evaluation. Each of these phases is designed to apply to any type or level of operation. Collectively, the phases address important considerations and include the necessary activities for the proper integration of MISO with the CCDR's military strategy and mission.

Planning: Phase I

CCDRs are required to obtain approval prior to conducting MISO. A MISO program provides the required SecDef guidance for execution. MISO objectives, usually determined by the highest-level MIS authority involved in the operation (e.g., CCDR) provide the framework for developing the MISO plan. The goal of MISO planning is to integrate MISO into the commander's vision and concept of operations. Staff planners adjust the MISO plan as necessary to support the commander's objectives.

Target Audience Analysis: Phase II

During this phase of the joint MISO process, foreign groups or individuals are examined carefully and closely for their ability to be influenced. This provides insights on

Series Development: Phase III

how best to persuade the TA to change its behavior to one that is more favorable to US interests.

The information learned as a result of TAA is used in the development of products and actions. MIS personnel design a series of products and actions, determine the appropriate mix of media, and develop an execution plan. Series are reviewed for their suitability, length or duration, potential to affect the intended audience, accuracy of persuasive arguments or techniques to influence behavior change, and the resources available to execute them.

Product Development and Design: Phase IV

The work completed during the planning, analysis, and series development phases are vital for designing the prototypes of MISO products. Evaluating the TA's understanding and acceptance of the arguments conveyed in a MISO product is a key task. Pretesting products also helps establish a foundation for conducting post testing of entire series after dissemination occurs.

Approval: Phase V

A judicious and efficient approval process for MISO series and the management of the series development and approval process are fundamental in providing supporting MISO to emerging, ongoing, and future operations.

Production, Distribution, and Dissemination: Phase VI

MIS units from group to detachment level may deploy with organic production assets or utilize reachback to fixed assets at higher levels. Once production is complete, products are transferred to the disseminating unit or agency in accordance with a predetermined timeline. The most appropriate dissemination means are determined through TAA, and intelligence about the operational area. Radio and television broadcasts, the Internet, aerial leaflet drops, and loudspeaker transmissions are some of the means used throughout the world to disseminate MISO messages. Messages also are communicated through planned face-to-face contact with the local populace.

Evaluation: Phase VII

Assessing the effects of MISO product series on TAs relies on MISO impact indicators and analyses produced in earlier phases. MISO assessment criteria are focused on the achievement of supporting MISO objectives by TAs. The results of the evaluation are thus two-fold as they yield substantive information about the trends toward achieving the supporting MISO objectives and contribute data that are relevant for the commander's overall measures of effectiveness (MOEs).

Employment

Support to Unified Action

MISO are integrated in joint and multinational military operations as well as actions conducted by other designated governmental agencies. To be effective, MISO must be fully integrated with the supported organization's planning and decision-making activities. MISO are a key capability in furthering US endeavors to deter aggression, and to maximize the commander's efforts to shape the operational environment, insert combat forces, neutralize the threat, and secure the region. When authorized, MIS forces may be used domestically under a designated lead federal agency's or other US civil authority's public information efforts during domestic emergencies.

MISO and the Range of Military Operations

Employing MISO in conjunction with other activities to further national security goals in specific locations may prevent escalation of hostilities, shorten the duration of hostilities, or hasten a return to normalcy.

Military Engagement, Security Cooperation, and Deterrence

As an information activity in military engagement, security cooperation, and deterrence, MISO are employed to shape environments and influence relevant audiences to discourage armed conflict. MISO can reduce the need for a lethal response to adversary actions.

Crisis Response and Limited Contingency Operations

During crisis response and limited contingency operations, MISO are executed to mitigate the effects of the crisis and stabilize the operational environment.

Major Operations and Campaigns

MISO are planned and integrated throughout all phases of operations or campaigns. During major operations, MISO are integrated with both conventional and special operations (SO) activities.

MISO and Special Operations Activities

SO are relevant across the range of military operations and the eleven core activities, including MISO should be integral parts of a theater strategy, OPLAN, or campaign plan. SO usually are most effective when integrated with operations conducted by conventional forces.

Direct Attack Support

MISO can be integrated in all **direct attack** activities, employing within the physical and political risks, operational techniques, and use of force to achieve specific objectives.

Special Reconnaissance Support

MISO can be integrated in the four **special reconnaissance (SR)** activities by providing an additive capability to special operations forces conducting SR actions.

Unconventional Warfare Support

When conducted independently, the primary focus of **unconventional warfare** is on political-military and psychological objectives. MIS forces are employed to advise, assist, and train indigenous or surrogate forces in developing and implementing an effective MISO capability.

Foreign Internal Defense and Security Force Assistance Support

MISO are employed to prepare key audiences for US **foreign internal defense and security force assistance** operations, and to directly assist the host nation in establishing an environment that promotes internal stability and security through democratic systems.

Counterterrorism Support

MISO are a critical capability in conducting **counterterrorism** through the application of the direct and indirect approaches in support of DOD's global operations against terrorist networks. When authorized, MIS forces support national security or disaster relief within US territory to reduce civilian casualties and suffering.

Counterproliferation of Weapons of Mass Destruction

USG strategy to **combat weapons of mass destruction** (WMD) consists of three pillars: nonproliferation, **counterproliferation** (CP), and consequence management. MISO can facilitate USG CP informational activities directed at state and non-state actors to prevent and dissuade the production, acquisition, and delivery of WMD.

Civil Affairs Operations Support

MISO can be integrated with **civil affairs operations** activities to increase support for the HN government and reduce support to destabilizing forces.

Information Operations Support

MIS forces can be employed in conjunction with other **IO** capabilities and provide a critical means of communicating with foreign audiences to inform, direct, and influence.

Interagency Coordination

Military operations are synchronized with operations of other USG departments and agencies as well as with foreign forces, non-governmental organizations (NGOs), intergovernmental organizations (IGOs), and regional organizations for the purpose of accomplishing objectives. Success depends on the ability to blend and engage all instruments of national power. Interagency and MISO coordination occur at all levels of warfare to ensure synchronization of activities intended to influence TAs.

Multinational Operations

MIS units should be integrated into all multinational operations to ensure that MISO are coordinated. MISO must begin early, preferably before deployment, to prepare a population for the arrival of multinational forces and develop communication channels that can be used from day one of an operation. When the Armed Forces of the United States are integrated into a multinational command structure, peacetime MISO policies and wartime conduct should be coordinated and integrated to the maximum extent possible for the attainment of US and multinational security objectives. However, US MISO normally will be approved in US channels regardless of the composition of the multinational force chain of command.

Civil Authority Information Support Within the United States and Its Territories

MIS forces can provide a civil authority information support element within the US and its territories. When authorized for employment in this manner, MIS forces utilize their media development, production, and dissemination capabilities to deliver public and other critical disaster information to populations in the impacted area. Their role is to assist in dissemination of messages developed by civil authorities.

Enablers

Intelligence Operations

Ongoing intelligence support is critical to all phases of the MISO process. During phase I (Planning) of the MISO process, planners identify information requirements and use the intelligence process to request needed information used in conducting TAA in phase II. Phase II (Target Audience Analysis) includes thorough examination of the political, military, economic, cultural, religious, and psychological or social conditions that make up the operational environment, and impact the behavior of the audiences within that environment. Intelligence plays a critical role in phase VII (Evaluation) by confirming or denying MISO MOEs. **Development of MISO-related information should be predicated on a detailed collection plan** with specific collection requirements to exploit all available sources and techniques.

Threat Identification

Any factor that presents a recurring and identifiable obstacle to achieving success of a MISO program is deemed a threat. The early identification of threats and opportunities increases the potential for successful fulfillment of MISO program goals and objectives.

Intelligence, Surveillance, and Reconnaissance

MISO rely on theater intelligence, surveillance, and reconnaissance (ISR) operations to provide intelligence products based on a whole of government approach that occurs within the intelligence community. ISR assets also are critical in collecting data to confirm or deny MISO MOEs.

Communications

Communications between commands that are planning and executing MISO are necessary for effective use of capabilities. A joint MISO communications plan should be prepared to ensure that communications systems are compatible and adequate.

Logistics

The execution of the joint MISO process in sustained operations requires critical logistic support. MIS units are dependent primarily on the supported unit for all classes of resupply, maintenance, base support, commercial item restock, and dissemination contracting support. Early identification of host nation support is critical to the establishment of agreements or contracts to provide needed supplies, equipment, and facilities for MISO.

Capabilities

Service Inherent Capability

Each Service has the inherent capability to support achievement of US national objectives by using organic assets for production and dissemination of MISO products.

Studies Programs

CDRUSSOCOM, as the supporting CCDR, manages the MISO Studies Production Program, issues taskings, and monitors production. Products of the MISO studies program primarily are designed to support the operational requirements of the combatant commands and of US MIS forces worldwide, although they also are used by a variety of other organizations (e.g., DOS). MISO studies are unique in format; however, other military intelligence products can contain this type of intelligence information. In general, they profile the salient features of a country or its people; provide an analysis of the influences that lead different social, occupational, and ethnic groups of thatcountry to act as they do; discuss issues that elicit strong responses from the indigenous population; assess attitudes; identify vulnerabilities; and suggest ways and means to influence people.

United States Army Assets

In addition to dedicated military information support units, conventional Army units can also support MISO. With routine interaction with target audiences, they are in an ideal position to support MISO product dissemination and collect limited measure of effectiveness indicators for transmission to MISO planners.

Army Service MISO assets provide a vital instrument of engagement across all military phases in support of the full range of military operations and interagency coordination in a foreign setting and under special circumstances during domestic emergencies as well.

United States Army Special Operations Command is the Army component command of United States Special Operations Command. Its mission is to command (if directed), support, and ensure the combat readiness of assigned and attached Army MIS forces for worldwide use.

Army Active Component Military Information Support Group organizes, equips, and collectively trains assigned and attached forces to rapidly deploy anywhere in the world and conduct MISO and other specified communication tasks in any environment in support of CCDR and the interagency as directed by the President and SecDef.

Reserve Component Military Information Support Groups organize, train, and equip assigned and attached forces to deploy anywhere in the world and conduct MISO and other specified communication tasks in any environment in support of CCDRs and the interagency as directed by the President and SecDef.

United States Navy Assets

The **US Navy** employs a wide range of dissemination assets, product reproduction capabilities, and planning resources that can support joint and Service MISO missions. Navy afloat and ashore IO cells coordinate with joint MISO experts to identify maritime audiences, develop themes and products, and plan dissemination. The Navy has ultrahigh frequency, very high frequency, and high frequency broadcast capabilities to deliver MISO messages to afloat and ashore target audiences. Boarding parties can disseminate products to crews of civilian vessels to achieve MISO objectives. Several Navy aircraft support MISO.

United States Air Force Assets

United States Air Force (USAF) MISO is focused on the employment of air, space, and cyberspace capabilities as the Air Force's primary means of preparing, shaping, and exploiting the cognitive dimension of the operational environment. USAF MIS forces support JFC objectives through a variety of operations and activities that include development of psychologically informed targeting strategies. Many USAF platforms are used to execute missions in support of JFC MISO objectives. Air Mobility Command IO and MISO planners uniquely postured to observe and support MISO in addition to supporting the operational-level MISO efforts of a single geographic combatant command.

United States Marine Corps Assets

The Marine Corps has the capability to conduct MISO at the tactical level via MIS teams using loudspeaker broadcasts, print media, and face-to-face communication. The Marine Corps expeditionary MIS capability is found within the Marine Corps Information Operations Center (MCIOC). The MCIOC coordinates and integrates the conduct of MISO programs that complement IO with the JMISTF, CCDRs, interagency, DOS, intelligence community, IGOs, NGOs, and others as necessary.

CONCLUSION

This publication provides guidance for the planning, execution, and assessment of MISO in support of joint, multinational, and interagency activities across the range of military operations.

CHAPTER I
OVERVIEW

"In this war, which was total in every sense of the word, we have seen many great changes in military science. It seems to me that not the least of these was the development of psychological warfare as a specific and effective weapon."

General of the Army Dwight D. Eisenhower, 1945

1. General

a. Today's global information environment is complex, rapidly changing, and requires integrated and synchronized application of the instruments of national power to ensure responsiveness to national goals and objectives. Key terrain has undergone a fundamental shift from exclusively geographic to now include relevant populations. This has created an increased need for a broad set of capabilities and policy to engage local, regional, and global audiences. The informational, cultural, social, moral, political, and physical aspects of the operational environment are as critical to operational success as the traditional orientation on adversary military capabilities has been in the past. In the current operational environment, effective influence is gained by unity of effort in what we say and do, and how well we understand the conditions, target audiences (TAs), and operational environment.

b. Within the military and informational instruments of national power, the Department of Defense (DOD) is a key component of a broader United States Government (USG) communications strategy. DOD communications strategy and the separate and unique capabilities of military information support operations (MISO), public affairs (PA) (to include visual information), and defense support to public diplomacy (DSPD) address a variety of communication roles and specific audiences as permitted by operational parameters and policy. DOD informational activities can be used to inform, direct, or persuade. To be effective, all DOD communications efforts must inherently support the credibility, veracity, and legitimacy of USG activities.

See Chapter II, "Roles, Responsibilities, and Relationships," for additional clarification of DOD information activities.

c. MISO play an important role in DOD communications efforts through the planned use of directed programs specifically designed to support USG and DOD activities and policies. MISO are planned operations to convey selected information and indicators to foreign audiences to influence their emotions, motives, objective reasoning, and ultimately the behavior of foreign governments, organizations, groups, and individuals in a manner favorable to the originator's objectives. Military information support (MIS) professionals follow a deliberate process that aligns commander's objectives with an analysis of the environment; select relevant TAs; develop focused, culturally, and environmentally attuned messages and actions; employ sophisticated media delivery means; and produce observable, measurable behavioral responses. **It is important not to confuse psychological impact with MISO.** Actions of the joint force, such as strikes or shows of force, have psychological impact but they are not MISO unless their primary purpose is to influence the perceptions and subsequent behavior of a TA. Regardless of the mission set, all MISO are conducted within carefully reviewed and approved programs and under mission-tailored product approval guidelines that flow from national-level authorities.

d. MISO contribute to the success of both peacetime engagements and major operations. The combatant commander (CCDR) receives functional and theater strategic planning guidance from the Joint Strategic Capabilities Plan (JSCP), Unified Command Plan (UCP), and Guidance for Employment of the Force (GEF). These documents are derived from the Secretary of Defense (SecDef) *National Defense Strategy*, which interprets the President's national security policy and strategy, and the Joint Chiefs of Staff *National Military Strategy*.

(1) In peacetime, MISO are planned and integrated to further national defense strategies through the geographic combatant commander's (GCC's) theater campaign plan (TCP). CCDRs incorporate MISO programs and integrate them into the broad range of activities required for military engagement, security cooperation, and deterrence (i.e., Phase 0). For example, in steady-state geographic combatant command TCPs, MIS units can deploy to support approved counterinsurgency (COIN), demining, or foreign humanitarian assistance (FHA) programs under either a joint force commander (JFC) or US diplomatic control.

(2) MISO reinforce US policies that center on preventing hostilities and advocating peaceful resolutions when possible. MISO are key in furthering US endeavors to deter aggression and to maximize the JFC's efforts to shape the operational environment. MIS units communicate well-orchestrated and planned information to international audiences to clarify intent, prevent escalation of tension, ease concerns, and mitigate the potential effects and capabilities of adversary information activities.

(3) When diplomatic and other measures fail to deter conflict and lethal capabilities are employed, MISO can assist the JFC by setting conditions for the insertion of combat forces; neutralizing threats; facilitating efforts to contain conflict; stabilizing the operational area; and enhancing efforts to achieve conditions that allow a return to steady-state operations. MISO can inform, direct, educate, and influence targets to increase US combat power and decrease enemy hostile aggression. Proper integration of MISO may reduce operational risk and collateral damage, as well as military and civilian casualties.

(4) MIS forces can also be used to provide civil authority information support (CAIS). CAIS are DOD information activities conducted under a designated lead federal agency or other US civil authority to support dissemination of public or other critical information during domestic emergencies.

2. Legal Framework and Authorities

a. Introduction

(1) The employment of MIS units is governed by explicit legal authorities that direct and determine how their capability is utilized. This legal foundation establishes MISO as a communications means and allows their integration with those strategies that apply the

instruments of national power. Leaders and planners interpret relevant laws and policies to conduct MISO in any situation or environment, internationally and domestically. The outcome is the incorporation of MISO as an integral component of US measures designed to achieve national objectives.

(2) MIS units are employed during military operations as well as operations led by civilian agencies. They can be a vital asset to government departments and agencies in many situations when DOD is not the lead. The legal framework for MISO allows this DOD capability to be integrated with national-level strategies and support other USG departments and agencies.

b. **Law**

(1) The legal authorities for MISO are established in a number of documents and are in place to enable the proper integration of MISO. The legal framework for MISO applies to:

(a) Establishing the capability.

(b) Authorizing execution.

(c) Approving messages and actions.

(d) Establishing authorities for use of MIS forces in civil support operations (domestic operations) and for use of MISO in sovereign territory, air, seas, and airways.

(2) Although the following list is not all-inclusive, consideration should be given to the following specific legal issues when conducting MISO:

(a) The requirement that US MISO will not target US citizens at any time, in any location globally, or under any circumstances.

(b) *Geneva and Hague Conventions*. These international conventions preclude the injury of an enemy through "treachery" or "perfidy." It is also a violation of Geneva Convention III to publish photographic images of enemy prisoners of war.

(c) International agreements with host countries may limit the activities of MIS units (e.g., status-of-forces agreements).

(d) Domestic laws including copyright law and broadcasting law.

c. **Policy**

(1) Policymakers develop realistic and relevant policies that are within the capabilities of MISO to support. Executive- and agency-level policies reflect the laws and provide the necessary guidance to place MISO into action to achieve objectives. DOD policy, for instance, addresses the intent of the organization, guides decision making, and prompts action to integrate MISO into military operations and other USG strategies.

(2) Military leaders and planners consistently refer to and interpret both broad and specific policies on issues that affect our national security. They study US positions formulated to address a number of issues, such as terrorism, trafficking of illegal drugs, and proliferation of weapons of mass destruction (WMD). An in-depth understanding of MISO, and how they are best integrated with other US capabilities, is a prerequisite to determining how MISO contribute to US communication objectives in dealing with these and other global issues.

(3) MISO can assist USG mitigation efforts of issues that arise from unintended consequences.

d. **Strategy.** The Chairman of the Joint Chiefs of Staff (CJCS) and the CCDRs refer to national strategies as they establish guidance that provides the necessary strategic direction for employment of MISO. CCDRs' analyses of the national strategies' objectives are a critical step in determining MISO requirements. Understanding other government department and agency approaches in executing national strategies is another important step for decision makers for determining how MISO are to be employed, i.e., MISO contributions to strategic communication (SC) efforts.

3. Levels of War

a. Joint MISO support policy and commanders' objectives from strategic to tactical levels. The impact of these operations at one level may have significant implications at other levels. Although military leadership and local key communicators are examples of TAs engaged at the operational and tactical levels that are capable of affecting the accomplishment of a strategic objective.

b. MIS forces normally plan and execute operations in support of operational and/or tactical-level headquarters with a defined joint operations area. However, MIS forces may support USG departments and agencies, GCCs, or multinational partners. This is often the case when supporting a broad USG approach designed to achieve strategic objectives. MISO that support strategic objectives are often transregional in character and normally involve detailed coordination with one or more GCCs and interagency partners.

c. Commonly, MISO conducted at the operational level support regional policies and military plans.

d. Typically, tactical MISO are conducted in support of local military or civil authorities. Most commonly, they are designed to create immediate, localized effects, which together, support broader operational objectives.

> *"To seduce the enemy's soldiers from their allegiance and encourage them to surrender is of especial service, for an adversary is more hurt by desertion than by slaughter."*
>
> **Flavius Vegetius Renatus**
> ***The Military Institutions of the Romans***, c. 378 AD

4. Purpose

a. Every activity of the force has potential psychological implications that may be leveraged to influence foreign targets. MISO contribute to the success of wartime strategies and are well-matched for implementation in stable and pre-conflict environments. MISO are applied across the range of military operations and, as a communication capability, constitute a systematic process of conveying messages to selected foreign groups to promote particular themes that result in desired foreign attitudes and behaviors. MISO are used to establish and reinforce foreign perceptions of US military, political, and economic power and resolve. In conflict, MISO as a force multiplier can degrade the enemy's relative combat power, reduce civilian interference, minimize collateral damage, and maximize the local populace's support for operations.

b. MISO are integrated with US ambassador and GCC's theater-wide priorities and objectives to shape the security environment to promote bilateral cooperation, ease tension, and deter aggression. MISO convey the intent of the GCC by supporting public diplomacy efforts, whether to foster relations with other nations or to ensure their collaboration to address shared security concerns.

5. Missions

a. The purpose of joint MIS forces is further clarified by the application of their activities across the range of military operations.

b. Missions performed by joint MIS forces include:

(1) **MISO in Support of Combat Operations.** MISO are planned to influence the perceptions, attitudes, objective reasoning, and ultimately, the behavior of adversary, friendly, and neutral audiences and key population groups in support of US combat operations and objectives. Operations supported by joint MIS forces support include the following:

(a) Offense.

(b) Defense.

(c) Stability operations.

(2) **Military Information Support to DOD Information Capabilities in Peacetime.** This support can shape and influence foreign attitudes and behavior in support of US regional objectives, policies, interests, theater military plans, or contingencies. Operations or activities supported by MIS forces may include, but are not limited to:

(a) FHA/disaster relief.

(b) Noncombatant evacuation operations.

(c) Maritime interception operations.

(d) Support to USG country team or host nation (HN) civil programs (e.g., counterdrug, demining, human immunodeficiency virus awareness, security institution building, ethnic tolerance, and reconciliation).

(3) **Defense Support to Civil Authorities.** MIS forces provide support to public information efforts when authorized by SecDef or the President in accordance with Title 10, United States Code (USC). This support is provided during natural disaster relief following domestic incidents. Per Chairman of the Joint Chiefs of Staff Instruction (CJCSI) 3110.05D, *Joint Psychological Operations Supplement to the Joint Strategic Capabilities Plan FY 2006,* MIS forces do not provide their full capability. MIS forces deliberately exclude their development capability and support dissemination of messages developed by civil authorities. The National Response Framework establishes command relationships and responsibilities of DOD forces in support of domestic operations. Command of federal military and civilian personnel and resources is retained by SecDef when supporting civil authorities.

(4) **Support to Special Operations (SO)** (discussed in Chapter VI, "Employment").

6. Key Considerations for Effective Military Information Support Operations

a. **Early Planning and Sustained Employment**

(1) Military information support should be integrated into all plans at the initial stages of planning to ensure maximum effectiveness. This enables the JFC to shape the cognitive dimension of the information environment and set terms of initial and subsequent engagement. Early planning of MISO and employment of MIS forces will maximize the potential to influence foreign audiences within the area of interest.

(2) MISO require sustained application as part of a broader USG communication strategy. Effective MISO are proactive and set conditions for obtaining subsequent phase objectives. MISO are a critical component in all phases and in some phases may be the JFC's main effort.

b. **Integration of MISO.** MISO must be planned, coordinated, and integrated with the communication strategies of the USG and multinational partners at all levels from strategic to tactical. The synchronization of MISO with all other actions of the US and multinational forces precludes messages or actions at one level from contradicting or weakening the effectiveness at another.

c. **Use of Indigenous Assets.** Planners consider the use of indigenous resources, production assets, key communicators, and dissemination platforms to increase TA receptivity to messages, reduce military footprint, and facilitate credibility of the HN government, allies, and other agencies. While organic MIS assets are essential to the execution of joint force operations, their use may be limited by footprint restrictions or desired to be limited to specific phases of an operation when indigenous assets are disrupted or inappropriate.

d. **Command Emphasis and Resourcing.** Active involvement by the commander will emphasize the importance of MISO. MISO-relevant concerns may be included in commander's critical information requirements as priority intelligence requirements. Allocation decisions and logistics support of concept of operations (CONOPS) will also reflect the emphasis a commander places on MISO.

e. **Responsive MISO Approval Process.** Once delegated, the MISO approval process belongs to the commander. MISO approval authority should be delegated to the lowest practical level authorized by the Office of the Secretary of Defense. A time-sensitive process is crucial to providing responsive MISO.

f. **Assessment**

(1) Quantifiable and timely assessment criteria to determine measures of effectiveness (MOEs) are required for every MISO program. The assessment criteria should be established early within each planning phase, evaluated often, and adjusted as necessary throughout the campaign to ensure the joint task force (JTF) objectives are met.

(2) To create measurable effects in the human environment, commanders need to ensure that the information requirements for MISO and other information support activities are reflected in the collection plan; allocation of intelligence, surveillance, and reconnaissance (ISR) assets; and the codified output of selected staff elements and processes within the joint force battle rhythm.

CHAPTER II
ROLES, RESPONSIBILITIES, AND RELATIONSHIPS

"Psychological warfare has always rested as an uneasy activity in democracies, even in wartime. It is partly to do with the suspicion that using the mind to influence the mind is somehow unacceptable. But is it more unacceptable to shoot someone's brains out rather than to persuade that brain to drop down their weapon and live?"

Dr. Phillip M. Taylor
***Munitions of the Mind*, Manchester University Press, 1995**

1. General

The UCP and JSCP provide direction and guidance to CCDRs concerning joint operation planning and their respective responsibilities. The roles, responsibilities, and relationships contained in this chapter reflect general guidance derived from a combination of this strategic guidance as well as directives, instructions, joint and Service doctrine, and current practices within the MISO community.

2. Roles and Responsibilities

a. Secretary of Defense

(1) Participates in the establishment of national security policy and objectives.

(2) Recommends to the President the mobilization of Reserve Component (RC) assets, as necessary.

(3) Provides strategic MISO advice to USG departments and agencies and multinational partners.

(4) Approves all MISO programs submitted as part of a CCDR's operation plan (OPLAN).

(5) Through an execute order, delegates product approval and dissemination authority to the appropriate level for operational- and tactical-level products during contingency and wartime operations.

b. Under Secretary of Defense for Policy (USD[P])

(1) Approves and oversees all MISO policy and programs not delegated to the Assistant Secretary of Defense for Special Operations and Low Intensity Conflict and Interdependent Capabilities (ASD[SO/LIC&IC]).

(2) Delegates product approval and dissemination authority to the appropriate level for peacetime programs.

(3) Retains approval authority for strategic-level and politically sensitive products during contingency and wartime operations.

(4) Approves all MISO programs not submitted as part of a CCDR's OPLAN.

For a full description of MISO program and product approval authorities, see CJCSI 3110.05, Joint Psychological Operations Supplement to the Joint Strategic Capabilities Plan.

c. **Under Secretary of Defense for Intelligence (USD[I])**

(1) Ensures appropriate intelligence support and coordination are provided for MISO plans, programs, and activities.

(2) Oversees the integration and support of MISO into information operations (IO) plans, programs, and activities, and capabilities, as appropriate.

(3) Ensures that MISO are supported by other IO capabilities, as appropriate.

d. **Assistant Secretary of Defense for Special Operations and Low-Intensity Conflict and Interdependent Capabilities**

(1) Acts as principal staff assistant and civilian advisor to SecDef, Deputy Secretary of Defense, and USD(P) on MISO matters.

(2) Provides guidance on the planning and conduct of MISO activities and their integration into USG activities during peacetime, and more specific guidance for the planning and conduct of these activities across the range of military operations.

(3) Develops, coordinates, and oversees the implementation of DOD policy for MISO activities.

(4) Reviews, evaluates, coordinates, and oversees MISO plans, programs, and resources to ensure adherence to approved policy and planning guidance.

(5) Reviews, analyzes, and evaluates the various policies, processes, and programs of the DOD components that impact on the capability to plan, resource, prepare forces, and execute MISO; initiates and coordinates actions or taskings that enhance the readiness, capabilities, and effective use of MIS forces.

(6) Provides policy guidance and recommendations to consider and incorporate MISO in contingency planning.

(7) Makes recommendations to the USD(P) for all matters concerning the CCDRs' MISO plans, programs, activities, and requests for deployment of MISO personnel and equipment.

(8) Ascertains where shortfalls in intelligence support to MISO exist and recommends activities to the USD(I) that support the capabilities and plans of DOD components to conduct MISO programs and activities.

(9) Represents the USD(P) and SecDef in interagency deliberations and international negotiations dealing with MISO, as required.

(10) Establishes standing departmental and interagency working groups, as appropriate, to facilitate the conduct of effective MISO activities.

e. **Assistant Secretary of Defense for International Security Affairs** reviews MISO plans and programs, and provides recommendations to the ASD(SO/LIC&IC) on the development of specific MISO programs affecting the GCCs.

f. **Assistant Secretary of Defense for Public Affairs** provides PA guidance for MISO plans and programs.

g. **General Counsel, DOD,** conducts legal reviews of all proposed MISO plans and programs for consistency with US public law, regulations, and internationally recognized legal standards as applicable.

h. **Chairman of the Joint Chiefs of Staff**

(1) Advises the President, SecDef, and National Security Council on all MISO matters.

(2) Represents SecDef on the North Atlantic Treaty Organization MISO Working Group and in other multinational military forums.

(3) Coordinates and directs the preparation of multinational MISO plans and US participation in multinational MISO training programs.

(4) Provides MISO representation to the interagency organizations and their working groups.

(5) Provides the general policy and establishes production priorities for the MISO Studies Program.

(6) Provides the guidance for MISO conducted by the CCDRs.

(7) Prepares strategic plans and issues policy for the use of MISO across the range of military operations.

(8) Reviews the MISO plans and programs of the CCDRs to ensure they are adequate, feasible, and consistent with USG and DOD policy.

(9) Provides MISO plans and programs to the Office of the Secretary of Defense for review and approval.

(10) Reviews the CCDRs' peacetime MISO plans and programs.

(11) Establishes, in conjunction with the Commander, United States Special Operations Command (CDRUSSOCOM) joint doctrine for MISO.

(12) Provides a joint, prioritized statement of military requirements for MISO capabilities to meet the needs of SecDef, the Service Chiefs, CCDRs, and the CJCS.

(13) Provides an integrated statement of joint MISO training requirements and ensures that these requirements are appropriately addressed.

(14) Apportions MIS forces to the combatant commands through the JSCP.

(15) Prepares integrated logistic and mobilization guidance for MISO capabilities.

(16) Provides a unified, prioritized list of MISO intelligence and counterintelligence requirements to meet the needs of the CCDRs, Joint Staff, and Services.

(17) Ensures integration of MISO into the CJCS Exercise Program and Joint Experimentation Program.

(18) Incorporates MISO instruction into joint professional military education programs.

(19) Ensures integration of MISO into military planning.

i. **CCDRs (to include CDRUSSOCOM when designated the supported commander for MISO)** have the following responsibilities:

(1) Ensure that staffs and organizations within their commands have sufficient representation and working proficiency in the planning and conduct of joint MISO.

(2) Request liaison officers from other USG departments and agencies when appropriate.

(3) Working in coordination with the Joint Staff and the United States Special Operations Command (USSOCOM), develop plans and programs to support MISO requirements identified by supported CCDRs.

(4) Develop and submit to the CJCS additional MISO requirements necessary to support CCDR plans and programs.

(5) When directed by SecDef, accept the attachment of MIS forces and employ those forces as directed.

(6) Designate specific staff responsibility for maintaining MISO planning capability, coordinating MISO actions, and ensuring that regional plans, activities, and operations support national objectives.

(7) Develop intelligence and counterintelligence requirements necessary to perform MISO analysis, planning, and execution.

(8) Plan, support, and conduct MISO in support of theater military missions and US national and regional objectives.

(9) Coordinate military information support with the chiefs of US diplomatic missions within the GCC's area of responsibility (AOR).

(10) Prepare plans and, upon approval, conduct MISO to support the execution of operations.

(11) Foster cooperative MISO policies among multinational military forces and regional security organizations.

(12) Ensure advance contingency planning for use of non-DOD informational and related capabilities in MISO.

(13) Establish a reporting system to provide relevant information about adversary propaganda, measured impact of MISO, and any anticipated changes to ongoing activities.

(14) Integrate MISO into the preparation and review of joint OPLANs to ensure appropriate collaboration and deconfliction of IO, PA, and civil-military operations (CMO).

(15) Recommend regional-specific MIS forces training requirements to USSOCOM.

j. **Commander, US Special Operations Command,** is the designated joint proponent for MISO, which includes leading the collaborative development, coordination, and integration of the MISO capability across DOD. CDRUSSOCOM exercises combatant command (command authority) (COCOM) over assigned MIS forces. CDRUSSOCOM has the following responsibilities in addition to those detailed in the JSCP:

(1) Prepares program and budget to fund approved MISO programs for assigned forces. In fulfilling this responsibility, CDRUSSOCOM coordinates with the CJCS, Service Chiefs, and the other CCDRs to ensure that all MISO and support requirements are addressed.

(2) Provides trained and ready MIS forces to support SecDef and the other CCDRs with MISO support.

(3) Performs as joint proponent for development of MISO in joint doctrine; training and education for individuals and units; joint capabilities; joint mission-essential task lists; and identification of critical individual skills, training, and experience.

(4) Prepares and provides assigned MIS forces to the other CCDRs and USG lead agencies, when directed by SecDef.

(5) Supports the IO responsibilities of the geographic and functional combatant commanders, as well as their MISO planning, coordinating, synchronization, and execution efforts.

(6) Develops joint MISO programs of instruction, and when directed, trains DOD and foreign military personnel in MISO techniques and procedures.

(7) Recommends MISO policy guidance to the CJCS, Service Chiefs, and US military commanders, as required.

(8) Develops and validates priorities for MISO training, intelligence, and military requirements and provides these to the CJCS to support Service, combatant command, and Joint Staff responsibilities as they relate to MISO.

(9) Provides visibility of MISO issues, activities, tasks, and capabilities to the CJCS, Service Chiefs, and commanders at other US military command levels.

(10) Coordinates with the Joint Staff and combatant commands to integrate MISO activities into joint training and experimentation plans and programs.

(11) Develops concepts to support national security objectives, reviews Service MISO doctrine development for consistency with joint doctrine, and ensures that joint and Service MISO training supports national objectives.

(12) Observes and evaluates MIS forces in exercises to develop joint tactics, techniques, and procedures for MIS forces.

(13) Manages the MISO Studies Program and coordinates MISO input to the Defense Intelligence Production schedule.

(14) Coordinates and synchronizes transregional MISO when directed by SecDef or CJCS.

(15) Coordinates with the Service Chiefs for planning and providing sustainment of MIS forces assigned to the other CCDRs for conduct of MISO.

k. The **Joint Staff** supports transregional MISO programs and activities as well as the programs and plans of GCCs with integration and coordination of applicable strategic IO capabilities assigned to the Joint Staff under the UCP.

l. **Commander, United States Transportation Command (USTRANSCOM)**, supports the deployment of forces, distribution, and dissemination requirements for MISO through USTRANSCOM joint mobility assets.

m. **Military Departments and Services**

(1) Provide civilian and military personnel with appropriate MISO training and planning skills.

(2) Provide capabilities organic to Service forces to execute MISO actions and develop such dedicated MIS forces and equipment as directed by SecDef and CJCS.

(3) Develop Service MISO doctrine relating to the primary functions assigned to the particular Service.

(4) When directed by SecDef, provide global force management of MIS forces (not assigned to CDRUSSOCOM or under the operational control [OPCON] of a GCC) to support the regional MISO plans, programs, and activities of the combatant commands and other USG departments and agencies.

(5) Provide departmental intelligence and counterintelligence assets that are trained, equipped, and organized to support planning and conduct MISO.

(6) Incorporate MISO instruction into Service training and education programs.

(7) US Army Reserve Command provides RC MIS forces for the Department of the Army to the combatant commands or other USG departments and agencies when directed by SecDef.

(8) **US Army Directorate of Military Information Support Operations and Civil Affairs.** The principal staff directorate that advises the Commanding General, United States Army Special Operations Command (USASOC), on all matters pertaining to MISO. It coordinates with all Army major command staff elements and other special operations forces (SOF) as required to ensure MISO is properly organized, trained, equipped, and resourced to meet USASOC Commander's Title 10, USC, responsibilities and USSOCOM's UCP responsibilities. It provides subject matter expertise for coordination with external MISO-related organizations and agency initiatives. It maintains situational awareness on all MISO staff actions and requirements within the command.

For further detail concerning Service MISO capabilities, refer to Appendix A, "Capabilities."

n. **Director, Defense Intelligence Agency**

(1) Establishes and implements a plan to satisfy MISO relevant intelligence requirements.

(2) Assists in the preparation of intelligence and counterintelligence estimates and appraisals of foreign groups designated by USD(P), CJCS, Service Chiefs, CDRUSSOCOM, and other CCDRs.

(3) Provides training for intelligence analysts to ensure a capability to respond to intelligence production requirements in support of MISO programs.

(4) Recommends employment of MIS forces in support of US policy.

(5) Provides indications of potential vulnerability to adversary information or foreign intelligence service activities.

o. **Director, Defense Information Systems Agency,** provides computer systems support for the transmission of MISO products from the continental United States (CONUS) production facilities to overseas MIS forces.

p. **Director, National Security Agency/Chief, Central Security Service,** provides intelligence information to satisfy intelligence collection requirements.

q. **Joint Force Commanders Serving in Multinational Commands**

(1) Implement multinational MISO plans to the extent consistent with international law, including the law of armed conflict, and treaty/international agreement obligations in relations with the governments of countries where US forces are assigned.

(2) Request guidance from SecDef on implementation of multinational policies and objectives, as appropriate.

(3) Coordinate joint MISO planning with appropriate multinational commanders and national forces of HNs.

r. **Other United States Government Agencies**

(1) During peacetime, the Department of State (DOS) provides overall direction, coordination, and supervision of interdepartmental activities overseas. In peacetime operations or in conflict, the DOS may restrict MISO messages and themes used within specific countries or areas.

(2) Other government departments and agencies impacted by MISO, including peacetime MISO activities, may provide recommendations to joint planners to ensure consistency of effort.

3. Relationships

a. **General.** There are a variety of functions and capabilities that help a JFC formulate the command's message and communicate with local, international, and US domestic audiences as part of broader policy and in support of operational objectives. DOD information activities include IO, MISO, PA (to include visual information), and DSPD. See Figure II-1 for additional details concerning DOD information activities.

(1) PA and MISO are separate and unique activities that are governed by policy and practice in terms of audiences, focus, and scope. SC integrates various instruments of national power with other activities across the USG to synchronize crucial themes, messages, images, and actions. SC is policy driven and generally conducted under DOS lead. DOD SC activities are designed to support the continuity of DOD strategic- and operational-level messages and activities with overall USG policy and SC themes.

DEPARTMENT OF DEFENSE INFORMATION ACTIVITIES

INFORMATION ACTIVITY	PRIMARY TASK	FOCUS OF ACTIVITY	PURPOSE	DESIRED OUTCOME
US Government (USG) Strategic Communication (Department of State Lead)	Coordinate information, themes, plans, programs, and actions that are synchronized with other elements of national power	Understand and engage key audiences	Better enable the USG to engage foreign audiences holistically and with unity of effort	Create, strengthen, or preserve conditions favorable to advance national interests and objectives
Department of Defense (DOD) support to Strategic Communication	Use DOD operational and informational activities and strategic communication processes in support of Department of State's broader public diplomacy efforts	Key audiences	Improve the alignment of DOD actions and information with policy objectives	The conduct of military activities and operations in a shaped environment
Information Operations	Integrate information operations core, supporting, and related capabilities as part of a military plan	Adversary audiences	Influence, disrupt, corrupt, or usurp adversarial human and automated decision making while protecting our own.	Optimum application of capability to desired military outcome
Military Information Support Operations	Influence target audience perceptions, attitudes, and subsequent behavior	Approved foreign audiences	Shape, deter, motivate, persuade to act	Perceptions, attitudes, and behavior conducive to US/multinational partner objectives
Public Affairs	Provide truthful, timely, accurate information about DOD activities (inform)	US, allied, national, international, and internal audiences	Keep the public informed, counter adversary information activities, deter adversary actions, and maintain trust and confidence of US population, and friends and allies	Maintain credibility and legitimacy of US/multinational partner military operations with audience

Figure II-1. Department of Defense Information Activities

(2) Although each of these activities is distinct, commanders must ensure that there is a general compatibility of messages within the broader communications strategy. This must be accomplished without blurring traditional lines of separation between PA and MISO and their respective audiences. To this end, **it is critical that all DOD military information activities are conducted in a manner that reinforces the credibility, veracity, and legitimacy of DOD and USG activities.** In very narrow circumstances, MISO may support military deception (MILDEC) operations designed to preserve operational surprise and the safety of friendly forces, but this is done only after the commander and staff carefully weigh the likely benefits of a deception operation against a potential short- and long-term loss of credibility with the media or local audiences.

b. **Military Information Support Operations and Strategic Communication**

(1) SC consists of a focused USG effort to understand and engage key audiences to create, strengthen, or preserve conditions favorable for the advancement of USG interests, policies, and objectives through the use of coordinated programs, plans, themes, messages, and products synchronized with the actions of all instruments of national power.

(2) MISO are a key capability that supports SC by influencing foreign audiences in support of US objectives. Given its focus on foreign TAs, MISO personnel should possess a good understanding of the language and culture of the TA and ensure this knowledge is effectively used in the preparation of MISO products and related activities.

c. **Military Information Support Operations and Information Operations**

(1) **General.** MISO play a central role in the achievement of the JFC's information objectives through their ability to induce or reinforce adversary attitudes and behavior favorable to these objectives. MISO can be particularly useful during pre- and post-combat operations, when other means of influence are restrained or not authorized. Because of its wide ranging impact, it is essential MISO be fully coordinated and synchronized with relevant activities and operations. This is normally facilitated through the combatant command IO cell.

(2) IO is the integrated employment during military operations of information-related capabilities in concert with other lines of operation to influence, disrupt, corrupt, or usurp the decision making of adversaries and potential adversaries while protecting our own. MISO must be coordinated with other information-related capabilities, such as computer network operations (CNO), electronic warfare (EW), operations security (OPSEC), and MILDEC, to ensure deconfliction control measures are in place, and that all capabilities within IO are coordinated and synchronized in time, space, and purpose to achieve the objectives established in planning.

(3) In order to ensure all aspects of IO are properly integrated and synchronized into the combatant command planning process, an IO cell chief is chosen (in accordance with Chairman of the Joint Chiefs of Staff Manual [CJCSM] 1630.01, *Joint Information Operations Force*). This cell chief convenes meetings of the IO cell periodically in order to facilitate the integration of information-related capabilities. Within the IO cell, the MISO

representative integrates, coordinates, deconflicts, and synchronizes the use of MISO with other IO capabilities. Specific examples of this kind of interaction between MISO and the other information-related capabilities follow:

(a) **Military Information Support Operations and Computer Network Operations.** CNO support MIS forces with dissemination assets (including interactive Internet activities) and the capabilities to deny or degrade an adversary's ability to access, report, process, or disseminate information. These capabilities support MIS by providing access to digital media within the information environment to reach intended targets and denying TA information that does not support objectives.

(b) **Military Information Support Operations and Military Deception.** MIS forces provide the JFC the ability to reduce the allocation of forces and resources required to deceive the adversary and facilitate mission accomplishment. MISO create and reinforce actions that are executed to deliberately mislead adversary military decision makers about US military capabilities, intentions, and operations. MILDEC operations that integrate MIS unit's targeting input provide the JFC with the ability to influence the adversary to take specific actions (or inactions), giving the joint force an advantage. MISO support to MILDEC operations must be carefully considered by the commander and staff, weighing the likely benefits of a deception operation against a potential short- and long-term loss of credibility with the media and local and regional audiences.

(c) **Military Information Support Operations and Operations Security.** It is essential that MISO plans and messages are protected prior to execution through the proper use of information security, information assurance, physical security, and OPSEC. Additionally, it is essential during the effort to influence foreign audiences that MISO not reveal critical information or indicators of friendly operations to the adversary.

(d) **Military Information Support Operations and Electronic Warfare.** EW platforms provide a means of disseminating MISO messages and shaping the information environment through the electronic dissemination of MISO products. The joint restricted frequency list deconflicts these two capabilities. When appropriate, EW platforms can also provide a means of denying enemy forces the ability to disseminate adversarial information. These platforms can also degrade the adversary's ability to see, report, and process information by jamming selected frequencies. EW validates the assessment of MISO effectiveness by providing information on threat responses to broadcasts.

For further guidance concerning IO, refer to Joint Publication (JP) 3-13, Information Operations.

d. **Military Information Support Operations and Public Affairs**

(1) MISO are used to influence the attitudes, opinions, and behavior of foreign TAs in a manner favorable to US objectives.

(2) Military PA forces plan, coordinate, and synchronize public information, command information, and community engagement activities and resources to support the commander's operational objectives. Through timely dissemination of factual information to

international and domestic audiences, PA puts operational actions in context, facilitates the development of informed perceptions about military operations among information consumers, and undermines adversarial information efforts. PA operations and activities shall not focus on directing or manipulating public actions or opinion.

(a) PA and MISO activities are separate and distinct, but they must support and reinforce each other, which requires coordination, synchronization, and occasionally deconfliction. These planning activities are generally accomplished in the IO working group, the IO cell, or other planning groups. In the event that formal planning groups are not established, informal coordination should be accomplished between these two capabilities as well as with other related capabilities. JFCs must ensure that appropriate coordination between MISO and PA activities are consistent with the DOD Principles of Information, policy or statutory limitation, and security.

(b) PA is normally the source for official information for the media. Information disseminated by the joint force regardless of source or method of distribution will reach unintended audiences. Efforts of one capability must not undermine those of another. While PA will have no role in executing MISO, PA can use MISO products to educate the media about MISO missions, as appropriate.

Made in the USA
Las Vegas, NV
05 May 2022

48447533R00149